THE TREE MYSTIC

A BOOK TO HELP YOU FIND
MEANING AND PURPOSE

AUTHOR'S NOTE

FILM - ART - HEALING -TRAINING

You can see photographs that inspired some of the characters and various scenes in the book at www.TheTreeMystic.com or on the Amazon book page – Author Central.

THE TREE MYSTIC - YOUTUBE CHANNEL
Videos and secrets from the book.

EXPERIENCE OUR HEALING
1-1 and group healing online, and at our camps - See www.TheTreeMystic.com

BECOME A SPIRITUAL HEALER
Gain a certificate in Tree Mystic Spiritual Healing – See our website.

PUBLISHING

First Published 2021 by Rich Minds Publishing.

Paperback ISBN: 978-1-9168901-0-7
E-Book ISBN: 978-1-9168901-1-4

DEDICATION

To My Mother – The Bird Table. To My Father – The Shepherd.
Thank you for saving me.

ACKNOWLEDGEMENTS

Heather and Malcolm Day – For their help with the logic that passed me by.

Moira Milne – For all the illustrations given from the heart.

James @ CRE-ATE for all the help and clever stuff to support the book.

Paul Baillie-Lane – Typography and Interior design

Andrew Dawson – Copy editing

Gabrielle Ragusi – Cover art

THE HATCHLING

When a baby turtle is born, their path towards the safety of the sea is full of trials. It must take a hazardous journey across the sands where predators and baited-traps lay in wait. It has been said that some turtles lay their eggs so that the babies hatch on a full moon; illuminating their path towards the sea. I do hope that this book can do something similar for you.

GINKGO SEQUOIA

WHY I WROTE THIS BOOK

One night in the city of Bhopal, India, I witnessed a tragedy. It was in the city's streets, in a shadow cast by the darkness of the human heart. As the shop shutters went down and the sky blackened, from hidden doorways and secret passages came an endless stream of old ladies. They were just a thimbleful of India's homeless widows, wafer thin, like the pieces of cardboard that they were about to sleep on. They didn't chatter, I suppose they didn't have a lot to look forward to. As quiet as dormice, they lay down on the cold, hard floor and huddled together. In the litter-strewn streets, soon they would be nibbled and scampered over.

I asked myself, 'How would I feel if one of these frail old ladies was my own mother?' Later, when I returned to England, I uncovered their story; these widows had been cast out onto the streets by their own families. Their fate sealed in ancient religious texts, their ragged clothes shaming the streets of every city in India.

What I witnessed gave birth to this book. A novel that hopes to be the catalyst for the disappearance of this human misery and suffering. I know that this is what my late mother and father would have wanted me to do. I hope you don't mind that I am asking for your help too … donations to the project at www.TheTreeMystic.com

Ginkgo Sequoia

THE GREAT MYSTERY

Ask yourself if it is logical that something that can transform itself into a butterfly can do nothing more than flutter, or that a bird that can migrate without map or compass can do nothing else but sing.

SOLLIE AS A BOY

Fear – Love – Inspiration – Miracles

He arrived with frozen feet. It would take 20 years to remove the numbness.

The giant looked down at the little boy. An arctic wind bit at his ears and turned his bare legs purple. He shook the snow from his hair. Somehow he had to gather the courage to clamber up the giant. This would not be easy. He might love trees, but he was also fearful of climbing them.

Sollie's ascent began encouragingly. Only when he was halfway to the top did his legs feel like those of a newly-born foal. Despite this, he continued to haul himself up the trunk. What was driving him on… courage, gain, pride? In fact, it was none of these. It was love. Not just for the birds and the trees but for everything that needed a helping hand. In the morning he had seen a mother bird killed as she returned to her nest of chicks. Now he was scaling the tree with a life-saving food parcel.

A little further up, his foot tested the strength of an old, knobbly branch that he would need to walk across; it creaked. He held onto the bendy branch above him for support and inched along it. Eventually, the bird's nest was directly above him. He looked up, then down at the ground... 30 metres below. For a minute he was despondent as well as queasy: 'I won't be able to hold on with one hand and feed the chicks in the nest with the other… If I slip and fall, I am sure to die.'

Then something quite astonishing occurred; he learnt that his kind thoughts made him capable of miracles. Suddenly, there was a hustle and a bustle overhead and an avalanche of powdered snow fell on his face. Then big bright eyes, furry tails and speckled breasts began to hop and scurry around him.

"Are you here to frighten me off?"

The reply was delivered in a chirp, a squeak and a warble: "No…we are here to will you on."

Then his new friends hopped onto his shoulders and ran up and down his arms. It seemed that one little boy's selfless actions had inspired them to make a contribution.

Slowly, he took his left hand off the branch and put it into the bottom of his jacket pocket. Here, twisting and turning in a bed of mushy fungi and red winter berries was a handful of wriggling worms. The other pocket, packed with playing cards, tobacco, lollipops, coins and matches, remained buttoned up. A minute later, eager beaks and ferreting paws scooped up the wriggling worms and took them to the starving chicks.

He could have started to make his descent after that. Instead, he climbed a little higher. As he did so, he experienced what it was like to sit on the shoulders of a giant. Now he was floating above everyday life. Love had conquered his fear. It was this that would transform his life.

GETTING YOUR LIFE BACK

Intuition

The Tree Mystic

Sometimes he even imagined himself to be a tree, with a tingling desire to push through the soil, spring his leaves and open his buds. With time, the birds came to trust him. When he took a walk through the woods, they passed their messages to him. One day they shared one of their greatest secrets and wishes. Such was his love for them, he took it upon himself to give them a helping hand.

Now Sollie was an adult and a Tree Mystic; someone with the gift of turning your grey clouds blue. A man wearing a poncho and a childhood scar on his forehead. A spiritual healer in possession of benevolent brown eyes that framed good intentions as well as passionate desires. Wavy locks of hair wafted around him like sacred wind chimes. Bare feet and ankle bracelets, studded with coal black jewels, completed the mystical aura of a man that bellowed, laughed and whispered.

Today he was in a small backstreet London art gallery, studying a copy of an ancient painted scroll, commissioned by a Chinese emperor. It was a mesmerizing 12 metres in length and laid out on a large table. However, before he had completed his first circuit of the display, the art suddenly came to life; leaves from the trees began to fly towards him. When the spices and scents rolled up his nose, he had to sit down in the curator's chair. Within a minute his intuition was on fire and all his plans were in flames. Now it seemed there was only one option left; he had to head for China and see the original art.

He quit his job. His comfortable retirement plan disappeared... but so did his worries and anxiety. In walked his life...now he could find his purpose. Two weeks later he was looking out of the window on a very long coach journey; a voyage alongside yellow rivers that cut through towering gorges and endless seas of rice.

Sollie's visit to the Liaoning museum in Shenyang was the crowning glory of his two-week cultural tour of China. It was here that he saw the original scroll. When it was rolled out, he was shown how to examine it from a variety of perspectives. By the time he left the museum, the ancient piece of cloth had bewitched his mind. Now his plan was to return home and start his new life. However, as he was preparing to climb aboard the coach, someone sitting on a nearby green bench caught his eye. It was an old man dressed in an ancient, red silk robe. On his head was a funny black hat with side flaps. The old man's expression was clear; it said that he had something in his possession that he wanted to share.

The driver of the sky-blue tourist bus honked her horn. The old man on the bench said nothing; he just maintained his gaze. This was enough. Sollie made the decision to join him. Before the tour guide could shut the boot, he offloaded his suitcase. One minute later, he was sitting on the bench next to a man with 200-year-old eyes and no wrinkles. The coach pulled away without him.

> The intuitive mind is a sacred gift and the rational mind is a faithful servant, but we have created a society that honours the servant and has forgotten the gift.
>
> Albert Einstein

EMPEROR HUIZONG – ART NOT WAR

Fate - Ancestors - Changing the past

True Facts

Emperor Huizong was a painter and a calligrapher who ruled China during the golden age of the Song dynasty. He also set out the procedures for the most sophisticated tea ceremony in Chinese history.

After a minute of silence, the old man stood up slowly and shuffled towards an old oval door at the rear of the museum. Sollie followed. The door creaked open. Immediately he could see his breath in front of him. Then there was a pitter-patter of what sounded like dainty silk slippers running ahead. Sollie followed and soon found himself in the centre of a dimly-lit, dome-shaped room. In front of him, resting on an antique easel, was a hypnotic painting of Manchurian cranes landing on the roof of an imperial palace.

The old man pointed his finger towards it: "The painting is called *Auspicious Cranes*. It is the work of Emperor Huizong, a painter and a calligrapher who ruled China during the golden age of the Song dynasty. Most scholars know this. However, few know about his teachings on walking and talking with those that you have loved and lost. I am Fei Hung, a descendent of Emperor Huizong, and with your help, it is my intention to bring his work back to life."

A CALLING

Before Sollie could reply, around the perimeter of the room, a circle of red candles began to light up the darkness. It seemed that they were not alone; an old lady came into view. A large birthmark covered the right side of her face. She was dressed in a plain green kimono; pale and thin from years of washing. When all the candles were lit, she knelt down on a cushion and carefully rolled out a scroll on the floor.

EMPEROR HUIZONG

Sollie knelt down beside her: "What is the story detailed on the scroll?"

Instead of answering, she continued sewing. The old man spoke for her: "This is Ying Yue. She is a descendent of Li Yu.

True Facts

Li Yu was a great contributor to Chinese art who championed the importance of practice and patience. He published a manual of instruction for landscape painting called The Mustard Seed Garden.

"Ying Yue is working on your calling; a calling that also honours Li Yu's work. The details of your mission are explained on the scroll. She will also give you a copy of *The Mustard Seed Garden Manual.* There is a supplement at the back with instructions for planning a spiritual home and garden with shrines and idols."

Sollie leaned over to read the instructions. Then he turned towards Fei Hung: "It says that I need to recruit five helpers."

"Yes…human pollinators; they will include those who have been overlooked, those that feel they are not valued, people who can no longer trust and those searching for a sense of belonging. Some might be anxious and feel that they have lost their way. Others may just want to feel that they are loved. It is possible that some of them need a few kind words or a hug. However, some might need a hand to haul them out of a swamp. They might even need a miracle. When you arrive in India, lots of other people will help you too. You will find them sitting at the roadside, in cake shops, schools, art shops and prisons. This is what happens when your cause is good."

MAKE TEA NOT WAR

Thoughts

In the same way that the boiling of the water is the first stage of a heavenly-tasting cup of tea, you must know that meditation is the precursor towards a heavenly consciousness. It is this that wakes up your awareness and changes your thinking.

AUSPICIOUS CRANES

Whilst Ying Yue continued to sew, Fei Hung entertained Sollie with a completely different distraction; an ancient tea-making ceremony. It started with the banging of a small, bronze gong and the clinking of three china drinking bowls.

Then Fei Hung closed his eyes and took a bow before whispering, "I am performing the tea-making ceremony that follows the guidelines set out in the *Treatise on Tea* by Emperor Huizong himself."

After which, Fei Hung ladled boiling water into one of the ornate drinking bowls. While he was waiting for the bowl to warm, he offered Sollie a sugar fish: "This will sweeten you before you enjoy the bitterness of the tea. It is another reminder to love ourselves first, before taking on our challenges. It also asks us to, **Accept that life can be painful and joyus; sweet and sour at the same time.**"

When the old man was satisfied that the tea was the colour of white jade, he passed Sollie a bowl of the frothing, scented liquid: "Now drink this. Then ask yourself if Emperor Huizong was right to spend his time mastering the art of calligraphy, painting and setting out the rules for tea making. The alternative would have been to marshal his armies in preparation for war."

SOLLIE'S MISSION

Don't go searching for a purpose. Know that you are here for a purpose.

While continuing to sip the magical tea, Sollie studied a further section of the embroidery. The first task was underlined: 'Bring Emperor Huizong's ultimate dream to fruition – help make the poor rich.' The second sounded religious: 'Teach people how to find the God within them.' The third one addressed miracles: 'Pass on the secrets of eternal life. Show people how they can walk on water.' The fourth was beguiling: 'Teach people how to change the past and transform their problems and anxiety into joy.' Finally, 'Help people discover their purpose, in order that they can enjoy a meaningful life.'

BOOM! … Fei Hung regained Sollie's attention by banging down a lacquered, red box: "You will also need to put people on a spiritual path and prepare them for a calling. This is important, because in the future, one of your students will receive a calling like no other."

"What must I do when I leave China?"

"There are some people that you must meet in Siberia, France and Australia. After that, head for India. Which town or city you settle in is up to you. Just choose a place that needs a helping hand." Then Fei Hung rummaged in a wooden tea chest: "Take these, at some point they will help you." He handed Sollie a conch and what looked like a rolled-up dressing gown. Sollie bent down, placed the gown on the floor and rolled it out. In fact, it was a djellaba; a hooded head-to-toe coat favoured by men of the desert; a coat of many colours with vertical stripes of yellow, indigo, navy, blue and grey. "Please try it on."

Sollie pulled the djellaba over his head and shook the cloth to his feet. As he did, Fei Hung blew the candles out and followed Ying Yue towards the oval oak door. Sollie was worried that he was about to be left behind or ... possibly locked in: "Come back! I still don't know enough about what I am meant to do?"

"Just follow the rest of the instructions on the scroll, and try and avoid stepping on any ants when the elephants begin to swing their trunks."

"Are you sure that's everything?"

Fei Hung spun around in a manner that defied his years: "Oh, there is one more thing... The light that is on your side is painted on the cave walls, flying with the cranes and moving with the stars. However, there are also dark and ungodly forces working against you; wickedness lying dormant in and around the caves, circling with the albatross and poisoning leaders' minds. These ignoble forces do not want you to succeed with your mission or spiritual teachings, for fear of losing their power and riches.

"Therefore, your journey will be full of perils, risks and sorrow. Know that your enemies will try and seduce, infiltrate and deceive you. Along the way, they will carry out acts to weaken your resolve and strike woe and misfortune on those that you care for. Be careful who you kiss and enter into partnerships with. Do not become distracted with other causes. Never let your guard down... even when you assume you have passed the finishing line. Know that the fortunes and happiness of many rest upon your shoulders. If you fail, things will be worse than they were before you started. Those that could have been saved will die. Innocent souls will commit the foulest of crimes, and hopes of a better future for the poor and the maligned will be incinerated. It will be as if every bird has fallen from the sky and every tree has uprooted... the darkness will take precedence over the light."

ARRIVING IN INDIA

Visions - Needs

Sollie St-Martin dawdled through the customs doors at Delhi airport. He was met by a sea of expectant faces and jarring colour. His name was smudged in crimson lipstick on an old soap powder box. Sollie paused for a moment to suck in the full splendour of his greeter's appearance. He wore an orange and yellow bandana and a vivid orange linen kurta. It was complimented by a white goatee beard. He certainly didn't resemble the Indian taxi drivers he had seen in London.

"It is a pleasure to meet you Mr Sollie. I am Souvik, please follow me, I will take you to Bhopal."

Then Sollie saw the taxi. Souvik pretended not to see his apprehension: "Its age, sir, is testament to its durability and powers of recovery." Then some helpers appeared. They secured Sollie's bags on to the roof of the car and attached an old wooden trailer to the back.

"What is that?"

Souvik lifted up the trailer's lid so that Sollie could examine its contents. Scattered on the floor of the trailer were lots of small, shiny metal parts and a wheel. "Those, sir, are the missing parts of an incredible vehicle fit for a king to make a royal entrance."

Sollie stared at Souvik and waited for an explanation.

"You pay so little money, sir. I need more than one paymaster to make my journey worthwhile."

Sollie accepted this; he had wondered how the taxi fare could be so unfathomably cheap for a 14-hour trip.

True Facts

Bhopal is just like many people; it is stuck with a bad name. The Union Carbide chemical leak in 1984 attacked the livers, lungs and kidneys of the city's inhabitants and left 25,000 dead in the world's worst industrial accident. A further 120,000 suffered from ailments, including blindness, birth defects and brain damage.

However, it is also a city of lakes, hills and maharajahs. There are ancient caves and a huge national park teeming with wildlife and rare birds. Its heritage is also vast. There are extraordinary pilgrimage trails, an old walled city and magnificent mosques and temples. Its greatness, its name and its history descend from a legend and a great 11th century ruler - King Bhoj. In fact, Bhopal possesses everything that any city aspiring to be a kingdom would want.

Sollie was renting a bungalow until he could find some suitable land and buildings to rent. It was located in the Shyamalan hills overlooking Bhopal's two great lakes; waters that had diminished in size significantly after a year of drought. Also waiting here for him was a large copy of Emperor Huizong's painting, *Auspicious Cranes*. The taxi pulled to a halt outside the real estate office and Sollie handed the taxi fare over to Souvik: "Can you wait for me? I may need another taxi ride."

VOLUNTEERS APPLICATION

Visions - Madness - CVs - Difficult pasts - Success - Recruitment - Self-love

"He sees the mermaid's head but not the dragon's tail."
Emerson

In his first real job, Sollie worked alongside Gabriel St-Martin, a man of Caribbean descent with a mop of unruly hair. They shared an unusual surname but little else, except the desire to help those in need. Gabriel was logical and consistent. Sollie was saintly but mischievous.

Within a week of arriving in Bhopal, Sollie invited Gabriel to come and see his venture. Gabriel looked over Sollie's shoulder at the drawings and papers scattered on the table: "What exactly is the vision?"

"An opportunity for people to get their lives back. A place where people can find out who they really are. Freedom from approval, striving and trying to become something."

"What about your gambling, risk taking and womanising?"

"I have given those up."

"Come on. You are not happy unless you are taking risks and cavorting."

"Trust me. I am focused on this mission."

"You have never been focused on anything Sollie."

Sollie paused for a moment before deciding that it was probably not a good idea to mention Fei Hung's warning about the perils of being distracted.

"Do you still intend to have a thousand wives?"

"Yes. I am working on a plan to finance them."

"Why? Such a desire will be the ruin of you, mark my words."

"They will give me comfort. I can't bear the thought of being left alone again, and I would be surprised if they all leave me."

"Don't bet on it. You get duped easily. You have a history of choosing the wrong type of women. Additionally, you constantly give people second chances… and they always let you down. Now tell me, why did you choose to come to Bhopal, a place with such a tragic history?"

"I chose Bhopal because, **I would like to demonstrate that any difficult past can be transformed into an incredible future.**"

"What type of helpers do you need?"

"People who can help us move along a spiritual path: knitters, gardeners, nature lovers, teachers, yoga instructors, storytellers, artists and dancers."

"Tell me Sollie, what type of person do you think might apply to work in a snake-infested forest, without pay, for a mission yet to be determined?"

"You came Gabriel. I have no doubt many others will apply too. There are a lot of crazy people out there."

"Then make sure that you take references… Now, did your master tell you what will happen if your mission fails?"

"He did. It is not something that I want to think about."

Before they left for a break, Gabriel picked up a conch that was sitting on the table. He put it to his lips and blew. No sound came out. "Sollie, can you blow this thing?"

Sollie put the conch to his lips and woke up Bhopal. He was good at things like that; he wasn't so good at taking advice or following procedures.

BRUNO THE PROPAGATOR

Talking plants - Mental health - Diet - Love

> The most painful love is not the one that you had and lost, but the one that never existed. The one that never germinated; like a dry seed sitting in a box. A love denied to you as a child, which makes you fearful of searching for it as an adult.

With his mop of dark, curly hair, bark-rough hands and colossal frame, Bruno had the appearance of a mighty oak tree in bloom. A peaceful but troubled

BHOPAL LAKES

soul, he was a man who moved around at wheelbarrow pace. He had left Italy to work as a chef in a sleepy little English village. However, now he was retired from the kitchen. This was not because he was old; it was because he could no longer kill the things that he loved - vegetables, particularly tomatoes. He was a chef who used to cross himself every time he chopped a courgette. A cook who cried every time he put a tomato in the pan. So instead of cooking them, he decided that he would find a way that he could devote his life to them. One might think that this was strange behaviour, but it didn't seem that way to Bruno. For here was a man that had neither heard the words of love or felt its arms around him.

Bruno also had a secret. He had known for a long time that his plants listened to him when he spoke. Now he had discovered something life-changing; a way for his plants to talk to him. This was exciting but also unsettling. He wondered if he had turned insane. Wasn't that what the kitchen staff had said when he returned unused vegetables back into the soil each night? He reasoned that whilst a vegetable might not be fazed about being buried alive, it surely would not be happy about the thought of being cooked alive.

Bruno's baritone voice, earthy fragrance and aubergine-coloured cheeks had not escaped the attention of his neighbour, Miss Heather Blythe. When she invited him for Sunday lunch, he wrongly assumed that she was interested in his tomatoes. Miss Blythe had other intentions. The pleasantries didn't last long… When the cooking pot lid was lifted, it revealed a dish of mixed vegetables bubbling in a creamy sauce. Bruno duly fainted and had to be resuscitated with a tall glass of water. After recovering, he made it clear that he would not be seeing her again.

In his application letter, Bruno told Sollie that Miss Blythe didn't like rejection. He said that she dug up his potatoes and strangled his tomatoes. After that, she recorded him talking to his plants, embellished the evidence and reported him to the authorities. "Before the nightjar had even started to sing, a large windowless van pulled up outside my cottage. They sectioned me for my own good."

* * *

Was Bruno mad? Possibly… his mother had experienced severe mental health problems. However, it was not clear if his unusual thoughts and behaviour were the result of a chaotic upbringing or the inheritance of his mother's illness. It was whilst Bruno was waiting to see the psychiatrist during his imprisonment that he discovered a small advertisement in a magazine.

Human pollinators wanted - Get muddy and breathless
Join us as a volunteer in India and get your life back

He escaped from the mental hospital in the back of the baker's van a week later. Now he would have to step out of the shadows, share small talk and join in – all things that would normally drain the colour from his cheeks. However, this was insignificant when compared with his real fear; that one day his mother's demons would completely engulf him.

TOM THE BEEKEEPER

Belonging - Self Sabotage - Relationships - Loneliness
Happiness - Career - Rejection - Pasts

We need meaning in our life. However, what we yearn for more than anything else is human connection and to feel that we are loved.

Tom the beekeeper was a tall, pale and wiry Canadian. He dressed in a way that suggested he had never been shown how; trouser lengths too short, t-shirts too baggy, hair cropped with gardening shears. However, he did have listening ears and a shoulder built for resting on. And, he could dance wildly and make everyone laugh… if he was drunk. After which, he could be embarrassing and uncouth.

At the age of nine, Tom had been sent to live with his grandmother in Scotland by the couple who no longer wanted him. Now he was an adult, living alone amongst the heathery hills but desperate for human connection and love. However, this was unlikely to happen; he sabotaged any friendships that dared to point towards his heart. He needed a new beginning but was wedged in a painful past.

Plagues come in multitudes - don't they? Tom opened a letter that made him swallow a plum stone. A month after his grandmother had passed, he was informed that the landowner of his farm had also died. The new owners intended to sell the farm and the cottage that Tom lived in. Tom had never thought to ask for a contract. No one had ever told him that there was no such thing as security. He had no idea what to do next. Even if he did, he wasn't very good at change. In fact, the seat of his trousers was frayed with indecision.

Tom was assisted on the farm by Rhona. When Rhona heard Tom's news, she tried to help him. On the first night this included some toffee pudding and a gardening magazine. On the 33rd page of that gardener's magazine, an advert thickened his custard.

Human pollinators wanted - Get muddy and breathless
Join us as a volunteer in India and get your life back

After that, Tom poured a very large glass of whisky into his tumbler ... and then another.

LING THE ADMIN ASSISTANT

Identity - Belonging - Careers - Yoga - Opportunities

Monticello, New York isn't the first place that springs to mind when one thinks of angels. However, if angels do exist, they probably look like Ling - sweet and dreamy and tiny enough to fit on the end of your pencil. Those close to her knew that the colour of her headband on her short, dark hair usually matched her mood. Those seduced by her sweetness often mistakenly interpreted her kind nature and little hops for a timid bird. However, Ling was also ambitious. She would usually move on quickly, if she outgrew someone or something. On occasions, she could also peck and stamp her tiny feet.

Ling's birthplace was Kaifeng, an ancient Chinese city that had been prosperous during the Northern Song dynasty. As a little girl, she had loved painting and craft work. However, when her parents divorced and her mother moved to the U.S., her passion was buried. Art was substituted for extra English lessons; pleasure was substituted with pain. This left her feeling as if someone had uprooted her without taking the care to pat the soil down when they had re-potted her.

Surprisingly, despite her alluring looks, Ling had never been kissed. Not because she wasn't desirable but because she didn't see herself as so. Her mother was responsible for that; eroding her confidence and lowering her expectations. During the day, Ling reluctantly worked as an office admin assistant. In the evenings she worked as a part-time yoga instructor. It was in the latter job that she came to life.

Things changed at Christmas. On her last day at work, she picked up a gardening magazine that had been left on the subway and took it home with her. Then, on a crisp and snowy Christmas morning, she and her mother opened their presents. The gifts that Ling received from her mother each year were very similar; something that would conceal her natural beauty. This year it was matching green woolly hat and gloves, complimented by some brown, woolly winter leggings.

"Try them on."

Ling did as her mother asked and paraded in front of the mirror. She shrieked, "Oh my God, I look like a stick insect with a green head."

After lunch Ling began to read her magazine. It was here that a little advert at the foot of the page suddenly started to glow.

Human pollinators wanted - Get muddy and breathless
Join us as a volunteer in India and get your life back

Ling touched her brown leggings and pulled the green hat over her head. Within an hour, she had taken them off and thrown them into the dirty washing basket. Two minutes after that, she was in the bath scrubbing the old Ling away. By the time she stepped out of the bath and wrapped herself in a soft, fluffy towel, she felt emboldened. The full-length bathroom mirror was in front of her. She stuck out a tiny tongue and touched the cold glass. Now it was time to practise her proclamation: "Mother, I am going away for a while!"

Then every day for the next two weeks, **Ling practised her speech and victory in her mind's eye**... She knew that this was a critical part of the 'Formula for Success'.

Two weeks later, Ling was accepted. She put a red headband on and confronted her mother: "I am going to live in India. I would like to find out 'who I am' and find my purpose. I want to improve my light, my rhythm and my beat."

Now the little bird was about to jump off the fence post.

APOLLINE THE TEACHER

Overlooked - Anxiety - Valued - Fate - Discipline

The school bell rang and the children ran for the door. A young lady with velvet eyebrows called after them in a clear, audible voice: "Remember, practise, practise, practise." Apolline Rippe was an unhappy, married schoolteacher, with easy tears, living in a riverside village in Bergerac, France. She wore tousled hair, plain sneakers and no makeup. The soft, slender and beautifully manicured hands suggested she was musical. Only the thinnest of nose rings hinted at rebellion. As a child, she believed that her sisters received all the attention and that she was overlooked. Consequently, her early years had been spent looking for praise and displays of affection. When this was unrequited, she settled on the pursuit of perfectionism and the hunt for a loving father figure. The former had given her good grades and anxiety. The latter meant that she was good at flirting but always searching. Apolline also had a dream; to put her apostrophes away. She wanted to be a storyteller and a dance teacher… she wanted to flutter.

* * *

Apolline studied her new term timetable for the first time. There were some changes; a smidgeon more French grammar to teach but considerably less English. On Monday morning she had no lesson at all. Now there was no need to take the 7am early train to her school at Sarlat-la-Caneda a few miles further down the Dordogne river.

On the later 12pm noon train, things were different. There were rows of empty seats and unobscured windows. The conductor smiled, and the station master's whistle could be heard. On the opposite side of the aisle sat an elderly lady with rose-petal skin; someone clearly still in love with the idea of beauty. The green ribbon on her floppy hat matched the colour of the over-sized buttons on her jacket. The blue, jewelled broach suggested intrigue. Despite the fact that the lady had numerous bags, she kept them packed tidily around her feet and off the other seats. Very quickly the seats around the lady were filled. Apolline enjoyed the pleasure of stretching her legs.

LASCAUX – FRANCE

True Facts

In 1940 Marcel Ravidat discovered one of France's greatest treasures - the Lascaux cave paintings. Like the Bhopal rock shelters in India and the Kakadu caves in Eastern Australia, the 17,000-year-old cave art is now a UNESCO World Heritage Site. Later, a few miles away, at the beautiful village of Les Eyzies, further caves were discovered.

The Lascaux caves were a place of worship and sacrifice. The cave paintings incorporate prehistoric star charts of the night sky. One shows three bright stars known as the 'summer triangle'. One of the most unusual cave paintings is a bird on a stick known as *The Birdman of Lascaux*. In 1963 the French government said that it was alarmed by signs of mould and crystals on the paintings. It shut the caves to the public and introduced extensive security measures to prevent any entry. At great expense, it constructed numerous replica visitor caves. It continues to do so, with the latest opening in 2016.

When you leave Lascaux and Les Eyzies and head west along the Dordogne river towards Bordeaux, there is one of the largest crane migration points in Europe. Here, a monumental gathering of cranes perform one of the most mysterious ritualistic bird dances the world has ever seen.

APOLLINE MEETS OLIVIA

Careers - Discipline - Inspiration - Action

The following Monday, Apolline took the same 12pm train. The elderly lady was sitting in the carriage again. As before, she sat upright and kept the table and seat by her side free of any baggage. Her carriage felt warm and velvety, and Apolline was unable to resist sitting down opposite her.

The lady smiled and her eyes sparkled: "Hello I am Olivia. I live in Lamonzie-St-Martin and mount the train at the stop before you."

Apolline was immediately captivated by what she assumed was a meadow-flowered English accent: "Hello. I am Apolline."

"Tell me where you go every Monday Apolline?"

Apolline lowered her eyes, touched by the fact that she had been noticed: "School. I am a teacher. What do you do?"

"I am the curator for the famous caves of Montignac, Les Eyzies and Lascaux. Do you know anything about them?"

"I went on a canoeing trip to Les Eyzies when I was a child. We stopped off at the nearby Lascaux caves on the way. The ones that we visited were reconstructions. I can remember my father saying it was strange that the government had spent such a vast sum of money replicating the originals."

"Not really strange; they are, after all, a national treasure. Now tell me, what subjects do you teach?"

Suddenly, Apolline felt very inadequate and her voice became faint: "French, English and sometimes the violin and cello." Then she blushed, before attempting to move the focus away from herself: "How long have you been speaking French?"

Olivia paused to blow her nose on a handkerchief embroidered with a long-legged bird. Then she carefully folded and gently pressed the edges in a manner that suggested she cared for all the fragile things in the world: "Fifty-seven years. I came here from Australia at the age of 20."

"Do you speak any other languages?"

"I recently started to learn how to teach deaf and blind children. I subscribe to the view that it is never too late to start anything and that every disciplined action will be rewarded at some time in the future."

"Why did you want to learn how to teach deaf and blind children?"

"I wanted to develop my communication skills. When the day arrives for me to tell the world that I have something very important to say, I will not say it with words. I will say it with an action. One that I hope will inspire you too."

STATEMENTS OF INTENT

Who am I - Happiness - Sadness - Beliefs - Conditioning - God - Salvation

The aim is to find paradise here on earth

On the train the following week, Olivia dropped some apple-green-coloured papers in the aisle. Apolline leant over and picked the papers up.

D706
A 89
Clermont Fd
SARLAT
ST CYPRIEN
MONTIGNAC
TERRASSON
Pôle International
de la Préhistoire
Centre d'accueil
LES EYZIES DE TAYAC
LASCAUX

LASCAUX

"Oh, thank you Apolline. It's my inventory."

"An inventory? Are you moving house?"

"Oh no. It's my personal inventory and a statement of intent."

Apolline twitched her nose. Olivia realized that she needed to expand: "It's just a few columns and lists. There are three pages. The first is to help me discover who I am. The second is about discovering what I was born to do. The third is to help me find joy."

"What about what makes you sad?"

"Oh, you don't need that one. **Fill your life with light and the darkness can't exist**."

Apolline sat up and took on the alertness of a disturbed deer in the forest.

"How do you discover who you are?"

"Simple. First you scrub and then you polish. You put on the table all the beliefs that your teachers, friends and parents conditioned you with. Then you scrub them off."

Olivia peered down her glasses at Apolline: "Then you go inside yourself; **On a journey that focuses on the development of your spiritual being.**"

"Will I find God on this journey?"

"The goal is not to find God; the goal is to find yourself and the God within."

"Will I also find salvation?"

"**The aim is not to find salvation. The aim is to find paradise here on earth**."

That was a lot to take in. Apolline decided to change the subject to something that she was a little more familiar with; vocations.

A CALLING

Passions - Careers - Happiness - Skills - Roles
Communism - Risk - Fear - Rejection

If you want to power yourself to a destination, use will power, your experiences and logic. It is like travelling on a boat with an engine. Or you can travel to your destiny on a voyage of discovery by sailboat. The former leaves whenever you want, the latter dictates that you must wait for the wind.

"How do I find a career that will make me happy?"

"Make your skills available to something higher than your own needs. Some call this a calling or a meaningful life."

"Is it just a matter of waiting and hoping after that?"

"Absolutely not. This is not where you just light a candle and hope. This is where you polish and practise your skills so that you are in a state of readiness."

"A calling sounds ominous. Is it dangerous?"

"No, for you must not take unnecessary risks with your life. **The only risks that you must take are emotional risks, like overcoming the fear of failure and the fear of rejection**."

"Will a calling prevent me from enjoying a normal life?"

"Not at all. It will consider your circumstances and your measure. Karl Marx said, 'From each, according to their abilities, to each, according to their needs.' He may have been referring to communism, but he could have been referring to a calling. No one will be expected to abandon their families. Don't think of a calling as something that will require you to hold the world on your shoulders. Just think contribution; it doesn't matter if it is a small stream or a large river."

Apolline let out a little sigh.

"Why are you sighing?"

"A meaningful life sounds wonderful. However, I don't think that it is for me; I'm just a grammar school teacher. It seems that I'm destined to be no more than a comma in someone else's story."

"Apolline, our maker hasn't designed life so that a few enjoy incredible things and the rest of us live in the shallows. Life is designed so that we can all play a part in an incredible story. Whether we are the principal player or a supporting role is not important. Of course, if you were the one chosen to lead, others would be chosen to support you."

Such was the serious tone of Olivia's statement that it made Apolline laugh nervously.

Somewhere in an ancient forest a tiny beetle is breaking down some old wood. Their contribution, however small, matters... ultimately it can save the world. You are no different, your contribution matters too.

THE PURPLE BOOK

Creating space - Goals - Surrender - Vessels - Mystery - Humility - Hobbies

Take the time to make sense of your wings. Let yourself be pulled by the moon and warmed by the sun. Look to swish like a fish, nap like a cat and swoop like a bird.

"What is the purple book for? Is it another inventory?"

"Oh no. This is something different. It is my book entitled, *Empty Spaces and New Beginnings*."

She handed the book over to Apolline, who flicked through it.

"It is just four empty pages. Haven't you started it yet?"

"Actually, it is complete. The empty pages are there to remind myself to empty my mind, throw away my goals and build more free time and space into my life."

"How can you be satisfied if you do not pursue goals?"

"**If you pursue goals, you will always be looking outside of yourself for happiness and joy.** Try and make sense of the wings that you have been given instead."

"How do I empty my mind?"

Zen masters say, **'You must empty your cup and put aside your experience, knowledge and egotistical mind.'** This is because, on matters of importance, these things will limit you. However, it is not enough to empty your cup; you must surrender and become a vessel. **Surrendering means putting your own desires and goals aside and making yourself available to God. Now God works through you and with you. Together you carry out his work.** This way, something higher pours the tea. Now something pure and wonderful can flow through you; this will be your calling." Then Olivia reached down into her bag and passed Apolline a little verse to read.

SPACE AND TIME

How easy is it to fill your day with tasks in the hope that you will achieve your goals? How easy is it for your goals to steal your life? For your ambition to fill you with anxiety and stress instead of joy? What would happen if you set out to do less instead of more? Created space instead of ideas? Set aside time for mystery to visit you, instead of pursuing your desires?

Know that the forest only comes to life when you have gone to bed. Only when you step out of the space do the owls step in and begin to hoot. Only then do the deer walk fearlessly through the bracken and the field mice come out to play. It is in the space that the wild mushrooms appear in the morning and the dew comes on the grass… Only in the space can mystery do its work.

"If you follow this advice, you will have plenty of time for hobbies and the sweet and lighter things in life."

"Like what?"

"My favourite hobby is making dolls' houses."

"Oh, that sounds fun."

"It is not meant to be fun; it is to make you humble and childlike. For it is this that will bring you closer to God."

Then Olivia reached for her bag and pulled out a box of chocolates: "The light and sweet moments that I enjoy most are eating these. Please take one."

"You only have two left."

"Don't worry. I only ever buy boxes with two trays. The bottom layer is all for me, it represents the secret and mysterious layers of my life. If there is no mystery and no secrets, surely there is no excitement?"

Olivia watched Apolline choose her chocolate and wondered how well their bonding was progressing … for the success of their friendship was beyond important.

Adult problems can be removed with childlike behaviour.

HANDS, HEARTS AND MINDS

Schooling - Careers - Self-development - Sabbaticals - Caring

Compassion - Detached - Desensitized - Early love - Success

The train stopped at the next station for five minutes, allowing Olivia enough time to prepare for her next lesson: "Are you happy being a teacher?"

Apolline looked down: "No, but I'm not sure that I am ready to empty my cup."

“Then perhaps you should take some time out from your teaching job. Maybe it is time for a sabbatical and some self-development. Maybe it is time to discover who you are.” Olivia peered over her glasses to gauge Apolline’s reaction.

Apolline laid her palms down flat on the carriage table: “What type of self-development?”

“**Spiritual development… so that you can teach using your heart, body, mind and spirit.**”

Apolline looked at her arms and hands for a moment: “In truth I am tired of standing in front of a class. I would love to teach dance and write stories.”

“**You could do more, if you attach your heart to your hands**. You could heal, soothe and rescue, as well as performing other miraculous acts.”

“I think that I am too detached and desensitized for the caring professions. Maybe it’s because I didn’t experience love as a child. Compassion is not a behaviour that was passed down to me.”

“Compassion does not have to be passed down. It can be discovered. **Compassion is a decision to work in union with your higher self and find the God within**.”

“Then perhaps you should tell me what type of miraculous acts?”

“Show other people how to find their wings and teach them how to fly. Is that something that you might be interested in?”

The lesson was over. Every Monday after that, Olivia taught Apolline something new. It was as if she was preparing her for a great journey. One day, after stepping off the train at St. Cyprien, she left an English gardening magazine on the train table. Apolline picked it up and started to read it, not because she knew anything about gardening; but because it was in English. A slow smile emerged as Apolline recalled Olivia telling her, **At some point in the future, every disciplined act is rewarded.** This appeared to be true; today she was utilising English skills learnt when sacrificing her youth. Then, on page 33 of Olivia’s gardening magazine, a small advert jumped up and begged her to take notice. One that could only be seen and understood because she had studied English for so many years.

Human pollinators wanted - Get muddy and breathless

Join us as a volunteer in India and get your life back

* * *

Apolline's application was successful. She decided to take some time out in her bedroom to consider the offer. Like Ling, she confronted the mirror: 'Is this as good as it gets?' The mirror didn't answer. This was good; it informed Apolline that things needed to change. **Change, she reasoned, would require new thinking, decisions and actions**... and maybe a heaped spoonful of courage.

Then she shouted out a proclamation: "Apolline Rippe, it's time to stop surviving. It's time to start living!" Her eyes met the mirror in a standoff. '**Now I need to take some action that will mean there is no turning back!**' The mirror agreed with her... In the evening she told her husband that she was leaving. Later, she shared her successful application with Olivia.

"Apolline, will you travel to India with your husband?"

"No."

"Please don't go alone; at least take an umbrella. I would never go anywhere without one. I would take one to my own funeral if I could."

In Asia people carry an umbrella to protect them from the sun. In Europe they use one to protect them from the rain. Rich and poor might have different problems but most have the same worries.

SLUGS AND SNAILS

Projects - Ego - Possessions - Attachment - Purpose
Missions - Vessels - Freedom - Callings

Sollie never imagined himself completing all his tasks. In his vision, later down the line, someone else would take over. There was even a mantra at the top of his book for such a strategy: **'Think incompletion. Leave before you finish. Pass the baton... Leave space for other people to add their brush strokes.'**

As he had expected, there were hundreds of applications for the job of pollinator. However, only four had been selected. He reminded himself of some of the key things that he had looked out for: 'A beekeeper, a language teacher, a gardener, an artist, a yoga teacher and someone who is Chinese... I will also need to recruit a local administrator who can organise me.'

Satisfied with his recruitment, Sollie lay on his bed and put some calming music on. Now it was time for some uplifting thoughts before he closed his eyes. A snail came to mind... 'What is the difference between a slug and a snail?' he imagined someone asking him.

'They are very different. The slug represents someone who has made themselves available to a cause greater than their own. Now it has purpose but not its own purpose. This makes its shell and possessions fall away. Now it is light. It can take rests and holidays, as well as giving attention to other important things. When it goes to bed at night, it is free to lie on its back and marvel at the twinkling stars.

'However, I do appreciate that many people prefer snails to slugs; their shell gives them the appearance of being a little cuddlier. They often represent freedom because they can take their house with them on their back. However, all is not as it seems; the snail becomes attached to its possessions, lovers, learning and skills, as much as it does to its house. Although in theory the snail is free to roam, in truth it is weighed down by its possessions and its ego. Everywhere it goes, they must go too. There is no time to twirl the buttercups. Unlike the slug, it is unable to lie on its back and enjoy the twinkling lights.'

APPOLINE ARRIVES IN INDIA

Destiny - Purpose

Apolline wanted a period of reflection and some time to think about her destiny. She decided to arrive in India a few days before the official rendezvous. Happy and whimsical, she walked out of the air-conditioned airport and quickly made her first error; to assume that now she was full of good intentions, everyone else was too… She asked the taxi driver to take her to a 'reasonably-priced hotel'.

Room 15 was at the end of a dark, narrow passage. She brushed past the grubby mattresses resting against the corridor walls and let out a little shudder... The bedroom was even darker. Apolline opened the door to the bathroom. The blue, glazed wall tiles were cracked and dirty. The toilet was a hole in the ground. There was another big hole in the wall above the sink. However, she needed to wash and turned the sink tap on. As she did, a shadow of fright slithered down her back. Something was behind her.

CLAP! A loud slap rang out. Then several more. Her heart pounded. She turned around slowly… there was nothing to be seen. CLAP! Suddenly, the venomous head and torso of a huge, scaly white lizard with bloodshot eyes appeared. It hissed and stared at her menacingly. CLAP! CLAP! Then, from a hole around the door frame, the remainder of its body forced its way out. Screaming wasn't working. Nothing came out. Now the lizard had completely barred her exit. HISS! She tried to scream again. Still no sound. There was no choice but to step back. Looking for something to defend her, Apolline accidentally put her hand in the dark hole by the sink. This scream did work; it was so loud that a succession of bedroom doors opened.

By the time that the rescue party arrived, Apolline had fainted and lay crumpled on the dirty bathroom floor. When she regained consciousness, her head was in the lap of a tiny chef. A curious crowd looked on. Apolline pushed everyone away and picked up her rucksack. Then she ran and ran, not daring to look back.

THE PRICE OF HAPPINESS

Three hours later Apolline did what the poor can't; she bought her way out of her horror and moved into the luxury Sunny Gardens Hotel. The bedroom was on the ground floor, and the full-length windows opened onto a vast lawn. This time the bathroom was opulent. After showering, she settled down with fresh linen and soft pillows.

The morning brought a balcony breakfast of freshly-squeezed orange juice, sunshine and almond cakes. Immediately, her worries began to retreat. Now it was possible to work on her future plans: 'I just want to be happy.' However, before she could ask how, three ladies dressed in green and blue saris appeared. They swept the hotel steps and then the leaves from the lawn in front of her balcony. As they swept, they laughed and made merriment as if they were schoolchildren. 'I wonder how much money they earn? What is the price of their happiness?' Then it dawned on her… 'They have it. The leaf sweepers have the happiness that I want.'

LEAF SWEEPING

Unlearning - Attachments - Surrender - Downsizing

Joy - Desires - Staring - Being mindful - Fun

When you become older, there are certain things that you must unlearn. There are other things that you must learn again, like having fun.

Apolline picked up her papers and decided to take a leaf out of Olivia's book and produce a little inventory. She wrote a heading… What Makes Me Happy? Then she mused, 'Olivia told me that, **Happiness is found within, through an inner search.**' Apolline scratched her head with her pencil; she wasn't quite sure what that meant.

The next trawl searched her memories for joy and laughter. 'What do I do for fun? This is what the children in the school playground ask each other.' It was this that made her realise that something in her life was missing. 'Now, as I recall, the next page is about my attachments; identifying what I need to stop clinging to.' Then she remembered what Olivia had told her about downsizing: 'Downsizing is not about moving into a smaller house with one less bedroom. Downsizing is about permitting your desires and attachments to fall away. However, **Don't try and give up your desires and possessions with willpower; they will fall away naturally after you have surrendered and made the decision to work in partnership with God.**'

Apolline wasn't sure what that meant either. 'Maybe I should stop thinking and practise being mindful instead.' This decision proved to be transformative. She made the tea very slowly. A sugar cube was placed on the teaspoon. Her eyes switched from watching to staring, until the sugar had dissolved. Her ears stood to attention as the teaspoon clinked the china cup. There were no mouthfuls; only sips. The tongue tasted. The nose sniffed. Only when her cup was empty did she allow herself to gaze across the lawn and observe the leaf sweepers again. This time something clicked. Now Apolline understood their majesty; **They had gone beyond themselves… they were no longer observers; now they were amongst the observed.**

To transform yourself from being an observer to being observed, you might need to do something significant. However, what is significant might be no more than sweeping the leaves.

LEAF SWEEPING

A NATURE LOVER

Identity - Direction - Problems - Travel - Migration - Sacred relationships

Ling had learnt that if you are not careful, other people board up your windows and pretend that there is nothing out there to see. However, now she had started to ask life-changing questions like: 'Why not? What if? Who says?'

She was also searching for someone who could switch her bedroom lights on. However, it is fair to say that the man sitting next to her at Delhi's departure lounge wasn't what she had in mind... He looked like an ancient butterfly catcher, complete with cream linen suit. A straw hat with pink ribbon cemented the image whilst complementing his white, curly hair, bushy eyebrows and ruddy cheeks. She noted he took off his hat when he was listening and put it back on again when he had something to say.

"My name is Hubert. I am from Norfolk in England." Then he pulled out a handkerchief and sneezed in a way that hinted he might be late and forgetful.

"Hi. My name is Ling."

After that there was a silent pause. For the first time in her life, Ling didn't know where to say that she was from... 'Am I Chinese, or am I American?' she asked herself.

Hubert rescued her in the most agreeable manner: "Don't worry Ling. Where you come from is not important. All that you need to know is who you are."

"Why are you heading for Bhopal?"

"I am recording bird migrations. This year's normal migratory patterns have gone askew. Right across the world, birds are visiting places that they have never been to before. Bhopal is the epicentre of these strange migrations. That is why I am heading there."

"Are you a nature lover?"

He clasped his hands in front of him and looked upwards: "It depends what you mean. Lots of people call themselves 'a nature lover'. They often mean that they like to go to the beach or walk in the forest. However, that does not make them a lover. Lovers give and take. They pine. They care. They protect. They take action. They put themselves on the line. I like to call myself a 'nature lover', and I pine. I love and live for birds."

At which point Ling immediately took a liking to Hubert and moved her chair forward: "Hubert, do you think that it is necessary to travel great distances to find what you want?"

"In my job, I travel because I am following my passion. I am not running away from anything. I am merely moving towards joy. However, if I was moving away from something because I was unhappy, then I honestly believe that's wrong. Move away before your problem is fixed and it travels with you in your suitcase. Fix it first. Then decide if you still want to travel. Only ever move towards joy. **Never run away from pain, unless you are travelling to a place of healing.**"

"What makes you say that?"

"Simple, it is what the birds do. They always migrate towards a place where things are better."

"Now I have moved from the city, I hope to become a nature lover too. What do you recommend that I do?"

Hubert gave a little quiver of emotion; his Adam's apple jolted, then he delivered the type of sermon that only a passionate lover could.

SACRED RELATIONSHIPS

You treat nature the same as anything else that you love deeply and unconditionally. You watch it grow and listen out for those things that may harm or help it. You identify yourself as being its carer and protector. You celebrate its birthdays and look forward to its arrivals. You cheer and will it on. You fill with sadness when it is threatened. You grieve when it is hurt and share its joy and its disappointments. You forsake your comforts for its well-being. You sacrifice and you make do. You become stubborn. You get up in the middle of the night and wait outside in the rain for it to come home safely. Most importantly, you make your relationship with nature sacred. Then you realise that you are sacred too."

THE FIRST GOOD OFFER

In Bhopal Sollie advertised for a land parcel with accommodation. He soon received a most enthusiastic call from a man called Durga. Everything that Sollie inquired about seemed to be on Durga's list and so they agreed to meet at a nearby truck stop.

Durga arrived on a motorbike with a garland of flowers wrapped around the handlebars. He was a fidgety little man with a roguish laugh, in need of some shampoo, dentistry and haberdashery. However, Sollie was only interested in what he had to rent. Durga quickly pulled out a rough sketch map of the land and laid it out on an empty oil drum. Sollie inspected the drawing. It matched his criteria perfectly: rural location, a main house, lots of outbuildings to develop and an unexpected bonus… a forest.

"Amazing! This has everything that I want. Is a 20-year lease possible?"

Durga slowly folded the map away: "Yes!"

They quickly agreed upon a price.

"Do you have a lawyer Mr Sollie?"

"Not yet."

"Leave that with me. I will find you the best conveyancing lawyer in the state. I will take you to see him and the property on my motorbike tomorrow."

Durga was due to meet him at 7am. He was late. It was 9.30am by the time they approached the land. They turned a sharp corner and a large lake appeared in front of them. In the middle of the lake was a large, white palace.

"Oh my, is that it?"

"Not exactly Mr Sollie. That is your neighbour's dwelling. It is the home of the incredibly rich Parminder, an angry man that they call the Honey Badger. A man who used his great wealth to purchase a royal bride."

FIT FOR A MAHARAJA

They drove a little further. Then Durga pulled up in a plume of dust and turned the engine off: "Let me show you the land borders."

They walked through jungle-green-coloured grasses until they reached the lake that overlooked Parminder's palatial dwelling. Then Sollie craned his neck, saw the clincher and sighed, "Wow, coconut trees. They were always in my dreams."

"Permit me to show you the main house Mr Sollie."

The whitewashed walls and exterior were crumbling. The rickety, red-tiled roof had bowed, and the lawn had ceased praying for water. However, Sollie looked beyond all of this; all he could see was snowy-white cranes, lemon-yellow butterflies, flamingo-pink lily ponds and Elysium wooden bridges.

Faded red steps from the lawn led to a large, open porch. Along the front there were Arabesque-shaped windows and wooden shutters. An old, Moorish blue door shed tears in hope of restoration.

Durga gave him a quick tour of the outbuildings at the back of the main house. "There is a well with a good supply of drinking water in the long grass and something very special Mr Sollie… There is a community of singing tree frogs living in that tree."

After that, they set off for the lawyer's office in the old, walled city of Bhopal. The building didn't look too impressive; neither did the lawyer. His name was Phanishwar. A man with a ballooning stomach and a tight, red shirt that was about to pop its buttons. However, such was Sollie's enthusiasm for the property, he only mustered one question: "Are there any restrictions?"

"Only one. You are not permitted to keep elephants."

After that, Phanishwar rubbed his hands together. It seemed that they had arrived at a conclusion.

A WIDOW LIVING IN A TREE

Interviews - Mindsets - Suggestion - Souls

Silence - Purpose - Leaders - Self-love - Empathy

Sollie also needed an administrator to help him. Someone who would work with people in the same way a bee buzzes from one flower to the next. Somebody who might even arrive for their interview on a magic flying carpet. Coincidentally, on the other side of Bhopal, there was a young lady who could convince people that she could work like that. However, she was planning to travel to her interview by bus.

Her name was Yutika; a homeless but relatively young widow. She only had one suitable dress for an interview. It was kept in a hollow tree, along with her few other possessions. The same hollow tree that she slept in. Sollie had never met a widow. He was also oblivious to their suffering in many parts of India. He saw an interviewee dressed conservatively in a smart, dark blue smock. A gold chain around her neck disappeared down the front of her dress without revealing its charms. A slender figure with ripples and curves, jet-black eyes and long, black hair lowered his voice, without him being aware of it.

* * *

Sollie passed her a cup and saucer in readiness to pour her some tea… The saucer trembled and the silver teaspoon took a little jump in the air. He pretended not to notice. He wasn't too interested in her past experience either; he was more interested in what she could do in the future, if given an opportunity. This is how the interview went.

"Hello Yutika. What do you think your best assets are?"

She replied in a whisper: "I am an optimist; I am aware that the sun always follows the rain. I do not allow the difficult times in my life to prevent me from imagining a bright future. Knitting has taught me that joy and sorrow are inseparably intertwined and come from the same ball of wool."

He grinned manically: "What would you like to know, Yutika?"

"Do I have an important role to play on earth other than passing on my genes?"

"I meant questions about the job… However, your question is wonderful… the answer is definitely yes."

"Why do you want to work in Bhopal?"

There was a pause and a shuffling of feet: "Unfortunately, I recently lost all my family in a tragic fire. I would like to make a new start."

Sollie straightened the papers on the desk and filed away any remaining questions. It seemed that what the new home needed had just walked through the door. Of course, had Yutika pointed out at the beginning of the interview that she lived in the hollow of a tree, he wouldn't have had to ask her any questions at all.

Afterwards, Sollie was as happy as a little bird taking a bath in a summer stream. Yutika, he decided, was someone who had the gift to open petals. Her alluring looks and northern eyes had not escaped his attention either. The next morning, despite the lack of fluffy pillows, his hair had curled and his cheeks were bright.

AUSPICIOUS CRANES

Self-Doubt - Approval - Acceptance - Greetings - Appearance - Hugging

In the taxi on the way to meet Sollie, Tom was feeling a mixture of joy and anxiety; joy that he was arriving, nervous about how he would fit in. He folded his arms and crossed his legs. This, it seemed, helped him worry: 'Will they like me?' Tom asked this question because his life was centred around the need for approval and acceptance. He had never afforded himself the luxury of being the accepter or the rejecter. On his arrival, Sollie greeted Tom with a bear hug that made him feel like a pair of bellows. By the time he had his breath back, Sollie had sat down on the porch.

"I don't think I could give anyone a big hug like that. I find it hard to say a big-hearted hello."

Sollie put his hand to his ear: "You don't need to. Just listen to the chattering birds. All they are doing is saying lots of little hellos. This is what compels all the other birds to join in… One day I want our home to be like this; just full of people saying little hellos to each other."

Instead of waiting for an answer, Sollie introduced Tom to Yutika. Whilst she didn't hug him, she did bathe him in honey.

"Follow me. I will show you your temporary sleeping quarters. You probably want a rest after such a long journey."

Bruno and Apolline arrived whilst Tom was sleeping. Later he joined them in the front garden. Then Ling's taxi pulled up. Bruno went to help her with her rucksack. There was an immediate crackle of shared energy. Ling's feet lifted off the ground. Bruno imagined his muddy gardening glove delicately holding her tiny stem.

An hour later they all clambered aboard Sollie's newly-acquired open truck to take a look at their new home. Here, Sollie made the first of many overtures.

"Our new home will be called the Mustard Garden. Please don't be concerned by what it looks like now. Imagine it with wind chimes dangling from the trees, high-pitched voices hanging in the air and old ladies' knitting needles clinking away. Expect calling birds from distant lands to come and inspect our work."

After they had all taken a good look around, Sollie asked, "Now tell me, what has surprised you most since you arrived here?"

Apolline's reply was instantaneous and unexpected: "I didn't expect the men to be so handsome," she said breezily.

Bruno and Tom both seemed to be thinking the same thing: 'Surely she isn't talking about me?'

The next morning they decided to leave the bungalow and move straight into their new home. On arrival, Sollie hung Emperor Huizong's painting of the *Auspicious Cranes* on the lounge wall. However, as he was explaining who the emperor was, he was interrupted by some high-pitched shrieks. They all looked out of the window. Birds were tumbling out of the sky and landing on the lawn like a platoon of parachuters. Birds of every colour and size. Had Hubert been there, he might have thought that the United Nations of Birds was holding its world summit. No one knew what to say... Had Sollie not just told them to expect calling birds from distant lands?

GROUP DEVELOPMENT WORK

Coping mechanisms - Sharing problems - Receiving compliments Anxiety Over-sleeping - Control - Comparison - Overlooked - Approval Perfectionism Dependency - Trust issues - Lost - Avoidance - Unloved/unvalued - Intimacy Chanting - Yoga - Spiritual growth

The hollow tree is the symbol of acceptance, admission and surrender. It leads to transformation. It is a space where you make an admission, find forgiveness and start a new beginning. Here, regardless of what your admission is, the woodpecker will still tap on your door and the fox and weasel will still come and visit you. No one will think any less of you.

The next day Sollie's work started in earnest. He decided that the quickest way to bring the group together was for them to share their history, worries and hopes. Of course, they had all their first impressions. Bruno's volcanic looks put Ling and Apolline on a collision cause. Ling saw Apolline as friendly but flirty. Apolline deemed Ling to be sweet and unthreatening. Tom and Bruno were instantly comfortable in each other's company, even if they didn't have much to say. Tom was attracted to Apolline; she found Tom attractive but socially unsuitable. Everyone found Yutika's mystery and Sollie's energy appealing. Sollie was delighted with his recruitment.

"I asked this morning if you would like to share 'your' personal challenges. That can sound as if they are yours. They are not. They are ours. There is no such thing as a personal problem, because each person's problem affects all of us. The bird lands on the tree and every branch and leaf moves. Therefore, whenever you have a problem, look for someone to share it with. **When we chant and sing, we share our problems without talking about them.** However, today we are going to verbalise them. Please say whatever is on your mind."

Tom volunteered to go first. Sollie ushered him forward and asked him to sit on the table before adding, "We don't want any half admissions."

Despite the instruction, Tom spoke mostly to his feet: "I suffer from anxiety and I worry. I am an overthinker. I also have difficulty dealing with quiet or relaxing moments. Usually, I either oversleep or work every minute of the day to avoid them. In the end, this just exhausts me."

Tom paused for a minute and scratched his cheekbone, whilst he thought what else to say: "In truth, I guess I am lonely. I am lonely because I don't feel I belong anywhere. I feel like a cuckoo. I shy away from people and they shy away from me. I guess that I worry that I will be rejected again. Consequently, I do all that I can to avoid that. If someone does try and save me, I run away. All gifts, compliments or kind words that do come my way slip through my fingers and go crashing to the floor.

"When I was a small boy lots of different people looked after me, but there was no one in my life who I believed truly loved me. They gave me shelter, took me to school and fed me. They held my hand, but it never felt as if they held my heart." As soon as Tom had finished speaking, he put his hands on the table in readiness to jump down.

"Hold it there a minute, Tom," said Sollie, who then turned around to face the others. "Where is your cheering? This is not a court room! Tom hasn't pleaded guilty! **Admission and sharing your challenges are causes for great celebration. They are one of the steps on the road to recovery.**" They received the message. Bruno whistled, Sollie banged his feet, Apolline and Ling clapped their hands and shrieked.

Apolline followed Tom: "As well as my desire for perfection, I know that I also look for things that give me control. This is because I constantly feel overwhelmed. Unfortunately, when I do find something that I can control, I take it to extremes. Before long it's controlling me. I also compare myself against other people unfavourably. I have no confidence. I always think that other people are doing a better job than me. This makes me work harder and ends in stress and gloomy moods."

Then, without warning, her speech took a turn. Despite the positive start, Apolline's shoulders suddenly dropped. From nowhere, a black, emotional cloud appeared in the room and dropped itself over her head. Now she was a ship being tossed on a stormy sea. There was a long silence whilst she tried to recover.

"As a child, I craved my parents' love. However, it remained unrequited... My parents were not very present. Even when they were at home, they always seemed distant. We could never discuss feelings in my house, which is why I can't express them now. They were unable to show me any real love or affection. My father only ever wanted me to be a success. I only ever wanted his love. I worked as hard as I could for his approval in the hope that approval would morph into love. However, it never came. I spent my childhood walking on eggshells to avoid setting off his temper. I grew up feeling very unloved and without value. It seems that my childhood has made me permanently fragile. Deep down, I just want to be loved. However, it seems that I won't let any man embed themselves in my heart until I have secured my father's affections. I am ashamed to say that I have a history of toying with men and discarding them unceremoniously. I suppose that I have still not broken free from my childhood unhappiness."

There was another pause. The others weren't sure if they should cheer after all. Until Sollie whistled and clapped vociferously. He reminded them that the tears that they witnessed were not Apolline's; those tears belonged to all of them.

Ling was third. She was sporting some blue streaks of hair colour that she knew her mother would never approve of. "Until recently, like Apolline, I had no confidence; my mother saw to that. My parents divorced when I was six years of age. After that my mother clung to me; she did everything that she could to keep me at her side. If that meant discouraging educational attainments or destroying my prospects for promotion at work, she would. If she felt that making me feel awkward and ugly would prevent me from finding a boyfriend, she would do that too.

"I think that when my mother bought me silly hats, scarves and leggings, it was just another way of reinforcing my unattractiveness. Unfortunately, her plan worked. I never feel good enough. I have always felt ugly." This time they didn't need to be told; the applause was unbridled.

Bruno was next. "Sometimes I worry that I frighten the life out of everyone. There are also times when the outside world terrifies me." Then Bruno paused to clear his throat: "Although I do not wish to frighten anyone, I think that there is something that you should all know... I applied to come here whilst I was a guest at a mental institution, a place that I subsequently escaped from."

Bruno's eyes swept the room to see if anyone would take cover or run. "On reflection, I think the balm that I have been using might be from the wrong jar… I tend to go and hide in my garden. Now I have been away from the real world for so long, I am finding it difficult to reconnect and feel that I belong."

Yutika was last. Considering that she appeared to be the most compassionate person that you could meet, her revelations probably surprised everyone the most. "The truth is, that although I lost five children that I dearly loved in a tragic fire, I lost a husband that I didn't love. In fact, I have never experienced love in an adult relationship. I am not even sure if I would know how to respond if someone showed me love. Therefore, I suspect I will never be in a mature, loving relationship.

"Maybe it's because my parents never hugged or touched me as a child... or maybe it's because they never hugged each other. They only fought. And shouted. And screamed. They only knew chaos. All I saw was mistrust, broken promises and betrayal. All I heard was noise. All I learnt was that relationships do not work. Now I cannot trust."

There was some silence. Nobody was sure if Yutika had finished. She took a little breath: "My marriage was arranged by my parents. It turned out even worse than I had expected. After that, I took extra precautions; I wrapped my heart in cardboard and packed it away. **What I didn't realise was that when you shut your heart away from relationships, you also close your heart on the other joys and celebrations of life.**

"Finally, I would like to share with you something that I told Sollie. I do worry that everything that I am enjoying here could be taken away from me. If that happens, I will be a homeless widow sleeping on the streets again."

They all clapped and whistled enthusiastically. Only when they had all finished did Sollie speak. "You are here to find your liberty. However, freedom is not doing as you please or living in your own house. It is removing any unhappiness or limiting beliefs from your youth. What is more, we want to go beyond freedom and healing; our real goal is spiritual growth. For this reason, I hope you will participate in Ling's art and yoga classes and follow the spiritual path that I have laid out for you."

Of course, not everything was shared and revealed. Certain individuals kept things hidden. Those that did have secrets went about their days worrying that they might be discovered. Although, this was not true of all of them. There was one of them who had a secret that they themselves were unaware of, a confidence kept from them but known by others. And there were also those that lied.

A WOODEN HOUSE WITH GOLDEN ROOMS

Art – Nature – Yoga

Environmentalists know the importance of creating wildlife corridors on urban land. This way, all those animals that need to pass through can do so safely. It also means that amazing wildlife will come and visit. We are no different; our body is a field, a forest and a river, and we must also create a corridor so that beautiful things will pass through and visit us.

Although they had volunteered to start a new life, they had no idea what they had signed up for. Sollie scratched his head…How should he tell them that he didn't have a plan; just intuition and faith? Would it disappoint them if he told them that they just needed to be patient and wait? Would it frighten them if he said that they just needed to create a space in which good things could happen? Would they leave if he told them that something higher than his own capabilities was working on the vision?

They all sat on the porch as Sollie shared his thoughts. Apolline sat unusually close to Tom; so close that he wasn't sure whether to keep his leg next to hers or move it away. Then Bruno lurched forward: "What will the rest of the house look like, when it is renovated?"

"Welcoming and tranquil... A simple, wooden house with golden rooms. The main house will be your sleeping and living quarters. The outbuildings behind the main house will be converted into flexible accommodation for paying guests attending healing courses and students taking gap years. Then we need to create some artistic and mindful facilities.

Ling raised her hand: "I think that we should build an arts and yoga studio as soon as possible. **This is a place that will take us out of our minds and place us in our bodies. It will disrupt any gloomy moods and lethargy. It will earth us and take us to a state of happiness. When we are all earthed, we can work on our energy and beat.**"

"I don't disagree. Perhaps someone could suggest an order of works for the renovations."

Apolline had been talking to Yutika about snakes: "What about fences to keep the forest wildlife out?"

Sollie tutted, "We must not fear the animals or try and keep them out. We need to establish whose little footsteps cross our land, who roosts in the trees and who is sleeping in the hollow. We must create a nature corridor. In fact, we will make the entrance gates wide enough for a procession of elephants to pass through if required."

RESIDENT STORYTELLER

Universal souls - Change - Empathy

Our soul is the collective or universal one. We go 'into our self' and, when we come out, we can reflect the goodness of the universal soul of which we are one with.

Then Sollie spun around: "Apolline, I have a special task for you. I want you to be our resident storyteller. It's important that we record feelings, expectations, hopes, disappointments and celebrations from the onset. Your stories will be used to entertain all our visitors."

"That would make me so happy. I would love to do that. I have always wanted to be a storyteller. I will start interviewing you all immediately, before you have forgotten your early feelings."

Sollie gave her a broody stare.

"Have I said something wrong?"

"I didn't mean us. I meant write the stories from the point of view of the forest; the birds, the plants and the trees and all the others who reside here. Can you imagine how they might be feeling now that we have arrived with our grand plans? Only when you understand that you are dependent on all things does your behaviour towards the universe change. Only then do you become truly loving."

A HOUSE WITH MANY SACRED ROOMS

House building - Security - Expectation - Prayer flags

Blessings - Spiritual activities - God

This is not a garden; it is where I plant my prayers. Our kitchen is not just a place to cook but a chapel of devotion. Our bedroom is not just a place to sleep but a place to honour God. We too are like our houses; a temple with many sacred rooms.

The next morning Sollie went into town with Yutika to look for someone that could help with some of the more complex building works. When they returned, it was clear that the others needed a clearer brief. He scribbled down some lists and headings.

Apolline picked the piece of paper up: "Who is all this dance equipment for?"

"It is for our older visitors."

"Are you expecting a lot of old people to visit us?"

"Let me just say this, **If we expect them and we make provision for them, then they are more likely to arrive.**"

Apolline continued, "Which heading does security come under?"

"Good question. Security comes under number four."

"There is no number four."

"Correct. **There is no security in life**. **It is the pursuit of security that gives you anxiety**."

Ling asked Apolline to read out the items on the activity list.

"Spiritual activities: poetry, music, chanting, singing, art, meditation, yoga, screaming, prayer, dancing, gardening, baking, love therapy, knitting and sewing, history and genealogy. These are the activities that will make our home fragrant and saintly."

Tom raised his eyebrows: "Why history and genealogy?"

"We are here to make Emperor Huizong's wishes come true. This will include bringing your dead parents and ancestors back to life. However, you will learn more about this later. For now I want us to focus on laying the foundations of a spiritual home."

"Do you mean a place for God?"

"God is everywhere, therefore God is already in our home. If we make a loving and spiritual home for him, we make a loving and spiritual home for ourselves."

"Will this make our home sacred?"

"We cannot make things sacred; all that God has made is already sacred. **However, we can allocate more space in our home for the areas where it is easier to appreciate how sacred things are… like the kitchen and garden.** We can also create more playful places to get to know God. For it is when we get to know God and have a sacred relationship with him that the sacredness in all things is revealed."

His last comments silenced everyone. He decided to change the subject:

"Enough of lists and logic for today. We have something more important to do. We are going to make some prayer flags. **Then we will hang them from the surrounding trees and rooftops, so that our good thoughts bless our neighbours.**"

We are at our best when we create space around us... our home is no different

STAGES OF PRAYER

Belonging – Self-love - God - Shrines

Places for prayer - Forgiveness - Unburdening

Despite the fact that none of the group were particularly religious, they were not frightened off by Sollie's comments about prayer. In fact, **The idea of a spiritual home with many sacred rooms gave them comfort**. They were all keen to hear more on the subject.

"We should create spaces that purify our inner temples; spaces that make it easier to pray, unburden, forgive and be loving towards ourselves."

Bruno's eyes looked up and across to the left: "I don't think that I have ever said a prayer as an adult. I am not sure if I would know where to start."

"**Start by creating a space in your home where you can pray and get to know yourself**. This can create a spark of divinity within you. **Your prayers build a bridge towards God**. **They awaken your spiritual side**. Prayer is part of faith and faith is something that you build gradually... in stages. **In the beginning, start gently... know that just kneeling down or putting your hands together will soften your shoulders.**

"Also be aware that, in the early stages of prayer, many people feel unworthy, unloved and without the expectation of a better future. If this is how you feel, don't pray for yourself; pray for God himself. If you are unsure why you should pray for God, think of it merely as a thanksgiving for the gift of life and all the beautiful things in the world.

"Prayer is humbling and is an act of self-love. It will take you towards your 'higher self' as a universal soul. **Prayer will not just help you feel closer to God; it will help you feel that you belong in this world.** We will complement our prayer with meditation. **First we will meditate on our small personal issues,**

and then we will progress to the big questions like, who am I? In the beginning we will pray by ourselves, and later we will link our prayers with others and pray for the whole."

FURNITURE SPACE AND POSSESSIONS

Attachment - Suffering - Relationships - Homes - Vessels

> Your home and your mind are of the same cloth. When they are not cluttered or occupied, they become welcoming.

After some solemn words, Sollie knew exactly what to do in order to make the room airy once again: "Now Apolline, can you tell us how to keep our house tidy?"

"Tidy things up as you go along."

"Perhaps. The clutter of our home is like the clutter of our mind; it is something to be avoided. The emptier our home and our minds are, the easier it is for God to work through us. The results of this will be evident in our cakes, paintings, music, writing, etc."

"I think that you are telling us that we should have as little furniture as possible."

"No. I am telling you that you need to imagine yourself being happy living in a simple home."

Apolline scrunched her nose up: "Does that mean that furniture and furnishings are not important?"

"No. The right type of tables will bring us together, sitting on mats will keep us earthed. Handmade stripy rugs will charge our bare feet when we walk across them!"

"If there is less furniture, does that mean that there will be less for us to be attached to?."

"No. You will be either attached or not attached to material things, regardless of how many you have. **Having possessions is not an issue; however, being attached to possessions will cause you suffering."**

"Focus on creating the right spaces, not collecting clutter. I said before that **'If we create space for unexpected visitors, they are more likely to arrive.'** We must also set aside some space for the things that we haven't thought about."

Eyebrows remained in a tangle. Then they took another break. Tom went to his room. Apolline followed him. He lay down on his bed. She sat down at the end of the bed by his feet. His heart quickened. Apolline spoke as if nothing out of the ordinary was taking place. Tom hadn't had a woman in his house for a long time, never mind one sitting at the end of his bed. He was unable to relax or find the right words to say. Instead, he climbed off the bed and offered to make coffee.

LOST AT SEA AND HOUSE RULES

Finding ourselves - Contribution - Drugs - Alcohol - Inhibitions

LOST AT SEA

Like land lost to the sea, we must reclaim ourselves. It is never too late to get our life back. Sometimes it just requires an admission, a decision and new action. Sometimes it requires the courage to leave old habits, beliefs and friends behind. At other times it just requires a question, like - Who am I? Why am I here? What is my purpose?

After the break Tom found his voice again: "Are there any house rules?"

Sollie replied without looking up: "Leave your shoes outside the house."

"Is that it?"

"No smoking, drugs or alcohol on the premises."

There was a brief period of silence.

"Our aim is to be awake and mindful. Hopefully, we can discover some better ways to relax and remove our inhibitions. If you want to get high, climb a tree."

A FORMLESS LORD

Faith - God - Expectations - Love - Momentum - Homes
Visions - Body as a temple - Inner light - Sharing

Ling went to the village. Sollie stayed behind with Apolline.

"Sollie, how do you think that we should lay out the five bedrooms?"

"I think that it is more important to ask where the spare bedroom should be!"

"Can we afford to build a spare bedroom?"

Sollie beamed, "Sit down for a second."

As she did, his voice became more velvety: "My mother told me that you don't need to wait until you can afford children before you have them. She also said that if you build a spare bedroom, it is more likely that an extra head will find a way to its pillow. This is what I was talking about when I mentioned preparing for unexpected visitors. However, in truth my mother's message about an extra bedroom is just a spiritual metaphor."

Apolline tucked her hair behind her ears.

"To find our godliness, we must build faith within ourselves. We must have faith that we can do incredible, God-like things. We must also expect. To expect, we must build momentum. The way we build momentum is to build the right things, even before we have worked out what exactly they might be needed for.

"However, we are going to do much more than just build a spare bedroom; we are going to build our home without fixed form. Then, like love, there will be no limits to its capacity."

Her brow crumpled; she was confused. His teeth gleamed: "We will do the same with our home as we do with our bodies; we will invite God inside. **Our home and our bodies will become amoebas; formless lords. They will be buses, whose route is not defined by predetermined stops**. Buses that will stop to pick up whoever is in need. Buses that will change their shape to accommodate whatever needs to be accommodated. They will be made for sharing."

SHARING

Group therapy - Admissions - Chanting - Love
Morality - Adoption - Space

Love sits higher than morality.

Apolline's smile returned: "I quite like the thought of sharing everything. I realise now that owning things makes us worry about losing things."

Sollie rubbed his hands together: "I am pleased to hear that you have embraced sharing."

"To be truthful, I didn't bring many possessions with me, so sharing hasn't been that big a challenge."

"Oh... I wasn't referring to possessions. The first thing that came to mind was airing and sharing our worries and darkness. **We do that here by singing and chanting together in the evenings.** This is group therapy without the need to make any actual admissions. When you said 'sharing', I also assumed that you wanted to share your partner, your house and your children."

Apolline wasn't sure how to reply to that.

"Imagine that you were gifted with good looks, good fortune and a good husband. Imagine that, in the area that you lived, other women were not so fortunate. That because of a shortage of men, as happens for example in times of war, these women were unable to find a partner or a husband. Could you share your husband?"

This time at least Apolline's mouth opened.

"Consider that these other women may be deprived of companionship, love, affection and shared experiences. Now ask yourself if it is right that you keep your husband to yourself, so that you have everything, whilst they have nothing. Is it right that you are blissfully happy, whilst these other women are desperately lonely? Ask yourself if loving your husband monogamously makes you a loving person or if it makes you unloving. Does morality supersede love, or is love something that melts morality? Are the teachings of your church moral or are they unloving?"

Once again Apolline had nothing to say.

"Now ask yourself if you should keep all your children for yourself. Could you share them? Could you give away some of your children to those couples who can't have any? Could you give some of them to the lonely ladies who can't find a husband, who then have their unhappiness compounded by also being unable to have a child?"

By this time, Apolline's arms and legs were in a twist. However, he still hadn't finished.

"If you have a happy family, could you bring an orphan who is all alone in the world into your house to share your happiness, knowing that their insecurities might bring disruption instead of joy to your family?"

He could see that her body had become limp and so he lightly touched her palm: "I say all this because it appears that only when we understand the true meaning of sharing can we understand the true meaning of loving. Know this too, **No one truly loves anything until they are happy to share it or even see it fly away.**"

SOMETHING GLEAMING IN THE SUN

It was time to find the water-well that Durga had mentioned. Then they heard a scream. Bruno had discovered it; in fact, he had fallen down it... It didn't look good. Bruno was lying halfway down the well, and he wasn't moving. Tom climbed down and pulled him out. Five pairs of eyes hovered over the motionless body.

Ling took the initiative; she unbuttoned Bruno's shirt. Her tiny hand moved slowly through his hairy chest like a mouse tiptoeing through the undergrowth of a dark forest. Finally, the heart was located. It appeared to be lifeless, so she pressed down hard on it. BUMP! His heart jumped, as if it was on a spring. Ling reeled back. He was alive, despite a huge red bump on his forehead. The other good news was that the well contained water.

The following morning, Yutika made another discovery as she peered out of the kitchen window: "I think that we have a visitor."

Sollie looked up from his desk: "Who is it?"

Yutika ushered everyone towards the entrance: "I am not sure. I can see their transport, but I can't see them."

It appeared that their visitor was a monster; a beautiful monster. Standing all alone, on top of a small, sandy mound, it gleamed in the sun. It had the style and design of the Second World War but the polish of a modern showroom; an enormous, super-powered motorbike, complete with a set of keys in its ignition. Tom rubbed his hand on the polished petrol tank: "I don't think that it will be long before its owner returns." However, he was wrong. For no one did return to retrieve it.

PERFECTIONISM

Identity - Rules - Comparison - Approval

> No matter how hard I looked, I could not seem to find the perfect one. Each flower was either incomplete on its approaching or part touched by its passing.

When she retired that night, Apolline spent some time thinking about their building strategy. **Sollie had steered them away from perfection and towards**

incompletion. Now she realized that building walls and putting things in boxes was how she ran her life. A place for everything. Everything at the right angle. This stressed her and other people.

As she started to think about this, there was a dawning: 'There are many types of prisons…It appears that I have made the rules of my life into a piece of hanging rope. If there were less rules, more things would be right and less would be wrong. If there were less rules in my life, I would have more freedom.' It appeared to be true. The rules may have started with French grammar, but they had invaded her life like a flowering wall creeper. Apolline understood that now. The next morning, she discussed her thoughts with Sollie: "Why do I like things to be perfect?"

"It could be several things. If you were brought up amongst chaos, you might strive for order. If you believe that you were overlooked, you might try to ensure that everything is correct, in order to receive the recognition that you yearn for. A person who believes that they can acquire love and acceptance by pleasing others sets themselves up for a difficult life. There will be no respite."

"What should I do?"

"**Reset your identity. Recognise that you are not an individual; you are part of something bigger.** When you view yourself as part of the universe, there are no comparisons to make: now you are a part of all things, and nothing is better or worse than you."

"What else?"

"You could try spending more time in the garden or in the forest. Then you will see that, on closer inspection, nature is full of imperfection."

"How will that help me?"

"It will help you understand that, **Beauty and imperfection are in fact the same thing.** If you accept that imperfection makes nature beautiful, it is easier to accept that it is what makes you beautiful too. When you understand you are beautiful because of your imperfections, you can relax and be more accepting. You will not need the approval of others either."

WEEDS INTO FLOWERS

Ego - Identity - Approval - Anxiety - Language - Sharing

Sollie and Apolline had been collecting fallen coconuts. She was about to leave when he pulled the strings of her apron: "Don't you have any questions today?"

"There is one small matter. What do you mean when you say that, **We need to surrender the ego?**"

"That is a big question! However, I can give you a brief explanation for now. Think of the ego as your 'I', along with the identity that you have created for yourself. If you use the 'I', you assume the position of an individual; you believe your work, your ideas, etc are the fruits of your own skills and creativity. If you do this, your work will be limited and heavy; a higher and lighter spiritual force will not be able to elevate your personal efforts.

"When you operate with the 'I', as an individual, you may receive recognition for your deeds. However, **With the desire for recognition comes the need for approval**. With this comes anxiety. However, remember what I said yesterday: you are not an individual, you are part of something bigger; the whole or the universe."

"Is it difficult to drop the ego?"

"The ego is not like one of these heavy coconuts that drop from the tree. It is part of your foliage; it falls away gradually, as you move towards your surrender."

"How do I know if I am moving in the right direction?"

"You will no longer take the credit for your best work. You will also find it easier to teach French. You will have one less conjugation to teach for every verb. You will no longer need to use or teach the letter I."

Apolline stared at him in bemusement.

"Imagine if you learnt a new language and the teacher wouldn't give you the word for the pronoun 'I'. You would not be able to say: "I know this. I am this. I believe this. I did this, etc. You would have to search for an alternative way to structure your sentences. Try it. See how the magic works, how the sentences change themselves and their meaning. Watch how the weed turns into a flower.

"Not using the 'I' is not denial or an abandonment of responsibility. It just means that you acknowledge your good work is a joint effort between your higher self and the sacrifices or work of others."

SPELLING AND FRAGRANCES

Perfectionism – Vocabulary

Better to be the flower than the bee

Apolline looked over Sollie's shoulder whilst he scrawled on some paper.

"It seems that you cannot spell, Sollie."

"This is true, Apolline. Perhaps it is because I never went to school."

She raised her eyebrows. He widened his eyes: "I have never lost any sleep over my bad spelling. Is it really important?"

"I believe so. What do you think that we should teach children to do instead?"

"Teach children how to flower. Surely this is more important than turning them into spelling bees?"

"Whatever do you mean?"

"It is the job of parents and teachers to help children learn a gardenful of beautiful words. For this type of vocabulary will change the children's thinking, feelings and actions. The fragrance from their vocabulary will also determine who is attracted to them."

"Can't we teach the children a lilting vocabulary and ensure that they also spell the words correctly?"

"No."

"Why?"

"Fragrance sits astride imperfection. Spelling lives alongside perfection; it can spoil enjoyment if it is wrong, but it does not necessarily give any pleasure if it is right. It is not the sort of thing that I can recommend you to pursue."

Focus on doing the right things, instead of doing things right

UNEXPLAINED SONNETS

Inspiration – Beggars – Faith – Gratitude – Sharing

As long as there is enough blue in the sky to make a sailor a pair of trousers, there is hope... my grandmother's sentiments.

Sollie, Ling, Tom and Apolline had been to see Bhopal's walled city. Here, extreme poverty was etched into the people, animals and buildings. There were many beggars. On the way, Apolline had been flirting with Tom. On the way home, she had tears in her eyes.

"What are you thinking?"

"I was thinking about the very old beggar sitting by the gates. Should I still feed him today if I won't be there to help him tomorrow?"

"Know that no act of kindness can be a waste of time. Know that others will be inspired by what they see you do. Sometimes other people just need someone to show them the way."

"What is the beggar thinking?"

"I can't be sure, however, the best gift that you could give to a person who has lost faith in themselves is a gift that says others have not. It may be the tiny bit of blue sky that they need to give them hope."

"I could not speak words of encouragement or tell him that I care, he didn't speak my language."

"The beggar doesn't have to understand your words or know who you are. A big part of being a pollinator is about composing sonnets and symphonies left unsigned by the composer. A gift from a stranger can stick to a heart for a long time. However, don't expect everyone who needs help to be grateful. Why would they be, when they are sleeping in a shop doorway or without peace of mind and love?"

* * *

A few days later Apolline asked Ling for some help. She placed a wooden box on the table. It was full of lollipops, brightly-coloured cards, ribbons and hearts.

"I am intrigued, Apolline. What are those?"

"They are my attempts at unsigned sonnets and symphonies."

"Oh. What's your plan?"

"I am going to carry a few of the items from the box in my bag at all times."

"Then what?"

"If I see someone down on their luck, I'm going to give them a lollipop. I know that it works because I tried it out. Even the very old people still lick their lips."

"What about the ribbons and hearts?"

"They go on the greeting cards. They are for people of any age who look forgotten or out of sorts. If they speak English, I am going to chat to them and find out their name. Then I am going to run around the corner and add their name to one of my greeting cards."

"Then what?"

"Then I will return, hand my gift over and disappear. The object is to let them know that someone cares. As Sollie said, it is not necessary for me to sign my sonnet or symphony."

"That is a beautiful idea. I think that it will make you feel better too."

"I haven't done it for that reason. It was something that Olivia said: **'Small acts of generosity prepare you for the day that you give yourself.'** I am not sure exactly what she meant. However, I feel that it could be important."

RELIGION

A spiritual path - Identity - Salvation - Resurrection and redemption

After dinner one night, Tom asked another question that had been on everyone's mind.

"What about religion? Where does that fit in with our mission?"

"It does not. I believe in God, but I don't believe in a particular religious faith. Why are you interested, are you searching for something?"

Tom gave a thoughtful answer: "I want someone to believe in me. I need something that I can hold onto tightly and someone to love me unconditionally."

"I think lots of people want those things. They also seem to want a saviour, forgiveness and something to take the fear of death away. Religion was created to control you and manipulate your fears. In truth, religion is no better than a bottle of whisky. It's not a solution, just a coping mechanism."

"What is the alternative?"

"People doubt themselves. They look for an external saviour. They fail to understand that they must take responsibility for their own salvation, resurrection and redemption. You do not need to seek a saviour; all the resources that you need are within you and around you. **Do not look to be saved; learn how to gain eternal life instead.**"

BELONGING TO THE WHOLE

God - Prayer - Spiritual path

> "Glorious indeed is the world of God around us, but more glorious the world of God within us."
>
> Longfellow

"So I don't need God."

"I didn't say that. **You must build faith in yourself by finding the God within you**. Those who follow a religion do the opposite; they go outside themselves to seek help from an external God."

"How can I acquire the faith to believe in myself?"

"**Don't pray to God; work alongside God. Pray for all things.** This helps you see yourself as being connected to the whole; not as an individual. Unfortunately, some people only pray for themselves or people that they know. Others only pray for those that share their identity or religion. A Jew, for example, might proudly tell you that they would never abandon another Jew to their fate. However, when you identify yourself as belonging to the whole, you will never abandon anything or anyone to their fate."

RECLAIMING RITES OF PASSAGE

Religion – Success – Commitment – Beliefs – Salvation

Mark yourself out as on a path towards God. Baptise yourself in meditation. Above all, understand the importance of a blessing. Bless yourself as the crowning act of self-love. Bless others as often as you can too.

"It seems that you are a passionate non-believer."

"Of religion, yes. One of the Ten Commandments states that you should not steal. Despite this, religion is the biggest thief of all. It makes out that it has jurisdiction over what is sacred and what is holy. It has tried to steal the copyright on important rites of passage, like communions and blessings. We must reclaim these. We cannot delegate those things that elevate our heart to something out of our control."

"Any questions?"

Apolline wasn't going to let this opportunity go a miss: "What about miracles?"

"What about them?"

"Surely we can't do miracles without religion?"

"Apolline, I promise you that miracles will happen here in Bhopal. However, because you appear doubtful, I am going to send you a personal miracle maker. What miracle would you like them to perform?"

"Someone who could walk on water."

SPIRITUAL GROWTH

Success – Change – Reaching out – Transformation

Look Inwards … Reach Outwards

Self-Development and Spiritual Growth

We are often taught that self-development is about developing our knowledge, skills and even our body. However, the self-development that matters is our spiritual growth. True self-development is mastering the art of being loving, steeping ourselves in self-love and then moving our thoughts and our actions away from ourselves and towards the health and happiness of all other things.

Ling sat quietly while Tom and Sollie discussed change and transformation.

Tom stoked the campfire: "Can you tell us a little more about spiritual growth and change?"

"I will, but I don't want to talk about religion anymore. Let's talk about nature and frogs instead… More than 300 million years ago, the early amphibians lived in stagnant water short of oxygen. Only plants lived on the land. Things needed to change. It required a great effort by these early amphibians to develop lungs and strong fins to hoist themselves out of the water. Sometimes, we must make the same effort to pick ourselves up off the floor.

"Through evolution, amphibians like the frog developed stronger pelvic bones to support them out of the water. Today many frogs start as tadpoles. Then they morph. When they do this, their gills disappear, the eyes are repositioned on their head and their tail is absorbed.

"I am not suggesting that you need to adapt in the same way as a frog. However, it is useful to know that when you have the desire to transform yourself, nature is on your side. First you must become curious. The frog decided to have a look over the rim and ask, 'What is outside of my pond?' Then it refused to accept a substandard way of living. The frog did not try and adapt the world to itself, it adapted itself to the world.

"Is the absorbing of tails and the repositioning of eyes relevant to me, you may ask. The answer is yes. Don't for one minute think that you cannot adapt and morph miraculously too. You just need to do it differently. For you, there will be no absorptions or repositioning of body parts. The morphing that you need to do takes place within… **Once you have made the effort to haul yourself up off the floor and love yourself again, you must simply reach out… this turns you inside out. Some call it morphing, others call it spiritual growth**. This is important, this is beyond change… this is transformation."

Then Sollie looked behind him to see if Ling had any questions. However, she had disappeared.

> Don't try to swim against the tide; find out what you must do to help you appreciate that you are part of the sea.

MOULDING CLAY POTS

Purpose - Loose ends - Self-love - Purpose

Faith - Spirituality – Higher self

You become spiritual when you shut one world out and open yourself up to another.

Thanks to Bruno, Ling now had an arts and crafts studio.

Sollie spoke to her there whilst she crafted some clay pots: "Why did you disappear yesterday?"

"I am interested in spiritual growth, but I hate frogs."

"Sometimes I tell the story of the frogs because the listener is in a swamp. However, that's not you. Therefore, I can share my views on spiritual growth without referring to any frogs… if it pleases you?"

She laughed sweetly.

"Spirituality is about a person's relationship with the transcendent; those things beyond the range of normal human experience. **The spiritual path is not a search for God but a search for our higher self**. The path will usually involve a search for the meaning of life and our purpose.

"A spiritual person's highest priority is to have a connection to something wider and higher than themselves; the whole. If you believe in God, it will also take you towards him. Eventually, this makes our sense of self fade away. However, we start the journey by learning to love ourselves; it is this that opens up our hearts. Along the path we do things that elevate us spiritually. We become 'mindful', we learn that everything that we say and think affects our spirituality. **We build faith in ourselves, and then we progress to building faith outside ourselves. It is these steps that take us across the bridge from man's secular world to the sacred.**"

Ling asked her next question without taking her eyes off the slithery, twirling pot that she was moulding: "What is our true purpose whilst we are here?"

"It is to understand the difference between the stone sculptor and the clay potter."

SCULPTORS AND POTTERS

The sculptor seeks to remove all the stone and marble that is not needed. The ugly and the unwanted are chipped away until all that is left is a beautiful design. However, the potter sees all their material as valuable; nothing is deemed superfluous or inferior, even the discarded and the irredeemable are added back. Now what remains is beyond beauty.

"Why are you telling me that?"

"I am telling you that because one day you might need to help make something wonderous out of something that someone else has discarded."

HAPPINESS AND SIMPLE PLEASURES

Happiness is an obligation. Acquire it and you will bring the sun out. Without it, you will cast a shadow on the rest of the world.

They were painting the roof and helping Bruno build a greenhouse. Sollie was concerned that they were rushing around too much. He made some leaf-sweeping brushes and handed them out: "I think that it is time for some spiritual activity."

Apolline turned to rush off: "Wait, I will be back in a minute."

Two minutes later she came back in her favourite dress.

"We are sweeping up, Apolline, not going to a party."

"Is that right?"

However, Apolline was thinking back to when she first arrived in India and her stay at the Sunny Gardens Hotel. Another drip had permeated. **Happiness didn't come from acquiring or seeking the unusual, it was to be found in the usual and being present**. Apolline hadn't just concluded it; she had witnessed it. 'The simple pleasures of life are not something to dress down for, they are the golden moments to celebrate and dress up for.'

A LOVING AND SPIRITUAL HOME

Uplifting purpose - Destiny - Spiritual cooking
Expectations - Calling - Entitlement

The dicing of a cucumber can reflect a loving heart.

Yutika was looking at the ground and appeared to be despondent, possibly left out: "What do you want me to do Sollie?"

"I want you to make our house a spiritual and loving home. Line the drawers with cherry-blossom-scented paper and make sure there is a love diary and a pencil next to the sweet jar. Tie pretty ribbons around our newly-laundered linen. Keep the windows open, so that we can always hear the birds singing. Create a home where there is a feeling of belonging but without any sense of attachment. Usher in beauty, prayer, simplicity and gratitude.

"Demonstrate to us the spirituality of cooking and baking…Waft the smell of bread through all the rooms, simmer apples with cinnamon and cloves. Teach us how to expect by stocking our cupboards full of cakes and treats to celebrate forthcoming events. Show us how the proving and the rising of the bread is relevant to the rising of our spirits. Help us clear away the clamour of the outside world and you will have set us on the path to inner joy."

"You make it sound as if a domestic helper's job has great importance."

"Hidden within the folds of all jobs are tasks of great importance. However, sometimes you must look at your job description with a fresh pair of eyes to find them. You can also use your day job to prepare you for a calling if you want to."

"Do you think that I might receive a calling?"

"There is no one that will not receive a calling, if they ask for one. It is the platter on which your service is presented. When we say that 'everyone is entitled to a better life', this is the entitlement that we should refer to. **The difficulty for many who receive a calling is for them to convince themselves that they are not deluded.**"

"What if my calling asks me to do something bad, like commit an atrocity?"

HEART-SHAPED BOXES AND CALLINGS

A calling is a gift so compelling that you might wonder if you are mad when you hear it. Your calling will always be an act of love. An atrocity is not an act of love, so it can never be a calling. If you are asked to commit an act of love, surely it doesn't matter if you are deluded. Therefore, before you unwrap your gift, simply check that it was delivered in a heart-shaped box. For if what you must do is not an act of love, then it is not your calling.

After that, Sollie disappeared. He seemed pleased with himself and felt that he had appeased her. In truth, he hadn't. She scowled and put a large spoon of salt in his soup. It appeared that she wasn't content with development; what she desired was some power.

PILGRIMAGES AND SEEKING FORTUNES

Religion – Visions – Purpose – Energy

A party is a place where you meet new people. A pilgrimage is a place where you go to meet yourself.

True Facts

In 1818 a British officer discovered one of the greatest ever monuments to the Buddha. It was hidden away under the undergrowth and vegetation at Sanchi, north of Bhopal. The hemispherical dome called a 'stupa' was built over the Buddha's relics by the Emperor Ashoka and his daughter. It dates from the third century BC and is one of India's oldest pilgrimage destinations.

Sollie had something important to say and planted himself at the far end of the table.

"One of the world's great pilgrimages exists at Sanchi, north of Bhopal. I would like to create another pilgrimage; one that the religious and those with no religion can enjoy."

Then he read out a little verse.

SANCHI TEMPLE

THE PILGRIMAGE

A pilgrimage is a place where you go to meet yourself. In truth, it is just another way to meditate; for the truth to arise, a place to go beyond your body and mind. A place to quieten the soul and release the spirit. Along the way there are connecting and charging points that will fill you with gratitude and demist your eyes.

Set out with no goals. Leave your books and mind behind. See what you can give away. Search for silence and put some in a jar. Empty your bags, and create space around you. Meander and travel backwards where you can. Raise welcome and blessing flags, and let them flutter in the wind. Make friends with all the little ones, and watch with no desire to understand.

When you come home and shake your bag, despite not putting anything in it, don't be surprised if it is overflowing. I will not spoil the end by telling you what you may find, save to say this is how you acquire your fortune and restore your peace of mind.

BEYOND OURSELVES

Pilgrimage desires - Imagination - Words - Approval

I seek mystery. To find it I must go beyond the limitations of my experiences, my logic and my memory. I must go beyond the 'treeline'; beyond the approval of my fellowmen. I must seek to observe life; not try to understand it. At the very point I try to touch it, like a forest deer it runs away and disappears.

Ling took out a drawing pad: "What will the pilgrimage look like?"

"I don't know."

Apolline was incredulous: "Are you saying that you have not tried to use your imagination to visualise it?"

"Correct. I think that it is a mistake to visualize things like this. If you do, there is often a succession of banging doors in the distance and other possibilities are shut out. If we use our imagination, all we will do is draw on our experiences and imagine them doing extraordinary things. If we would like to experience something beyond extraordinary, we need to go beyond our experiences, thinking and imagination.

"Some people say that the age of the Koran's text can make it difficult to follow if you are only trying to understand the words. They say that the book's true beauty is only revealed when it is read aloud. It seems that the book is more than its words. This has sense. If something is all that it could be, there will be no words to describe it. I hope that our pilgrimage will be like this too."

"What must we do?"

"Create the space, energy and light from which a pilgrimage is borne. A pilgrimage that all enlightened people will want to make, regardless of whether they are religious."

Now this was a big moment for Sollie. This was the point where the team might doubt their decision to come to India. Then Bruno said something that lightened the mood. He laughed, before saying, "I understand. That is what I do."

"Do what?"

"Pilgrimages. Every five years I travel on a pilgrimage to my favourite tomato-growing region in Naples, Italy. I am the only one on the pilgrimage, so there are no stampedes or over-priced hotels. It is not religious, but it is definitely spiritual."

BEYOND THE PLEASURE OF FOOD

Diet - Energy - Passions - Optimism - Fitness
Surrender - Yoga - Calling - Spiritual food

> Don't think of a vegetarian as someone who eats vegetables. Think of a vegetarian as someone taking responsibility for keeping the grass green and the seas blue.

They all watched as Sollie stirred his dinner over the flames. It swirled like a whirlpool, smelt like fried onions and was as dense and colourful as a Costa Rican rainforest.

Apolline decided that she needed to satisfy her curiosity: "What exactly is in that soup that you eat every evening?"

"It is my woodland soup."

"What is it made of?"

"I am not sure that you would believe me if I told you."

"Try me."

"It consists of tree bark, leaves, flower petals, nuts, flaxseed, sunflower oil, oats, rice, peas, coconut milk, lentils and lime."

"Why do you eat it?"

"I am committed to my cause – nature. When you are committed, you must become one with the colour green. You must do all that you can to turn your blood green and your inner organs into vegetable plots. Then, eventually, your composition will be green. If I stop eating meat, the world will be a better place and I will have made a contribution to ensuring the grass is greener."

"Is that the only reason? It has not gone unnoticed that you are rarely ill and you seem to have an endless supply of energy. There must be something magical in it."

"Tell me, have you ever met anyone with an unhealthy lifestyle who seems to have an endless supply of energy?"

"I have met quite a few. My last head teacher, for example, was so large that she could hardly fit through the door. She stocked up on a vast supply of fast food, cigarettes and alcohol. Despite this, she was always in the study when I arrived in the morning and was still there long after I had returned home."

"Where do you think that she acquired her energy?"

"I am not sure."

"Is it possible that she was clear about her vision, passionate about her cause and optimistic about her outcomes?"

"All three. She was totally committed to her cause and no matter what set-backs she experienced, she always remained optimistic. It seemed that nothing could deter her."

"Then, it appears that a significant proportion of our energy comes from passion and an optimistic mindset."

"Is that it? Is that the secret of success?"

"Oh no. That is not it at all. It just explains why some people can thrive for a period of time, despite doing their best to kill themselves. A healthy diet and a fitness regime are good for you, but a trip to the gym and a plate of vegetables is no match for an optimistic mind … in the short-term."

"What do you mean by the short-term?"

"Our bodies are quite resilient: we can survive a diet of bad food, harmful substances and lack of exercise for quite a while. However, although a poor lifestyle will catch up with you eventually, most of the time it is not our bad habits that cause our downfall. It is our passions and our causes, despite the fact that they can power us up in the beginning.

"It seems that, with time, the great energy giver becomes the great energy robber. In view of this, here in our garden, we will look for a more sustainable energy. **Energy not powered by goals or visions but powered by submission, surrender, kind thoughts, conscious food, reaching out and yoga.**"

Apolline still did not seem convinced: "Yoga? Are you serious?"

"**Yoga is also spiritual food; food for the mind, body and the soul. We need food, but we don't need to derive pleasure from food. We just need to relabel food as a source of fuel.** If we look to optimize the fuel for our body, we will be in the optimum state of health to carry out our spiritual work. If we look to eat the food that satisfies the pleasure of the senses, we may not be able to get up out of our seat! How can we carry out our higher purpose and calling then?"

MINDFUL FOOD

Souls - Vegetarians - Devotional food - Staring - Consequences

The next evening, Sollie gave Apolline a taste of his woodland soup and asked her, "Why do you think that vegetarians avoid meat?"

"Is it because they love animals and the planet?"

"I think you are right. However, once they have struck off the menu those items that are not in harmony with the world, many set about cooking a meal that satisfies their hunger and the pleasure of the senses. Just like meat-eaters, they eat food that makes them drool."

"What is wrong with that?"

"The order is wrong. **They look to satisfy the hunger in their stomach. What they should be doing is looking to satisfy the hunger of their soul**. This requires spiritual food; food that goes beyond the pleasure of the senses. Food that is nutritious, mindful and devotional. However, I will tell you more about devotional food another day.

"Eating mindfully is about remaining in the present. **Praying before meals is not about what you say; it is about who and what you engage with in your thoughts whilst you say your prayers.**"

"Eat and enjoy silent moments, eat slowly, savour and observe. Think about those that prepared your food. Be mindful of the consequences of your choices; for example, how they impact on the planet and all living things."

"How?"

"Staring at your habits or food mindfully makes you conscious. Stare deeper and for longer and you will see and feel the consequences of your actions."

BIG LOVE AND BELONGING

Relationships - Self-love - Belonging - Spiritual activities - Cults - Freewill

> First we take people out of their thoughts and bring them down to earth. Then we place them on a spiritual path.

Yutika placed some tea on Sollie's desk and sat down, arms crossed, without saying a word. It seemed that she was still dissatisfied with her responsibilities.

He sat upright: "What can I do for you?"

Her melodious interview voice had lost its softness: "I would like a deeper insight into my job."

"Before we can achieve anything worthwhile here, we need to help our little group acquire a sense of belonging. **We cannot permit the absence of roots or the feeling of being overlooked to stand in the way of happiness.**"

"What does that involve?"

"We start with earthing and anchoring. **The aim is to take the lost and the anxious out of their minds and place them in the present.** Here they can connect to their authentic selves and the authentic world."

"But you only asked me to bake apples and put pretty ribbons around the laundry."

"No, I told you that I wanted you to create a spiritual and loving home. **Our sense of belonging with the natural world deepens when spiritual activities become a way of life and not just a pastime.** It is your responsibility to immerse everyone in activities like baking, sewing, gardening, meditation and prayer… pastimes that are simple, inexpensive and within everyone's reach. This will move people in the direction of **Big love**; a love for all things."

"If you want me to create a place with a sense of belonging, does that mean that you want us all to stay here forever?"

"No. I want us to feel that we belong wherever we are. I have heard other people who live in ashrams and spiritual resorts say that they feel that these homes are the only places where they feel that they belong. However, if we feel that we only belong in one place then we must know we have more work to do on non-attachment. **Only when we can roam freely without anxiety have we found our true belonging.** Some people go away and feel that they miss their home and the people who live there. However, the real measure of their belonging is when they themselves are missed."

Look to feel at home on the path; not in a house.

WIDOWS

Love - Reaching out

If your conscience is pricked, you wake up. When you do something about it, you come alive.

"Yutika, I have a funny request. Would you mind bringing your sewing into the lounge and sitting on the floor with me?"

"Do you want me to sew something?"

"No. I would just like to be amidst the serenity that you and your sewing create."

Within a few minutes she was sat on the floor with her baskets and embroidery.

"Yutika, please don't leave here too soon."

She immediately dropped her needle, "I don't think that I will be leaving soon, Sollie. I am a widow, where would I go? More importantly, why would I want to go anywhere else? You have given me a home."

Sollie mulled this over… In England, he was used to his best staff moving on; either for more money or better prospects. He asked his next question innocently and without looking up: "Why does being a widow restrict where you can go?"

She remained quiet for a minute: "Let me just say that it is not so easy for people like me to acquire a job and a home."

"What do you mean? Why is life difficult for a widow?"

She took a very deep breath and bowed her head: "In India, when a woman marries, she often goes to live with the family of her husband. However, when their husbands die, Indian society sees widows as not worthy, cursed and devoid of status. When they become a widow, many Hindus, including their birth family, will shun them. Their adoptive family may also see them as a financial burden. Consequently, they are frequently removed from their husband's home, often violently and cast out.

"They are put out on the street with no food or shelter. They are not just denied what they need to survive but what they believe in. Orthodox religion forbids their participation in festivals like Holi, the festival of colour, which the rest of India celebrates. They are expected to give up all earthly desires and just wait for death. They can no longer wear jewellery or makeup. They may be expected to shave their head so that they lose their femininity. They can only wear a white sari, which signifies that the colour has been drained from their life. Their only hope is to beg from pilgrims or recite prayers and sing devotional songs for other people.

"Widows are prevented from eating fish, meat or eggs. Bread, cakes and sweets are denied because they may have come from a Muslim baker. Pulses, onions and garlic are outlawed because they are impure and may warm their blood. The washer men may not wash their clothes and the shopkeeper can't sell them goods. They are not only forbidden to attend the religious festivals that they crave to participate in, they can no longer attend any celebrations of birth, marriage or death. In some cases, even their shadow is deemed a curse and must be avoided. The widow is often referred to as 'it' or a creature and treated like a stray animal because it was only her husband's presence that gave her human status. This, along with the cutting of family ties and inability to celebrate their culture, results in loneliness. Being abandoned and betrayed by the ones they love also brings unimaginable heartache, despair and depression."

The ropes on Sollie's heart bells began to pull: "Is this a small problem?"

By now the tears were rolling down Yutika's cheeks. "Oh no. It is beyond comprehension. They say that there are 40 million widows in India. I am very lucky."

Sollie stood up, walked over to her and knelt down. He didn't plan his next action; it just happened. In the silence, he sucked up the herbal essence in her hair and lightly kissed her head before wiping her tears with his neck scarf. Then he made a solemn vow; one that chilled the air in the room. "Yutika, I want you to know that one day I will do something about this."

Sometimes, we can look back and remember the day that we fell in love or made a decision to reach out and help someone. It is often one thing. It can be an action, a touch, a look or some words. In this case, it was a simple sentence fashioned from a blacksmith's forge and seared onto a beating heart.

PASSIONS AND THE HARVEST MOON

Careers - Direction - Possessions - Parental pressure
Visions - Passions - Calling - Anxiety

We are often persuaded that we should be solid, move quickly, pursue goals and acquire security. Yet a Tree Mystic will steer you away from that. They will point you towards being hollow instead of solid, to reach out instead of moving forward, and to shed rather than acquire. Now your work will be bathed in the light of the harvest moon.

In the early evening, Bruno and Sollie were digging in the field at the edge of the forest when they were mesmerized by an unusual, milky light covering the wheat fields.

Bruno pointed to the sky in awe: "It is beautiful. What is causing it?"

"It is the luminous light of the harvest moon. It bathes the fields in a transparent, milky colour an hour or so before darkness sets. It heralds an end to one season and shepherds in a new beginning."

Bruno replied with the utmost sincerity: "How do you think that I should approach a new beginning, if I want to start a new career or life? Should I travel vertically and learn all the rules and mathematics of one subject, or should I strive for a broader education and move horizontally?"

"Think of what makes your senses come alive. If you were a flower, what would open your buds? If you were a salmon, what would make you want to swim up river? You must understand that we have similar instincts and feelings to plants and animals buried in our passion. Let me explain career paths further. I have seen five types of people.

"The first are those that don't know what they want. Usually, they have never inquired as to what their purpose is. These people usually end up in jobs that they do not like, if in fact they secure a job at all. The second are those that choose a career related to the things that they are good at, instead of what they are passionate about. Often their careers eventually bore them.

"The third are influenced by their parents' wishes and beliefs. They are often bullied into material success; canned like tinned sardines into professional careers that bring riches but leave a lid on their true potential. Or the reverse might be true; their potential might remain unfulfilled because their guardians gave them no encouragement or didn't want them to succeed. Then, they lack self-belief and often settle for mediocrity.

"The fourth are those that search for and unearth their 'passion' and then pursue a career in this field. Let us assume that you choose this fourth option. You might pursue your passion and create your own vision and your own business or project. You may think all will be well. However, what was once your friend can easily become your jailer. Before long you can find yourself being enslaved by a passion that consumes you, steals your freedom and sucks your friends and family away in the process.

"Fortunately, there is a fifth way. Here you make your skills available to something higher than yourself. You make the decision to connect to the universe, to make a difference and acquire meaning in your life.

"**With the fifth way, it does not matter if you use the skills that you are passionate about or the things that you are good at but not passionate about. This is because you will soon feel differently about them**."

"What do I do then?"

"Wait for your mission to arrive. Here you will find purpose and a reason for living."

"What will that be?"

"I have no idea. I can only recommend that you resist creating your own vision. However, if you make your passion and your skills available to a higher source, everything will change. Any enslaving will stop. Everything that was taut will loosen."

Sollie lifted his spade and pointed it at the sky: "Then, if you want to check if your calling is true, wait until the harvest moon is out. As it bathes the wheat fields in its luminous, milky light, so it will illuminate you."

Some people say, 'You can fail at what you don't love doing, so why not take the risk of failing at what you love?' This advice is incomplete.

BEFORE VARANASI AND VRINDAVAN

Leadership - Beyond religion - Human needs - Death

"Give me a lever long enough and a prop strong enough."
Archimedes

It was Yutika's official rest day. Sollie decided to give her something to think of. An intention that he hoped would pleasantly occupy her mind for the fullness of the day.

"I have been thinking about the plight of the widows, and I have carried out some research. It is as heartbreaking as you said. I can't believe that it is not mainstream news."

"There are reasons for that. It is a taboo subject; it has its origins in religion. Secondly, the widows' sorrow is buried alongside many other desperate groups in India: the other low castes, the orphans, the disabled and the poorest of the poor. It seems that there is only so much sympathy to share around."

"Well, fortunately, pollinators don't do sympathy, they do love and action. Archimedes said, 'Give me a lever long enough and a prop strong enough and I can single-handedly move the earth.' However, I don't need 'a lever'. I need access to the 'leader'. Then I will try and do something similar."

"What do you mean?"

"I mean that this is a leadership problem. Therefore, we must change the thinking of your country's leader. We must do whatever is necessary to persuade him to go beyond religion and liberate the widows."

Now he had her undivided attention, and she put down her sewing: "How are you going to do that?"

"I don't know, but I will find a way. I already have a starting point. It seems that huge numbers of widows have moved to the cities of Varanasi and Vrindavan. There are so many there that they are now called the Cities of Widows. I will go and visit Varanasi and see their plight with my own eyes."

"You sound very confident."

He laughed loudly: "I have a vision in mind and there are a lot of people laughing in it. Tell me Yutika, what do you believe the widows need in order to make them happy?"

"They need to be reconnected to society. They also require what everyone else needs; a sense of purpose, human connection, a sense of belonging, the expectation of a brighter future and an opportunity to celebrate life. Presently, many are sleeping in the streets, begging for their daily food and reverting to prostitution. There is no expectation or hope of a better future."

Sollie paused to allow all of Yutika's words to soak in, before saying, "If they have lived such a difficult life, we need to find a way of ensuring that they die on their feet dancing. I will take a trip to Varanasi to learn how we can help them do this."

"Why do you want to do that for them?"

"I would not be doing it just for them. I would also be doing it for you."

TROUBLESOME AND GOOD THOUGHTS

Meditation - Relationship with the world - Energy - Vibrations

Sollie and Tom were working side by side sweeping the entrance.

"Tom, what would you like to change?"

"I overthink everything. What is more, most of my thoughts are negative, which means I have sleepless nights."

"Good, at least you aware that**, Your thoughts are a matter of life or death!**"

"Is it possible to stop my thoughts from rising up or is it as pointless as sweeping these leaves, because more will arrive tomorrow?"

"You cannot stop thoughts from arising. Therefore, **Practise the art of watching thoughts pass through without attachment; without engaging with them.**"

"That sounds difficult."

"Not difficult; just an art to be practised and mastered."

"Will it take me long to master?"

"It depends if you treat it as a priority. It seems to me that many people are prepared to master the disciplines that will bring them wealth, fame or sporting success. However, not so many are prepared to take the time to master the management of those things that cause them great pain. Similarly, I have heard many people say that they have problems in their personal relationships, but I have never yet met a person who has admitted to having a problem with their relationship with the world."

"Where should I start?"

Sollie paused to peel an orange: "I did say that you cannot stop thoughts from arising. They are a river determined to find a sea. Therefore, I suggest that you work out what you must do to influence the type of thoughts that arise from within you. If your relationship with the world is a good one, a coral reef of beautiful thoughts with stripy fish will swim around your mind. If it's not a good one, it will attract the sharks."

Tom looked flummoxed.

"You create play lists and albums of your favourite photos and music, don't you?"

"You mean I focus on creating a bank of beautiful thoughts?"

"No. You focus on creating a blissful marriage with the world. From this relationship, beautiful thoughts will arise. The alternative would be to try and prevent troublesome thoughts arising. That would require you to erect a barrier or wall that could be held up in perpetuity. Even Samson could not do this."

"Then what?"

"Once you are experiencing better thoughts, you need to tune into them."

"How do I do that?"

"Meditate and practise yoga. Use your body as an antenna to tune you in and allow energy to flow through you. **Know that your thoughts affect your spirituality and your energy. It is this that creates your light and vibrations**.

"If you want to rock the world and shift it off its axis, don't try and push it; move it with the vibrations created by your thoughts. When I tell you to believe in yourself, what I really mean is believe in the power of your thoughts. Believe through your thoughts that all things are possible."

STIRRING HEARTS

Meditation - Life stories - Destiny

Yutika bought Sollie a train ticket so that he could visit the widows in Varanasi. However, on the morning of his intended departure, she was startled by something spluttering and vrooming outside the kitchen window. She ran outside and gasped, "Don't tell me that you are going to travel all the way to Varanasi on that! You don't even know if it works."

"You may be right. However, sometimes a sense of arrival is important; something that persuades people to put their washing out and come and have a look. I am also taking it because I would like to visit Vrindavan after Varanasi, if I have time."

"What are you going to do there?"

"I will film the widows. Then I will play the film back to everyone in their community."

"What will you ask the widows to talk about?"

He pulled a crumpled piece of paper out of his back pocket and handed it to her. Yutika studied the scrawl.

> Look through the eyes that you had when you were a little girl. Talk to us about your childhood joys. Speak of your thoughts and feelings when you were at school and in the fields. Tell us of the moments that melted your heart and your deepest sadness. Inspire us with your passions. Finally, share with us your greatest wish so that it can be heard.

"What will you do when you return?"

"I will write a book, tell their story and show their pictures. This will act like meditation; it will raise consciousness, bring clarity and wash up responsibilities on the shore. Some of those who read and see the book will hear their calling. Then they will know what they must do. They will help take the widows off the streets, change destinies and transform their own lives too."

VARANASI

If you wonder what an ancient religious city looks like, imagine Varanasi. It lies 800 km north west of Bhopal, is 3,000 years old and is one of India's holiest cities. Trying to describe the city is not easy, one can only give hints; it burns your nostril hairs and pinches your toes. It feels compelled to lose you in its ancient, winding streets. It spins your colour wheel and creates deep fault lines in your opinions and beliefs. You witness passages of joy that you wish you could partake in and scenes of pain that make you thankful for what you have.

Sollie arrived in Varanasi exhausted and minus his phone... he had inadvertently left that behind. His accommodation, a simple guesthouse, was at the top of a hill. The owner ushered him to his favourite type of resting space: a room full of emptiness with a squeaky, wooden floor. He was asleep within a minute.

At 6am, the light streaming through the thin, lining-less curtains top and tailed his dreams. Then, for the first time since leaving China, the colourful and striped djellaba was unrolled and given an airing. The minstrel's outfit, coupled with some loud revs of the motorbike and long blows on his conch, instantly attracted a large crowd. Before long it had turned into a procession; one that followed him down the hill. Parking the motorbike at the water's edge did not shake his followers off. Now they were curious, and they had questions to ask.

The procession accompanied him along the terraced ghats. His adventure also came with some unexpected success. Several in the crowd told him where he would find the widows' ashrams. One very happy-looking soul did more. He handed Sollie a letter of introduction for a lady called Cameli and told him, "You will find her at your next destination in Vrindavan. She is an angel committed to fighting the widows' cause, I think that you will like her."

VRINDAVAN

Mantras - Old age

Despite its proximity to Agra and the Taj Mahal, Vrindavan cannot claim to be one of the wonders of the world. However, it is one of the most unusual places on this earth. They say that it is the childhood home of Krishna, a deity that many widows love. The casual visitor would probably find Vrindavan intriguing but not necessarily holy and sacred. Those who do not worship Krishna might view it as dirty, dark and foreboding. Sollie found it beguiling. A place where great feasts of food are laid out for the Gods, just metres away from the lost and trampled. All in the name of faith and Krishna.

He started his tour by the riverside and headed for the Hare Krishna Iskcon temple. Dawdling along, he passed soulless eyes, famished cheeks and resignation. Most people looked like they were prophets or in need of a saviour. Here, friends did not shake hands when they said goodbye; they rested their heads on each other's shoulders and then crawled on their hands and knees to kiss each other's feet. Here, scantily-clad holy men sermonised at the roadside to enthralled disciples hanging on every word.

Sollie stopped at a bridge and observed a new world order. Here, ferocious-looking monkeys had commandeered the streets. They roamed their fiefdom in gangs, chasing starving dogs who were themselves fighting with bristly little pigs. At the bottom of the order, as well as the homeless widows, there were multitudes of starving old men. Most were fitted out in grubby saffron robes the colours of fire and sunset. They sat on the street pavements, begging and competing with the street cows for scraps.

At bedtime, he ran through his mind and heart all of the day's sights and sounds. It was all so unfathomable: 'Are these beggars in orange suits on the path to enlightenment or the road to hell? **Is everything really as it should be?** In the west, the elderly live in care homes, play card games and watch soap opera television. How can that be reconciled with the old people in Vrindavan? They chant mantras of devotion to Krishna but sleep in the streets alongside the cows and the pillaging monkeys.' He sat up straight in his bed: 'When I become old, should I continue the search to find out, **Who I am?** Or should I occupy my mind with puzzles? Is the **inner search** more important than a kind word and a shared piece of cake?'

MEETING CAMELI

Empathy - Dignity - Humility

On his second morning in Vrindavan, whilst the sun was still snoring, Sollie met Cameli. She was wearing large yellow earrings, a bright blue dress and a coral-coloured headscarf. Her presence filled the street with so much meaning and purpose that her movements appeared to have mellowed the surrounding brickwork. On the bright red tables in front of her stood large green pots of steaming tea. Like Varanasi, Cameli had an attractiveness that was difficult to describe. It was not a beauty defined by obvious characteristics; only by the gaiety that it swept in. One that caused little birds to swoop between her legs and butterflies to land on the refreshment tables.

Waiting to meet her was a very long queue of widows. As each one approached her, she poured them a cup of tea and placed a small garland of yellow flowers around their neck. Then Sollie witnessed a moment of lightness and empathy that humbled him. Instead of adjusting herself to receive a thank you, Cameli presented herself to each widow with her eyes closed before giving a curtsy and a bow. It was a greeting that said, 'I am honoured to meet you.' One that gave the widows dignity instead of cake to accompany their refreshments. A tea ceremony not unlike the one performed by Fei Hung.

When the last widow had been served tea, Cameli told him about her work, the challenges and her hopes for the future. Thirty minutes later, flames were shooting up from the kindling under his purpose.

CONQUERING FEAR

Love - Empathy - Injustice - Compassion - Comparison - Status

Cameli had arranged for him to visit one of Vrindavan's many ashrams. It was at the end of a quiet, muddy road. Before he could take further stock, a lady in a royal blue and red sari appeared and introduced herself… She had been expecting him.

"I am Geeta. Please step inside and meet Ashya, one of the elderly widows residing here."

Sollie entered a small, flimsy wooden hut in his bare feet. His toes and soles squelched in the warm mud on the floor. Lying in a metal bed were the smiling eyes and frail arms of a very old lady. Around the bed was a cooking stove, a toilet bucket and an assortment of clothes. In the corner was a small glittering shrine and a dish of banana slices for the Gods.

CRASH! Before he had even said hello to the old lady in the bed, an almighty commotion took place behind him. What a mistake! He had left the front door open. Two large, aggressive monkeys had run in. Now they were upturning all of Ashya's worldly goods. The monkeys were swiftly chased out. However, it was too late. The entire contents of Ashya's home were lying on the muddy floor.

"I am so sorry. Please forgive me."

However, Ashya wasn't angry. In fact, she chuckled and dismissed all that had happened with the wave of a bony hand. Then Geeta entered: "Don't worry, I will wash everything later. Just sit down. Let's take tea with your host, this is an honour for her."

Ashya could not speak English. Geeta told Sollie that Ashya was 94years old and bed bound. Then she informed him that they had both been cast out of their husband's family homes when they were young widows.

"It saddens me to say it, but as soon as I became a widow, my son looked down on me. My lower social standing appeared to elevate his. He starved and beat me before he threw me out."

Sollie whispered his next question: "Could you not go back to your parents' home?"

"When a Hindu bride leaves home to live with her husband's family, her own family ties weaken. When I tried to return to the village where I was born, my brothers shooed me away with a stick."

"How long ago was that?"

"Ten years ago. However, Geeta has been trapped here since she was 14 years old."

Sollie winced. Eighty years!' He gulped. A tear dropped from his heart. In fact, he hurt too much to continue talking while the subject of this sorrowful tale lay before him. Instead, he changed the direction of his questions.

"Who pays the ashram fees?"

"Wealthier people pay the ashram owner on condition that the widows in the ashram chant and pray for them for four hours every day. The wealthy believe that this will reduce their time in purgatory and ease their route to a better afterlife. So this is what the widows do. It provides them with basic shelter, but it is not enough for food."

"How do the widows pay for that?"

Geeta looked to the floor: "Those that can, go outside to beg. The youngest perform 'other duties', in order to ensure that everyone in the ashram can eat."

Before Sollie had time to take all of this in, he saw something out of the corner of his eye. It was sitting on the small shrine next to the banana offering. This time it wasn't a monkey; it was something beady-eyed. Then it moved. It was dark, wet and furry. It was the one thing in life that he was afraid of.

However, before he could think what to do, something bit him. He looked down at his bare feet. SHUDDER! A black rat was nibbling his toes. He quickly lifted them off the ground. His first thought was to run in fear. This would also mean running from the widows giving him hospitality. The same women who had to live in these conditions every day. A third rat appeared. "Oh my God," he said under his breath. However, Sollie didn't run. He stayed. He stayed out of compassion and transformed his empathy into love.

When it was time to leave, Ashya and Geeta didn't ask Sollie for anything; not a rupee or an orange. Why would they? They had given up on anyone saving them a long time ago. Yet they had given him something, a gift that he couldn't put into words. He asked himself, 'Is this why, in this strangest of places, good friends rest their heads on each other's shoulders and kiss each other's feet when they say their goodbyes?'

AN UNHAPPY OFFICIAL ARRIVES

When a set of screeching tyres stopped in front of the house, heads were sucked out of windows and beards were left untrimmed. A smiling official, immaculately dressed in white trousers and shirt, presented himself at the entrance.

"I am looking for Sollie St-Martin."

Yutika addressed him: "He is away. How can we help you?"

He took a document out of his briefcase, handed it to her and departed.

Yutika read it out: "Penalty charge - 50,000 rupees ... For not running the property in accordance with its operating license and for forcibly removing the residents. Repatriation to be arranged."

Apolline stood up: "I wonder who the residents are and how many there might be?"

The next morning a loud rumble and roar woke everyone up. The lost sheep had returned. When he woke up after a short sleep, they were all waiting for him.

Yutika assumed the role of interrogator: "Can you tell us how you acquired this property?"

"I leased it off a gentleman called Durga." Then he disappeared with a trailing leg and returned with a document.

Yutika opened it out. There was a moment of silence whilst she skimmed over it: "It seems to be a standard lease document with spaces for insertions, namely Sollie St-Martin and Durga Rastogi. There is an appendix with a secondary document detailing that the land must be run in line with its operating license NO 77754421." They decided to inspect the records of all the local land agreements and visit Phanishwar the lawyer for some clarification.

EXPECT THE UNEXPECTED

Tom and Sollie managed to collect a copy of the land register quite easily. Then they headed for the lawyer's office in the ancient walled city. It appeared shabbier than Sollie remembered. At a reception desk on the ground floor, a young boy greeted them.

"Would you like to rent an office, Sir? We can do long-term, weekly or by the hour."

Sollie paled slightly: "Is there a law firm called Tripathi renting offices here?"

The boy replied with an air of despondency: "No one is renting any of the offices this week. They are all vacant."

Tom gulped.

Back at the Mustard Garden, they all gathered around Yutika. She read slowly and carefully from the land registry certificate in her hand: "The aforementioned land has a permit to operate leisure and educational activities on the zones marked in brown. There can be no permanent dwellings in the area designated as forest and coloured green. No elephants can be kept in captivity on the land."

Sollie peered down the end of his reading glasses and stayed silent.

Tom breathed a sigh of relief: "That doesn't sound as bad as I thought it was going to be."

"I haven't finished yet." The room fell silent in anticipation of a bombshell. "The orphanage must comply with all state directives for a facility of that nature and pass an annual inspection."

"What?" they all asked in unison.

AN ARRIVAL

At 10am the following day, a cattle truck pulled up. The driver went to the rear of the truck and opened it up. Nothing happened. Then he grabbed a long stick and prodded it into the back. That brought a response…

Down the ramp trotted 14 sets of girdled roots. They looked as if they were between seven and 11 years of age. All were dressed in ragged, dirty clothes and mismatched shoes. There were floppy ears, sticky-out teeth and famished cheeks. There was also fear. It seemed that 'clarity of purpose' had just arrived.

They quickly established that the children could speak English. Yutika spoke as softly as she could: "Have you eaten?" The boy with the bucked teeth put his hand in his pocket and pulled out a small tin. He lifted the lid to show his selection of beetles. Then he popped one in his mouth and snapped it with his front teeth before gulping it down. Apolline shuddered.

Yutika and Ling went to the village to see if they could find out who the children were. Tom and Bruno were dispatched to buy some clothes. Ling cracked coconuts, peeled fruit and made soup. A few hours later Tom and Apolline persuaded all the children to take off their clothes and stand under a shower hose, which along with using a towel was obviously a new experience. When they were dry, new clothes were distributed.

Ling looked towards Apolline: "What shall we do next? I don't think that the children are ready for your French lessons."

MIGRATORY PATHS

Opening hearts - Flexibility - The unexpected - Success

Yutika arrived back from the village with information about the children.

"An old lady called Samira operated a small orphanage on the land. After Samira's death, it appears that Durga the landowner used the children as slaves. Apparently, when Sollie showed an interest in the land, Durga dumped the children in Delhi. However, it appears that, like migrating birds, the children found their way back."

Yutika looked towards Sollie: "Are we going to keep the children or send them away?"

"Some people celebrate passing their exams, some their birthdays. However, **The event that we should celebrate above all is the day that we open up our hearts.** When you first arrived, I told you that we needed to be an amoeba. One that could change its shape to accommodate any opportunity that presented itself... one like this. Now, let me tell you more about my longings...

A GENTLE OUTPOST

It is my hope that our home can become a gentle outpost and a migratory path; a place that all manner of wonderful things will be attracted to. A sanctuary where those with broken wings can rest and recover, before they take flight and inspire others to follow them. A place of pilgrimage that birds, animals and people will also want to visit. When we do this, our home will be full of colour. Our visitors will enhance our lives and hopefully we can enrich theirs too.

WHAT'S IN A NAME?

It is not who you think you are that is important. It is what you do. However, what you do determines who you think you are.

When they found out that the children only had nicknames, which in some cases were unkind, Ling came up with an unusual idea. She looked at Sollie: "Why don't we name them after islands? There are many beautiful ones to choose from."

He nodded, "I am happy with that… with one light condition. When they have come of age, they should feel free to change their name to something that resonates and vibrates with their new sense of purpose. One that confirms the removal of the limiting beliefs that were passed on to them as a child. One that in some cases is a proclamation that they are about to embark on a new path. A new name that says, **I am awake.**"

This was the list. Girls: Nirvana, Falsetto, Phi Phi, Batiki, Katikua, Coco, Cinnamon and Shimoji. Boys: Komodo, Bongo, Ascension, Stromboli, Curacao and Andaman. Ling painted each name on to a pile of wooden batons and gave them to Bruno to add a metal hook. He walked to the water well and jammed a large piece of wood a few feet down it. The name batons were placed on the wood. Yutika explained to the children that they should take the rope, lean over the well and hook themselves a baton that would have their name on it.

One by one, the children all hooked a piece of wood that would determine their name. Until there was just one little boy left. As the other children shouted encouragement, he walked around the well. Then the little boy toppled over. They all screamed. First he tumbled, then he rolled down the opening. They waited for the dull thud. Ling looked over the edge first… Bruno's strong arms were wrapped around him. She wiped her brow with relief.

Then they realized what they had missed. The boy may have been wearing glasses, but he was blind. Ling read out the name on the piece of wood that Bruno had rescued from the well: "Bongo." It was an apt name for a boy that would learn to love the drums. His funny hair quiff made him instantly recognisable. His bandaged knees and soily ears were testament to his love of climbing trees and unusual habit of listening to the ground vibrate! Above all, he was a boy who dearly loved the birds that he could not see. Bongo's best friend was Komodo; a boy with big, inside-out floppy ears and poached-egg eyes. A boy that liked to imagine himself as a ship with a noisy foghorn. Like Bongo, Komodo was a giver of joy.

CONSEQUENCES

Bruno and Tom had both lived alone for a long time. Both believed that having a happy family life with children was beyond their expectations. Until now, Bruno had only ever fathered his plants and been a husband to his greenhouse. Tom's love was still circling in his inner caves. However, the children's arrival would give them an outlet for their love that they had never imagined.

Yutika told everyone that the 1984 chemical disaster in Bhopal was not just about the 25,000 who had died; it was about the endless number of children who were subsequently born with disabilities. In impoverished places, disability can mean abandonment. Yutika said that this was the reason why such a high proportion of the children that they were now looking after had a disability.

It was only when the lessons began for real that the children's disabilities became apparent. Several of the children displayed behavioural challenges and struggled with paying attention, particularly Batiki. Komodo, the young boy with the most loving nature, displayed a form of autism. Sometimes he was boisterous, and he appeared insensitive to the other children's moods or needs. At other times, he bombed everyone with love and affection. It was apparent that he didn't comprehend the unwritten social rules very well. Stromboli was tough and all-knowing on the outside but seemed to be hurting on the inside; he was unable to make sense of the world that he had been left in.

THIRSTY WORDS AND COLOURS

Art - Diet - Language - Lightness - Stillness

Apolline listened carefully to an art class that Ling gave to the children. Ling explained that sometimes the Chinese referred to the colours of nature as dark, light, heavy and thirsty. Apolline had never thought about words in this way. She had looked for words to be right, not for them to bring lightness or darkness or to be of different weights. Then a thought crossed her mind: 'What would I have to do to make learning a language more fun?' This question gave rise to an idea… A language teaching project. Apolline called it 'Thirsty Words' to complement Ling's 'Thirsty Colours'.

Apolline and Ling developed their themes further; Ling with classes on silent drama, Apolline with a vocabulary of light and wonderous words that aerated the classroom.

When Sollie learnt about this, he was delighted.

CHICKS NESTING IN A TREE

Managing and motivating people - Compliments - Self-motivation
Conditioning - Love - Approval - Rejection

For the true meaning of motivation is love.

Now they were teaching the children every day. This presented Apolline with a new challenge.

"Sollie, I have a dilemma. It seems that the more recognition and compliments that I give out, the lazier the children become. It seems that they pay attention to the areas where I praise them and ignore everything else. They do what I ask, but they have stopped thinking for themselves."

"Sometimes I hear people say that a particular teacher or manager is good at their job because they pay compliments and give recognition. Are they really good, or are they just great manipulators? Are they teaching or merely playing the role of the zoo keeper feeding the performing seals? You must understand that great manipulators know that the world is starving from a lack of 'emotional food'. They take advantage of this and feed the famished with a diet of direct and indirect compliments. They say things like: Which one would you choose? How did you manage to do that so wonderfully? I wish I could do that like you. These exploiters also give out thanks, appreciation and individual responsibilities. Consequently, people working alongside them feel significant, valued and important."

"What happens then?"

"For a period of time, some people, particularly the overlooked and those searching for approval, will be happy. They might work harder too. However, you must know that when the zookeeper feeds fish to the performing seals, it is not long before the seals begin to expect. Soon they will be conditioned and dependent. Now their anxiety will increase in the same way that an addict always needs another fix."

"Are you telling me that I can't compliment the children or show an interest in them?"

"Just ask yourself, 'If I do a fantastic job of praising my students, what will happen when I leave? If the teacher replacing me does not give out compliments and praise, will all my good work be undone? Will all the flowers wilt? If this does happen, who is responsible for the cold winter that will follow?'"

"Me I suppose. What should I do instead?"

"Show a keen interest in their work and well-being, measure their performance, feedback on their progress and will them on. Point them in the direction of self-love and self-approval. Ensure they know that you are available to help them in times of need."

"I think that I understand... The flowers should water themselves and judge their own performance."

"Not quite... The flowers should water themselves and seek approval from their higher selves.

"Learn from the birds. Observe how the adult birds bring up their chicks in the nest. Then copy their behaviour. Flap your wings yourself, to show your chicks the way. Concentrate your efforts on encouraging them to jump out of the nest themselves. Convince them that they can fly. Clap, encourage, cheer and will them on. Know this: they don't need to hear compliments; they just need to understand where your heart lies, for the true meaning of the word motivation is love."

UNIVERSAL SOULS

Nature - Activists

After the children had been in their new home for a month, Sollie took Tom and Bruno aside: "I have a little task for you both. I would like you to take the children on a one-week safari to the Forest of the Emerald-Eyed Tigers."

"Why?"

"I want to encourage them to be activists. I want you to develop their relationship with the animal and plant kingdom and turn them a brighter shade of green."

* * *

Later, Sollie spoke to the children: "I want you to develop your relationship with the world; with all the lakes, mountains, forests, animals and people."

Bongo stood up: "How might we do that, Mr Sollie?"

"Every Sunday morning, we could dress up and organise a protest in the city centre. Every week we would campaign for a different good cause."

There was some kicking of the dust. Stromboli was first to raise his arm: "Mr Sollie, someone told me that Sunday should be a day of rest and enjoyment."

"Exactly. That is just what I want you to do. I want you to lie down in the road and rest whilst holding up the traffic. Then I want you to sing, dance and bang your drums in celebration."

There were more mutterings. The children, it seemed, were still not convinced.

"That is the good news. Unfortunately, there is some bad news too. To help you gain a better understanding of your relationship with the universe, Tom and Bruno are going to take you away for a safari. You will be staying in a forest with emerald-eyed tigers, hissing snakes and child-eating spiders."

Every Sunday after that, the children campaigned and protested on behalf of the forests, animals, widows, Hindus, Muslims, Christians, Dalits, rivers, seas and everything else that matters.

MUNCHING AND MOOCHING

Sport – Diet – Pace of life – Champions – The unexpected

If at some point you do lose your head, surely it is better that you enjoyed the journey along the way.

Bruno and Tom had been busy building some treehouses and a forest trail for the children. There was sheer delight when Sollie announced that there would be a 'dinosaur race' through the forest to celebrate its completion. The children were split into two teams. Stromboli and Komodo captained one squad and Phi Phi and Bongo the other. The rules seemed simple!

Sollie bellowed the rules out: "Each team should make a dinosaur. Which type you choose is up to you. However, it must be able to enjoy and sustain itself, return alive and keep something in reserve."

Komodo quickly persuaded Stromboli that they should choose a tyrannosaurus rex. To make his point, he stamped his feet whilst imagining his warrior stampeding through the forest: "It's huge. It runs at 20 miles per hour and is fearless. Nothing will stop it."

Not to be completely outdone, Phi Phi and Bongo also chose a large dinosaur; a stegosaurus, not quite as tall, but certainly fearsome looking.

Tom feared for Phi Phi and Bongo: "Why have you chosen a stegosaurus?"

"We wanted a dinosaur that mooches along slowly and enjoys the journey; instead of one that runs through the forest like a maniac."

They made their model dinosaurs out of papier-mâché and had them mounted on large wooden boxes with wheels. Sollie placed rocks in the boxes and explained that because the stegosaurus was four times slower than the tyrannosaurus, its box would be weighed down with four times as many stones. That would mean an awful lot of pulling and pushing for Bongo and Phi Phi's team. The route was clearly laid out with markers, and they were informed that there would be further instructions along the way.

At the start of the race the tyrannosaurus crossed the lawns and raced ahead. Behind them, Phi Phi's team pulled and puffed. Before they were even in their stride, the tyrannosaurus was out of sight and in the forest. However, five minutes later the first challenge appeared. The tyrannosaurus was a good bit taller than the stegosaurus. As the forest became thicker, it was having difficulty pushing its way through the tree branches. Despite this, it carried on at breakneck pace until the first set of instructions appeared on a tree.

1. Meat eaters must catch their dinner. (There was an arrow pointing upwards). 2 Herbivores should 'munch along' as they go.

Komodo and Stromboli's team looked upwards. At the very top of a tall tree, there was an orange papier-mâché monkey. They could not reach it. Sticks and stones would not knock it down either. Eventually, Katikua volunteered and shimmied up the tree to capture the dinosaur's lunch. As soon as they had secured the monkey on the dinosaur's back, they raced away. However, they had only moved a short distance when a second instruction appeared on another tree.

1. Carnivores must rest and digest their meat for one hour.
2. Herbivores should continue to 'munch along' as they go.

During the enforced 'meat-digestion break', the stegosaurus caught up and overtook the tyrannosaurus. However, all was not lost; encouraged by Komodo's trumpeting, a now headless tyrannosaurus was soon breathing down the neck of the plodding stegosaurus. As the finishing line came into view, the tyrannosaurus managed to overtake the stegosaurus before collapsing in a heap and breaking in two. The 'winning team' rolled in the grass, bereft of the energy required to jump for joy.

Then Sollie appeared and scattered the pigeons: "Why are you lying down? The race is not over! You must all return to the classroom. Here I want you to write and paint about what you learnt during the race." Bongo was first to read out his insights.

TRAVELLING LIGHTLY

Sometimes it is necessary to remind ourselves just how fragile this planet is. Therefore, we should do our best to travel lightly. It is for this reason that we chose the stegosaurus. They 'munch' rather than 'march', taking the circular route instead of the super highway. They may arrive late, but that is not important, for they have touched hearts and enjoyed tickles along the way.

However, not all the children had grasped the point of the race. Some descriptions talked of charging, frustration and exhaustion. Clearly they were only concerned with 'the winning' and not 'the journey'.

One of them included Stromboli: "Who has won, Mr Sollie?"

"That is a very good question. There is no doubt that the tyrannosaurus crossed the finishing line first. However, we did say that the winning team must enjoy itself."

"Does that mean it is a draw?"

"Oh no, it can't be a draw. One of the other rules was that you must come back alive. Unfortunately, it appears that the tyrannosaurus lost its head."

The first tears appeared: "That is not fair. We didn't know that the tree branches were going to be that low, and there were unexpected rules along the way."

"We must all learn to expect the unexpected in our lives, so please, never ever complain about it. It is the only thing that we can guarantee. What is more, if at some point in your life you do lose your head, surely it is better that you enjoyed the journey along the way."

GOYA'S ART STUDIO

Flowers - Art

We all have the potential to be great artists regardless of whether we can paint.

Sollie was not qualified to teach children. However, that didn't stop him trying. Here was a headmaster that loved to hear that one of his teachers could not make it to school. Today Ling was sick. He opened the classroom door and tutted at the wooden letters above the door - 'ART & YOGA STUDIO'. First he pulled the '&' off and modified it into an 'S'. Then he took the rest of the letters off and rearranged them so that they read 'GOYA'S ART STUDIO'.

"Ling is not very well today my little sunflowers, so she has asked me if I will take her lesson. I can't show you how to paint. However, I am sure that we can still enjoy ourselves. Now, do you have any questions?"

Coco's hand shot up: "Why do you call us your little sunflowers?"

"Young sunflowers track the sun. They start and end the day looking east, but throughout the day they head west. I call you my sunflowers because it reminds me that it is my job to help you follow the sun and be the light that others need. For the rest of the morning, I would like you to write a short story or poem on the life of sunflowers. In the afternoon we are going to do some modelling and biology."

BE AS YOUR MAKER INTENDED

Who you are - Personal potential - Limitations - Past problems

> Do not try and be whatever you want to be; seek to be what your maker intended you to be.

In the afternoon Sollie persuaded Tom and Bruno to join the class.

Prior to his address Sollie rubbed his hands together: "As painting is not my strength, we are going to work with some clay. I want each of you to take a piece of clay and make a model of yourself. Include all the good and all the bad. Tom and Bruno will do one too. You have one hour."

* * *

GONG! "Time up."

They all looked around the room and studied each other's models for a few minutes.

Sollie stood in front of the class with his hands behind his back: "Tom, would you please bring your model to the front of the class."

Tom did as he was instructed. His model was probably the best. If it had been hardened and painted it could have been sold in a shop. Sollie merely poked it with a curious finger. Then he handed Tom a rolling pin: "Now, Tom, I want you to flatten your clay model."

Tom reluctantly did as he was told.

Phi Phi gasped: "Why did Mr Tom have to do that?"

"I wanted to demonstrate that Tom is not a piece of broken glass that can't be put back together. He is simply a piece of clay that can be rolled out so that all his blemishes and cracks from his past can disappear. He can start his life again with a clean slate, whenever he wishes. **For you must know that it is not enough to recycle discarded materials; you must learn how to recycle yourself!** What is more, it is never too late to do so."

Suddenly Bruno's eyebrows untangled: "I think I understand it. Now we can be whatever we want to be."

Sollie tutted: "I don't think that you do! Please understand, the goal isn't 'to be whatever you want to be'. The goal is to remove your limited beliefs, religion, false identity, past experiences and your desires. Now you can be so much more than, **Whatever you want to be,** you can be, **What your maker intended you to be**.

The room was ghostly silent.

"Now I want each of you to bring your clay model to me."

They all reluctantly trudged to the front, seemingly far from convinced. Sollie ignored them and held the rolling pin high above his head, ready to execute each child's clay model as they passed.

CHOP! CHOP!

"Now, take a 10-minute break. When you come back, we will talk more about your form and your body."

WE ARE NOT OUR BODY

Identity - Spirit - Flexibility - Bodies - Form

Vessels - Transformation - Amoebas - Belonging

When he returned to the classroom, small pieces of clay were flying through the air.

"Stop! Stop! What I have to say to you next will determine whether you live your life as a small stream or a mighty ocean. He paused for effect... You must cast off the notion that you are your body, and identify yourself with your spirit. If you do this, you can imagine yourself taking on the appearance of a different form and shape. One that will enable good things to pass through and do their work."

Tom poked his finger into his piece of clay: "How might you describe this form and shape?"

"Like our home; like an amoeba. It should be flexible, adaptable and accommodating."

"Can you elaborate? It is not easy to imagine my form as an amoeba?"

Sollie took a piece of paper from his pocket, unfolded it and read it out.

MY FORM

"It would be light and shape itself in the direction of acceptance, rather than resistance; it would be made of faith rather than willpower. It would wish and wonder, as opposed to being knowing. I think it would run on its tiptoes, ballerina-esque across the stage; surrendering and collapsing itself whenever it was appropriate. It would be gossamer thin, if not transparent. It would be able to turn itself inside out or move to the sides like a human corridor when important things needed to migrate or pass through. A hollow vessel that others could use to do their work in. A frame that others could attach themselves to in moments of need. It would relinquish any desire to be solid and move towards being liquid. Finally, like a river searching for the sea, it would be looking for an open mouth in which to merge into."

SUNFLOWERS

On day two Ling was feeling much better and returned to teach the children.

"Children, I do hope that you all liked the lessons in my absence. Sollie told me that you are all destined to enjoy an incredible future. Perhaps you can tell me what you would like to do when you grow up?"

Coco stood up and turned her head slowly to the side: "I want to be like a sunflower."

"Why?"

"In your absence, we learnt that sunflowers can do all the things that we can do. They can also track the sun. Mr Sollie said that we must follow the sun like the sunflowers. Therefore, that's what I would like to do."

"Are you sure sunflowers can do everything that we can do?"

Coco stood up and read out her schoolwork from her notepad.

SUNFLOWERS

If the sunflower can turn itself towards the sun, it must be able to either feel or see. Therefore, why would it not be able to hear? It grows, so why would it not possess aspiration? It eats and drinks, so why would it not feel hunger and thirst? It dances in the wind and feels joy, so why would it not feel sorrow? It is born and it dies, so why would it not have purpose? When you see a field of sunflowers, can you be anything other than wistful and spellbound? For this is the effect that things have on the world when they try to do nothing more than make others happy.

Ling let out a sigh and a smile: "Did Bruno teach you that?"
"Oh no Miss, Bruno's crazy. He thinks that plants talk."

ART AND YOGA

Vessels - Depression - Teaching - Stress - Discipline
Success - Persuasion - Choices - Sport

At breaktime, on the way out of the classroom, Ling noticed Sollie's renaming of the yoga studio for the first time. She slammed the door. CRASH... the wooden letters from the sign came clattering to the floor. Then, bereft of her usual angelica, she found and confronted Sollie: "Why did you change the name on the studio door whilst I was away?"

"The studio is now named after Spain's most important romantic painter - Francisco Goya. He was also a man that used art to confront his demons. **Our studio is not just for exercise and hobbies; it is also to be a place of healing.**"

"Are you going to interfere every time I am away?" This time she slammed his door, before returning to the classroom. However, 30 minutes later she came back with tears streaming from her eyes. "I have lost control. There is no discipline. The children are throwing water bombs and paper aeroplanes. They will not do what I want them to do."

"Tell me, **If we cannot persuade ourselves to do the things that we should, why do we become disappointed when others will not follow our advice?**"

"But they are children. Surely they should be obedient?"

"Would it not be better if we could help children view discipline as something pleasurable?"

"How do you make discipline sound attractive?"

"Associate discipline with pleasure. The children need to understand that, **Discipline and delayed gratification are merely staging posts towards reward.** If you speak to winners, like great sports people, you will find that most are very disciplined. Their success was built on a rock of pain, persistence and restraint; there was no hardship that they would not endure to achieve their goals. They were motivated to train, day in and day out, because they imagined the rewards to be irresistible. People do not run through brick walls, get out of bed at 4am to train in their chosen sport, for fun. They only see what discipline will deliver them, and they imagine their victories in vivid detail. Without discipline, we cannot solve anything. With discipline, we can solve many things…**With surrender, we can solve all things**. Discipline must be viewed as something that can be found next to growth and success; side by side, like the slug and the lettuce."

"Out of curiosity, how do you monitor the children's progress in their mastering of discipline?"

"Oh, that is easy. I just watch them eat their dinner. In the beginning, I watch to see who eats what they like first and who eats what they dislike first. Then I note those that eat a bit of their likes and dislikes at the same time. After that, I monitor and look for progress. This is all that I need to know, to see how bright their future will be. How well we have taught them delayed gratification will determine their success at school, in relationships, at work… and even in the bedroom."

She was about to leave when he called her back: "One more thing; to celebrate the art studio's new purpose as a place of healing, I was hoping that you might encourage Tom and Bruno to do some painting."

"Why?"

"If we are in a dark place, painting is a way to bring some colour into our lives."

BIRD'S NEST SOUP

Sharing - Yoga - Art - Happiness - Security - Homes

Swifts and swallows return to the same nests. Blackbirds and song thrushes build a new nest each year. The cuckoo forces its way into the nests of others. The heron and the crane build communal nesting sites. The pheasant nests on the ground. But what of us?

Ling had been using her dressmaking skills. Today, to the delight of everyone, she was dressed like Emperor Huizong. A red robe cascaded to the floor. A black box hat with long, straight, horizontal flaps at the sides rested on her head. The costume was part of the lesson she had planned for the day. The subject was silence; she wanted to show Sollie that she had taken his comments on board.

The children giggled: "What are those funny flaps at the side of your hat?"

"During the Song dynasty, Emperor Zhao insisted ministers wore this hat in court. The hat flaps were straight and long to prevent officials standing too close to each other and disturbing proceedings with their whispering. I am wearing the hat to remind you about the beauty of silence."

Phi Phi raised her hand: "Mr Sollie taught us that silence stills the mind and stops the agitation of the soul."

"Did he!"

"Yes. **He also said that the importance of silence is not the absence of noise but the silencing of your thoughts**."

"What else did he teach you?"

"That silence can change our state so that we are conscious and awake."

"How do you think that will help you?"

"It will help us to be present and mindful. It is from this state that happiness arises."

For a minute Ling was silent herself. The children seemed to already know everything that she had planned for today's lesson. Komodo broke the silence.

"Can we all make a Chinese hat, like the one that you are wearing?"

Ling's reply was not sharp. However, it lacked her usual mellifluousness. "No... However, we are going to make something Chinese – some birds' nests out of the sticks that we have collected. What type of bird's nest would you like to build?"

"Mr Sollie said that there is no need to build a new bird's nest unless you want to eat some soup. Therefore, I would prefer to be a cuckoo. They don't worry about saving for a new home. They lay their eggs in the nests of other birds."

"Don't you want to save up and have a home that you can call your own?... Somewhere that gives you security and peace of mind?"

"**Mr Sollie told us that pursuing security will make us insecure.** He said that external security does not exist and only a fool would try and pursue it. We learnt that we must look for security within and place our emphasis on building a beautiful life; not a beautiful house."

"What might this beautiful life consist of?"

"Art, song and yoga. Mr Sollie said that is why you are so important."

"Did he now? Well then, maybe he is right after all." Then Ling turned her back on the class for a moment, whilst she wiped the tears from her eyes.

TEMPLE MAKING AND PILGRIMAGES

Shrines - Senses - Devotion - Give and receive love
Pleasures - Joy - Gratitude

Some religious people keep a mini-temple or shrine in their home. This keeps them connected to their faith on a daily basis. However, you don't have to be religious to enjoy the benefits. A small shrine and an area for prayer in your home can help you become spiritual. You might think that playing with something similar to a doll's house is a childlike activity. Don't let this worry you… being childlike will soften you and help make you humble. You don't have to buy one; you can make your own. You might even want to make yourself a smaller version to take with you on your travels.

* * *

Sollie welcomed Ling and Apolline with a big smile as they entered the house.

"That's perfect timing ladies. Come and sit at the table with me, I would like to discuss a very interesting project with you."

They both pulled a chair out and sat down.

"I would like you to design and make a mini-shrine or temple for our home. It should be about 50cm x 50cm in size."

Ling said what they were both thinking, "Oh. You mean a pretend one, like a doll's house?"

"No, I mean a real one … like a doll's idol house."

"Why? You said that religion was a hindrance to finding God."

"I did. However, this has nothing to do with religious faith."

"Is it so that we can make our home sacred?"

"No. I told you before, we can't make our homes or a building sacred. **We become sacred when we wake up and see the world and all that resides in it as sacred.** Our aim is to be as at home in our consciousness, as in the physical world. A shrine and a designated area for prayer in our home will increase our faith in those things outside of the material world and awaken the divinity in all that is sacred around us."

"What do we do next?"

"Visit all the temples in Bhopal to gather some inspiration. Then design and make your shrine!"

"What do we do with it when it is complete?"

"The area where we locate the shrine will become a special place in our home for prayer, kind thoughts, solitude, devotional offerings and connecting to our higher selves. We will also introduce some 'daily devotional temple tasks'. Small ones first; like cleaning the shrine, changing the flowers and lighting candles. These simple austere jobs will not feel like a hardship, they will feel like the kindling for devotion. When you carry out these tasks, they will not feel like chores; they are spiritual, and you will feel that you are helping God with his work."

"Why do we want to be devotional if we are not religious?"

"Don't think 'devout' means being serious; think of it as 'an outpouring of joy'. **Devotion is also another form of self-love. Devotion moves the desire for pleasure away from receiving and towards gratitude and giving.** The greater our devotional offerings, the easier it is to receive love in abundance."

As soon as Sollie left them, they began to discuss their preparations. Apolline scratched her head: "Who should we take some advice from?"

Ling squeezed Apolline's shoulders: "We should speak to Yutika, she knows about temples and rituals."

Then Apolline opened her mouth so wide that she had to put her hand over it: "Oh my… I know someone else that would be able to help us … My friend Olivia, she told me that her hobby is making dolls' houses. What a coincidence!"

LING'S TEMPLE PRESENTATION

Reasons for worship - Devotion

They waited until the sun had slid to the bottom of the sea… The children sang, and flickering candles lined the pathway. Then the curtains were pulled back to reveal Ling and Apolline's mini-temple. It had elements of Bhopal's Jain temple and the Taj-ul-Masajid Mosque. However, the principal structure was Olivia's suggestion. It emulated the 'stupa domes' of the Buddhist temple at Sanchi, including the stone walkway and some stone umbrellas.

When everyone had finished admiring it, Sollie began to question Apolline and Ling about what they had learnt on their visits to the various temples in Bhopal.

"We saw ritual, ceremony, prayer and chanting but alas, we saw little joy. We spoke to the devotees and asked them why they visited the temples. Some of them told us that they hoped that their worries would recede. Many came out of duty, tradition or social acceptance. Some admitted that they hoped it would secure their salvation."

Sollie directed his next question at Ling: "What did you conclude?"

"That most people came because they had been indoctrinated in their religion when they were too young to object or question it. They also came in the hope that they could free themselves of their worries and problems i.e. to take, rather than to give."

"Did all the houses of worship disappoint you?"

"No. In the grounds of one temple we experienced something truly joyous."

"What was that?"

"Visitors to the temple came with gifts of flowers they had bought at the night market. Then when they prayed, they spilled tears of happiness and joy. We approached a nearby monk and asked, 'What is happening here? What is it that makes these people look so joyful in their prayer?'

"He closed his eyes for a while, and then he spoke softly, 'They have not just come to pray for themselves or the people that they know; they have come to pray for the wider world. **They have not come out of expectation, they have come to share their joy.**'"

RUSSIAN DOLLS

Body as a temple - God - Nature

"Now I would like to tell you a little more about temples. However, before I start it is helpful if we can appreciate that, **If God is everywhere, God must also be present in our bodies and our homes.**

Then he passed a five-piece Russian doll around the room. "I would like to use the Russian doll to demonstrate the philosophy of 'interlinking the temples'. The first Russian doll represents our body; a temple that houses God, our spirit and loving heart. **It is because our body houses God that we should**

treat it like a temple. Formally inviting God into your heart and home can strengthen your faith in this realisation. **Our body or personal temple is also important because it can move; it can reach out and settle good tidings**. When a knitting circle, poetry class or a philosophy group meet on the road, for example in a coffee shop or park, personal temples extend the reach of spiritual activities.

"The second doll represents our home. Through spiritual activities like singing, cooking and gardening, our home also becomes a temple. When you are mindful that God is present in your kitchen, bedroom and garden, it will also impact on how you speak, what you wear and how you lay out your home.

"The third doll is the idol that we keep alongside our mini-shrine or doll's house. Loving the idol represents loving ourself. It also links us to the fourth doll; a communal temple. Don't think of a temple as a religious house of worship… It is a, **House of Energy**, also built to honour God… everyone can make use of it. The fifth doll represents the fifth temple… nature or the wider world.

"When you understand how all these temples are linked, you understand how everything housed in every temple is sacred and that your steps are saintly too." He lit a candle by the shrine: "**A small shrine or mini-temple in our home will help remind us to use our body as a temple to do God's work.** The little flower jar is there to remind us to show our gratitude and to share our joy. We light a candle as a reminder to put out positive energy and vibrations whenever we leave our house. In addition to all of this, I have a little request... Every day, I would like you to polish the shrine. This is a reminder that we must meditate to remove those things that obscure our authenticity."

VISIT TO A TEMPLE

Senses - Devotional food - Prayer ritual - Self-love

The tilac is the third eye. It is the signpost to the gate of your inner consciousness, where the desire to want to take your thoughts to a spiritual place will arise.

Each day someone tended to the flowers and candles that sat in front of the Mustard Garden's mini-shrine. **Now they had created a special place in their home to shine a light on the God within them.** When Sollie witnessed how much they enjoyed this new space, he planned the next stage of their spiritual education: a visit to a real temple. Here they would experience a 'puja prayer ritual'.

* * *

Sollie arrived at the temple a few hours before the others and decided to take a tour of the temple grounds. Later, someone helped him up the steep, stone steps of the temple, where he met up with the others. Here Yutika put a red tilac between everyone's eyes and a scented, yellow flower garland around their necks. However, before they entered, a temple guardian angrily waved his hands and insisted that they take off their shoes and place them in the wooden shoe store. Only Sollie was spared; he was just told to wash his bare feet.

Bruno looked down at the holes in his socks before turning towards Sollie: "Why did I have to take my boots off?"

"Some worshippers might say out of respect for God. However, your question is an important one, so I will answer it another day. Today, focus on how the five senses are brought together in the temple ritual."

Then the service started, and the sound of Sollie's voice was drowned out by a bell at the entrance gates.

Apolline tugged Sollie's arm: "What is the bell for?"

"The bell awakens the hearing sense and acts as a reminder to empty ourselves of negative thoughts. The bell's energy is also absorbed by the temple's idol."

Ling tugged his other arm: "What idol?"

"The idol is in the dark, over there by the priest. In the temple, it is believed that people become spiritual and closer to God when they talk to God through a medium. That medium is the idol."

As he said that, the crowd of devotees pushed forward in their eagerness to be nearer the idol. Ling was swept along with them, now the many-armed idol was right in front of her. It was wide-eyed and brightly-dressed in red and turquoise… She stepped back… fearing that it was about to come to life.

By the time the priest was ready to perform 'aarti', the air was thick with the scent of incense sticks. Then he encircled the idol with a flame. This activated the sight sense of those worshippers who had closed their eyes. After holding their hands over the flame, the congregation touched their eyes to activate the touch sense.

The priest rotated a plate ... now everyone's nostrils were full of camphor oil. Apolline tugged Yutika's sleeve: "What is happening?"

Yutika sighed, unconvinced it seemed in the sanctity of the message that she was about to deliver: "The circular movements of the plate are there to remind us that, **Our daily activities are secondary to our relationship with God; that if we put God at the centre of our daily activity, we will transform our lives.**"

Finally, the taste sense was activated when the devotees drank some of the holy water that the idol had been washed in.

Tom was at Sollie's side when they departed: "Can you summarise that for me?"

"Make God the centre of your daily activity. Practise spiritual activities ahead of earthly-based ones. Use the five senses in a spiritual way, not just as a means of pleasure. Participate in a puja ritual at home, similar to the one that you have experienced in the temple. It will help you with prayer, sharing your joy and showing your gratitude."

If God is not in your life and you feel something is missing, perhaps you should go and look for him.

BEYOND THE SENSES

Spiritual path - Clarity - Purity - Revealing God - Spiritual energy

It is our spiritual energy that will transport us to where we are needed.

On the way home from the temple, Sollie spoke more about 'what lies beyond the pleasure of the five senses'.

"Most people live in the familiarity of the five senses because they are not curious enough to ask what lies beyond them. To find out, **We must explore the world of meditative consciousness, and not just the physical world that we live in.**

"If you seek the senses exclusively for pleasure, they can turn into habits that will harm you. Desires for food, sex, alcohol, drugs, etc are rarely satisfied; it will not be long before you want some more. However, we do not go beyond the 'pleasure of the senses' to avoid entrapment; we go because something better lies beyond them. In the temple today, the sensory delights were not used as a source of pleasure. The bells, candles, camphor, idol water, etc were used to awaken the resources housed in our higher self.

"**Clarity is revealed in a state of consciousness. If we dare to go beyond the senses and the familiar world that we normally live in, we remove those things that are obscuring the purity of our loving hearts**. In a state of purity, we can treat our mind and our body as a vessel and a temple to pay service to God. **Now through our minds, hands and our hearts, God is revealed and can be seen, felt and heard in whatever we do.**"

A LOVING NATURE

Religion - Being loving - Anxiety – Higher self
Differences - Free will - Beliefs

They arrived home, and Sollie took some tea in the garden. When Apolline approached him, he was looking up to the sky.

"What are you thinking about, Sollie?"

"Whilst I was waiting for you all, I took a tour of the temple grounds. A young man approached me and we discussed his religion. I learnt that he was a volunteer who worked in the temple on his days off. I asked him why he liked to visit the temple… 'When I am here, my anxiety falls away and I feel closer to my higher self,' he replied. Then I asked him what happens when he leaves the temple and returns to the city? 'My worries return and I become less tolerant and loving,' he replied. 'Why is that?' I asked.

"The studious young man was silent for a few minutes. Eventually he replied, 'Outside of the temple walls there are injustices and differences that deflate my loving heart.' 'What differences?' I asked. 'In the city and at my work, not everyone shares my faith; there are also Muslims, Buddhists and Sikhs. These people subdue my loving nature.' 'Do you mean that you are only loving to those that share your religion?' There was a long pause, before a dawning: 'Actually, I become less loving to everyone, including those who share my religion. I can walk past a beggar of my own faith and fail to see the God inside them. All my worship fails me outside of these temple walls!' He paused for thought again… 'Perhaps we all need to share the same religion?' 'I don't think so,' was my reply. 'Why do you say that?' he asked. 'If everyone in the entire world shared one religion, it would not make people more loving; it would not solve anything.' 'Really?' 'Yes. We acquire a truly 'loving nature' when we identify with the whole universe, not when we identify with a certain section of the whole.'"

FOOD FIT FOR A BEGGAR

Devotional food - Mindful food - Thanksgiving - Beyond the senses
Fears - Sharing - Celebration - Feeding the soul

> Meditation stills us. Prayer is the spark that lights our divinity. Devotion and sharing are acts of joy that make us loveable.

Before the visit to the temple, the children and the adults had helped prepare a lip-smacking feast for a very special celebration. When they returned to the house, Sollie addressed them all.

"Today I would like to tell you a little of my visit to Vrindavan. I visited a frail 94-year-old widow called Ashya. On the day that I visited, Ashya had not eaten for two days. However, despite her hunger, she kept a dish of banana slices by the small shrine in her wooden hut. It was an offering to the God that she was devoted to: Krishna. She was able to smile and be joyful, despite the hunger in her stomach, because she had prioritised feeding her soul.

"There was more to learn; the bananas had attracted rats into Ashya's home. However, this did not appear to bother her too much … She chuckled as she told me, 'The rats are fatter than I am, but they do not scare me.' It appeared that devoting food to her God, Krishna, had taken her beyond her fears."

* * *

At the end of his discourse, the much-anticipated dinner gong did not ring. Instead, Sollie walked around the table and handed out a small paper packet to everyone. Komodo opened his. There was a limp-looking sandwich with the thinnest scraping of butter and a curled-up spinach leaf on it. Komodo sniffed it… He didn't think it smelt very good either! "What is this? Why can't we eat all that scrumptious food that we prepared for our buffet?"

Sollie stood back… with feigned shock: "Our buffet? Who said it was 'our' buffet?"

"I assumed it was for us. It took one whole day and a morning to prepare!"

"Oh. Then perhaps I should explain the thinking behind today's buffet. I have talked before about being mindful of the provenance of our food. Before eating, I would like to ask you to remain silent. This will help you enter a mindful state. Now instead of focusing on the pleasure of the senses, you can engage with those who provide your food: the farmers who worry about their harvest and the market traders who live in their fruit trucks.

"Ling and Apolline told us that some devotees arrive at the temple carrying a devotional gift of flowers. It is their way of demonstrating their gratitude for all of their good fortune. **They visit their temple, not to ask for their needs but to share their joy.** The flowers are no different than the devotional food that we see here today."

Komodo raised his hand, as high as he could: "Mr Sollie. You said share them. Yet I didn't make this mouldy sandwich. I helped make the buffet food. Does sharing mean giving everything away or having some yourself too?"

"Good question Komodo! What do you think?"

"I think that we should share the joy too. I think that perhaps we should feast ourselves on this mouth-watering buffet and then we can give the leftovers to the poor people." Komodo surveyed the room for approval. There was only silence. Something did not sound right.

"I do like your suggestion that we should share our food with those less fortunate than ourselves. However, because they cannot visit us, we are going to walk the streets of Bhopal and take it to them. After that, we will come back here and have the mother of all celebrations. We will dance all night and eat whatever food is left."

Komodo's hand reached the sky again, this time it almost tickled the sun: "There might not be any food left!" He took another look at his wilting sandwich: "We might go hungry!"

Sollie tutted, "**When we feed the needy first, we learn that devotional charity is something that we associate with our highest performance. We give our best first, not our leftovers.** When we share our food and our joy in this order, even if there is no food left, we cannot go hungry. For now, like the widow Ashya, we have already fed our soul."

MAKING AND PLAYING WITH IDOLS

Expanding the mind - Hindu Gods - Spiritual homes - Connecting to God Self-love - Anxiety - Loneliness - Humility - Surrender

When I am in the wilderness, I go for a walk amongst the tallest trees and talk to God. This humbles me and makes me feel small and insignificant. Other people use idols.

Sollie summonsed Ling and Yutika to his table.

"Ling, would you agree that there is no point in having a doll's house without any dolls?"

"Obviously!"

"Good, because now with Yutika's help, I would like you to make an idol to accompany our mini-temple."

However, before Sollie could continue, Yutika took charge of proceedings: "If we do make an idol, there are strict rules to follow. Idol makers must bathe at dawn, pray before commencing work and abstain from the pleasures of the senses. No work must take place, except for finishing, whilst the moon is waxing."

Ling wasn't sure if that sounded sinister or exciting, so she decided to change the topic: "What should our idol look like?"

Sollie intervened, "Like any one of the 33 million Hindu Gods."

"Thirty-three million different Gods! How could that be possible?"

Sollie laughed outrageously: "God's qualities and resources are limitless. So are yours. It is useful therefore to find ways of expanding your mind, to help you realise your true potential. The ancient Indians expanded the depth and width of traits and virtues by creating 33 million Gods. **Each God or idol helps us understand that what lies within us is much bigger than what we imagine.**"

"Thirty-three million Gods is a lot of choice."

"Don't worry about that. The real benefits are not to be gained from your choice of God. The reward is the development of your spirit and heart during the idol-making process."

"I don't understand why the idols are used to represent God. I was brought up to believe that idol worship was a sin."

"Devotees do not worship the idols. They worship the energy poured into the idol. **Idols are used as a medium to connect you to God because the**

human mind objectifies everything. Although devotees may point their devotion in the direction of a particular God, loving the God represents loving themselves. It is an act of self-love."

"How else will living with God change me?"

"**When we say that we feel alone with our troubles or that we feel lonely, what we really mean is that we haven't found the God within**. We should not attempt to deal with our problems as an individual… Don't imagine God to be your lone saviour either… Seek a union. Understand that God needs you, and you need God. Neither of you can do your work without each other. Talking to, dancing with and being loving towards the idols in your house are acts of spirituality that will take you closer to God.

"How?"

"**A return to a childlike state as an adult demonstrates your humility.** It softens up your ego in preparation for 'surrender' on your spiritual pilgrimage."

"How should I be loving towards my idol?"

"Dress it like a child would. Place flower garlands around its neck. Share your deepest secrets with it. Make confessions. Know that an idol is a living embodiment of God, it is not a lifeless puppet. God and idols remain wooden until we have a relationship with them. To bring our relationship with God to life, all our thoughts, prayers and plans must be centred on him. Similarly, the idol only comes to life when we worship it with love and devotion. It is this that awakens its divinity."

Then Sollie decided it was time to lighten the instruction: "So what type of idol do you think that you might want to chisel – one with slow-burning eyes or a devilish grin?"

"I quite like the idea of Ganesh's elephant head. I have heard that it brings good fortune."

"Mmm… I would prefer it if you chose another God. **Good fortune and freedom from anxiety will not come from having a lucky mascot or buying a lottery ticket; they will come from entering a partnership with the God within you.**"

* * *

That night the idol makers discussed their task. They decided that Ling would craft the idol from wood and paint it. Yutika would make the jewellery and clothing. However, the night before they planned to paint it, the idol went missing. They suspected that one of the children had taken it out of mischief. However, they soon forgot about that. When the next new moon arrived, Ling carved a replacement.

MUSICAL WASHING LINES

Relying on people – Trust – Disappointment
Giving up on relationships – Faith – Persistence

TIME AND MESSAGES

In the beginning, it may be necessary to show faith in what you have to say. Sometimes you will tell your story, and your audience will not understand what you have said. You may have to turn up and speak, even if your audience does not want to hear your message. There may be times when no one turns up to hear what you have to say. For disappointment is merely a call to action, a sign to blow your conch even louder. Never give up. If your message is worthy, it will only be a matter of time before it strikes the right note. However, know this: time does not strike the hour when you want it to. Time does not belong to you. Time belongs to God.

After two consecutive early nights, Sollie suspected that something was not quite right with Apolline. He caught her attention while Bongo was playing with the washing lines.

"Bongo has something to show you. Come and look."

She wasn't very enthusiastic: "What are you doing, Bongo?"

"Stromboli scared away all the birds. I have turned the washing line into a five-line musical stave as a peace offering. Now I am just waiting for the birds to return."

She laughed, and her better mood gave Sollie his cue: "I missed you last night. Is everything alright?"

Apolline dropped her head: "My father has died. My mother does not want me at the funeral. She blames my marriage break-up for my father's heart attack… I thought that we were meant to be able to rely on our family?"

Sollie touched her hand: "The great Roman emperor Marcus Aurelius said that we cannot rely on anyone, neither best friend or family, as both may let you down."

"What should I do then?"

"Don't give up hope of a reconciliation with your mother. Keep trying, leave the door open on your side. Know that just because you cannot rely on someone, it does not mean that you cannot have a good relationship with them."

Then Bongo nudged Apolline: "I am not sure that Marcus Aurelius is right when he implied that you can't rely on anyone except yourself. Besides, you can't rely on yourself. Don't you disappoint yourself sometimes too?"

Apolline nodded at Bongo's common sense: "Then who should I rely on?"

"Your higher self; the God within you."

Then there was a flurry of activity in the trees. One by one, birds of all shapes and sizes began to flutter down and space themselves out across the musical stave.

EMPEROR HUIZONG AND OUR LEGACY

Calligraphy/Art - Discipline - Meditation - Practice

Healing - Creativity - Transformative art

"Seas are the realm of dragons and skies are the homes of cranes."

Daoist text from the Song dynasty

Ling was painting: "Sollie, what should I do with the children who appear less gifted at art? Should I continue to encourage them or point them in the direction of something more logical?"

"Are you suggesting that those who can't paint, sing or play a musical instrument should be kept away from the creative arts? That would be unpardonable. I would have no choice but to chop off your little ears."

"Then help me, tell me what I should do?"

"You must change your view about what an artist is. I have told you before that creativity does not belong to the artist; a truly great artist is merely a vessel for creativity."

"I didn't know that. Remember, I have no formal art qualifications... I am not even sure why you chose me as a volunteer."

"You are of Chinese descent. I thought that this would make certain elements of our work more authentic."

"What elements?"

"During the Song dynasty, Emperor Huizong not only led his people, he found time to paint great masterpieces and develop the 'skinny golden style' of calligraphy. **Calligraphy is another form of discipline and meditation; it transports us to the present where our earthly desires fall away. It is this that brings us peace of mind**."

Ling bowed, "Do you know anything else about Chinese art, dear Emperor?"

Sollie ignored her impudence: "As a matter of fact I do. In ancient Chinese art, some incredible commissions of work were painted onto long, vertical silk scrolls. When the scrolls were unrolled, what you saw depended on which angle you looked from. You had to study the work very carefully to fully appreciate its splendour. The artist did not reward you if you only took a cursory glance."

"Why are you telling me this?"

"For now, I want you to use art as a healing tool to help all those that live here. However, later I might ask you to work as a vessel."

"What might that involve?"

"You might need to paint something that will make a particular action or mode of behaviour previously ridiculed or frowned upon, acceptable. Your art might need to influence an important person. It might even need to give rise to a miracle."

A BIG DANCE IS PLANNED

Happiness - Observation - Present - Patience

Anyone can hear if the birds are singing rock or opera, if they listen properly.

Bongo could imitate the songs of all the birds that visited the Mustard Garden. He was an observer; he listened carefully to what they said.

"The birds are happy when they are just 'coming and going'. This makes them want to sing and dance."

Tom scratched his head: "I have not seen them dance. I have only seen them swim, walk, jump and fly."

"Then you have obviously not taken the time to observe them as well as you could."

The birds do dance, of course. As Bongo had suggested, Tom had not been watching carefully enough. Bongo confirmed this when he returned.

"The birds are planning a big dance."

"How do you know that?"

"They are warbling in a different tone," he replied, matter-of-factly.

"You are very lucky Bongo. You may not be able to see, however, you can hear things that we can't."

"Actually that is not true, Mr Tom. Anyone can hear the nuances of the birds' songs if they take the time to listen properly. **Don't say that I am lucky. Say that I am happy. Know that being observant and 'in the present' is what makes me so.**"

* * *

Ling was hoping that there might be a dance soon too. A dance where she could put her arms around Bruno, before Apolline did! 'But how?' she asked herself.

THE SCHOOL INSPECTOR

Empathy - Belonging - Self-love - Development - Learning - Propagation Discipline - Silence - Belonging - Forgiveness - School curriculum

As they were new operators, they had to re-register the orphanage. This would result in an inspection. A few weeks later, the inspector arrived! The first thing that she asked to see was the children's work books. Unfortunately, none of the children had any writing books for English, science, maths or history.

The inspector wrote some notes in her book. She also appeared to be angry.

Apolline recalled one of her early conversations with Sollie: 'Please put those books away Apolline. We have more important things to do before we teach the children grammar and mathematics.' 'What might that be?' she had replied. 'We must help them feel loved and give them a sense of belonging. No theory or apostrophe will root properly until this task has been completed.'

Then the inspector asked to observe their teaching. Ling was taking the class. All the children were in attendance, regardless of age or disability. When the inspector walked in, the children were sat in silence rubbing each other's backs.

"What is the purpose of the back rubbing?"

"It is to remind us that, **We are all here 'to serve and be served' in equal measure.**"

"Why were you punishing the children with silence?"

"Please be assured the children do not see this as a punishment. They like silence, some of those with autism love it. They know that silence heightens the senses and is one of the first steps towards self-love."

"When do you teach mathematics and the sciences?"

"Those subjects have been substituted with gardening and nature watch. However, we are planning to teach them in the future."

"What about history and grammar?"

"Those have been replaced with subjects like kindness, forgiveness, propriety and meditation."

"Can you show me some exam papers and tell me who the brightest is?"

"We don't actually conduct exams. Each student is encouraged to improve on their personal best performance regardless of their starting point. We avoid comparisons. We inform everyone about their individual 'breakthroughs and successes' and what they must do to develop themselves further."

The inspector thanked them and told them that they would receive her report in due course. However, before she left, they were keen for some feedback.

"There are good points, and there are bad points. There are some areas where you score less than no points."

Apolline crossed her legs: "What happens if we fail the inspection?"

"Then the children will be taken away to a more appropriate institution. Oh... one more thing. For the safety of the children, all of the adults living here will need to report to the local police station to ensure they have no criminal record."

TREE PLANTING

Expectation - Entitlement - Bad news - Anxiety

The leaves are its tears. The fruits are its joy.

Sollie looked up to the ceiling: "I suppose that the time has come to balance our practical and philosophical teachings with some rudimentary education."

The next morning, lessons were suspended and they worked on a new curriculum. Was it too late though? Did they have enough time to improve before a possible second inspection? They were all worried.

Tom was particularly pale and unnerved: "We have done something very dangerous; we have given them a taste of a better life. Before they knew no better, they had no expectations, but now they have. If this goes wrong, we are culpable. We can't let that happen."

Every day after that was a challenge. The teachers became despondent, and the lessons became more logical and less fun.

Sollie knew that he had to act… He took the adults to the forest and made them all plant a tree. Over squash he explained his thinking.

"You may have heard the famous Martin Luther quote, **Even if I knew that tomorrow the world would go to pieces, I would still plant my apple tree,.** That is what we have just done and what we will continue to do… Luther's message is for all those that feel like giving up. It applies to your personal life, your business or if your favourite sports team is losing with a few minutes left to play. It also applies to our situation with the orphanage. When all looks lost, when the final appeal has been turned down, keep going, keep planting. As well as faith, you must remain calm. You must not panic. If we keep our nerve, there is more than enough time to score our goals and carry out our changes."

They all clapped and laughed at his optimism. Only Apolline seemed doubtful: "Where are we going to find a mathematics teacher?"

"I can do that. Watch me!"

DAISY CHAINS

Desires - Logic - Needs - Happiness
Mathematics - Problems - Transformation

Sollie was about to have some fun. The very thought of it lightened his steps and tousled his hair. He skipped into the classroom.

"The school inspector has told us that we must add mathematics to the curriculum. Therefore, this is what I am going to teach."

A loud chorus of boos rang out. No boo was louder than that trumpeted by Komodo: "Mr Sollie, you told us last week that you didn't know any mathematics. How can you teach that which you know nothing of?"

"I know one equation. I will teach that. Then we can go outside and play some sports."

He picked up some white chalk and wrote thickly on the blackboard: 'The sum of X must be eliminated in order to maximise Y. How do we do this?'

The classroom shrieked, desk tops clattered: "What does that mean?"

"It means that X (material desires and the pursuit of a sense of security) must be eliminated in order to maximise Y (your happiness).

"Executing this formula properly determines whether you spend your life toiling in a state of anxiety or living a wonderful life. This is the only mathematics that you need to know! As soon as you have worked out how to solve the equation, we will all go outside into the sunshine and play some sports. Oh… and there is one rule."

This time Stromboli raised his hand: "What is that, Mr Sollie?"

"You cannot remove X." (Your desires)

Sollie sat down. The children were silent. There were lots of attempts at the answer. However, every time someone shouted out what they thought the answer was, Sollie pricked and deflated it. What they thought would be a five-minute maths lesson, before a day of fun, wasn't turning out as the children had hoped. Now it was lunchtime, but Sollie had wrapped paper around the classroom bell and hidden it in the stationery cupboard.

Before long it was 2pm.

"Do you give up?" he asked them all.

"Yes. Yes. Yes," they all shouted.

"I am sorry, giving up isn't allowed. Please continue working on the equation."

Suddenly, Phi Phi stood up. She seemed very excited: "I think that I have solved the problem."

"I don't think that you have."

Stromboli decided to defend her: "How do you know? You have not heard her answer yet."

"**I know, because problems are not to be solved; they are to be synthesised.**"

Phi Phi did a little jump: "I still think that I have the answer."

She walked over to the blackboard, picked up the chalk and replicated the X 16 times and formed a circle. Now the Xs were all joined together; reborn as a chain of daisy flowers.

Then Sollie spoke in a tone of voice that did not hint at whether she was right or wrong: "Can you explain to the class what you have done?"

"You said that we cannot remove X – our desires and the pursuit of security. However, these wishes can be synthesised into something better. Therefore, I have converted X into something that has a positive impact on Y. It seems that after a course of self-love, we must turn our attention away from our own concerns and towards the things that other people need. **It appears that when we focus on the needs of others, our own anxiety melts away."**

Phi Phi placed her hands behind her back and looked up. Sollie walked over to the stationery cupboard. In complete silence, he slowly unlocked the doors. Then he filled his arms with cricket bats and footballs.

"Class dismissed!" he bellowed, louder than any bell could ring.

A HOUSE OF SOOTHING

Positive interpretations

The tree-planting speech relit their fires. However, it did not stop the inspector's report from arriving. They failed. The report said that the children must attend a nearby school during the daytime or they would be placed in a more suitable orphanage. Yutika wrote back and asked which school.

They received a short reply. It said that it was their responsibility to persuade the local village to assimilate the children into the village school.

They met with the village school head teacher and made a presentation.

Two days later, they received a letter. The school was sympathetic to their needs. However, there were not enough teachers to help them. Apolline and Ling were despondent. A few hours later they were in anguish...

Bongo popped his head around the door: "Don't look so worried. If the inspector will not let us stay, we won't be going to another orphanage. We have all decided that we will go and live together on the streets." With that he left. Apolline and Ling cried their eyes out. Then they shuffled away to see Sollie. They expected sympathy... there was none forthcoming.

"So what are you going to do about it? Remember what we said, **There is no such thing as bad news; only bad interpretations and a failure to plant some new trees.** The school's reply is not a rejection; it is merely a call to action to try again. Now please go away, and don't come back until you have a solution."

DINOSAUR INVITATION

Rejection

This gave Apolline the mother of all ideas: "Why don't I polish up the 'Thirsty Words' project and set up a language and cultural exchange that the village school can participate in? This might result in the children from the Mustard Garden being invited to attend the village school."

There were no dissenters. That encouraged Apolline to think up another fantastic idea... to invite the villagers to a welcome show at the Mustard Garden. "We could also invite our royal neighbour Parminder."

Sollie clapped his hands in agreement: "What welcome did you have in mind?"

"A theatre show in the forest. We could repair the dinosaurs and breathe a bit more life into them."

And so they did... The children went to work in the art room. A tyrannosaurus was given a new head and a stegosaurus a fresh coat of paint. Bongo and Bruno recorded some bird songs and shrieks! The ladies worked on some costumes.

* * *

Later, Bruno came to see Sollie. He was looking pale: "Sollie. I am worried. I don't think I can go to the police station."

"Why ever not?"

"Because I escaped from the asylum."

"But talking to flowers isn't a criminal offence."

"I know, but it is all a bit hazy. I also heard someone say that I set fire to my adversary's house."

"Do you think that your adversary could have been in the house at the time?"

"I honestly don't know. I wasn't feeling well at the time, and they filled me with drugs when they took me away."

Sollie wiped his brow: "I will need to think about this. I suggest you don't tell anyone."

Bruno looked down: "I will try, but it's not easy. Every time a visitor arrives, I think it is the police coming to take me away."

Sollie kept Bruno away from the police station and off the register of adult residents. However, he was unnerved by all that Bruno had said. He had never had to manage a second chance like this before.

Bruno returned to his room and tried to make sense of the menacing thoughts lurking inside him. The voices that had gained a foothold in his marrow.

THE DINOSAUR SHOW

Emotional stimulation

Approximately a thousand villagers turned up for the dinosaur show! On arrival they were led into the forest. Some sat on the floor, others sat on the branches of the trees. The sense of expectation was thrilling.

The big lights were dimmed. A lone forest horn called out. Yutika appeared, dressed as a woodland witch. She told the villagers that they were about to see the dinosaurs of the past come alive. However, before proceedings could start, the audience were asked to appoint four sacrificial adults. The village children shouted out some names, and four of the village elders were taken away.

Cracks of thunder and white lightning jumped across the sky. A huge cooking pot, lit by a flaming wood-fire, came into view. The strobe light moved up and down before settling on the four white-haired elders. Gasps of bewilderment ran through the auditorium… The elders were dangling from ropes a few inches from a bubbling broth of bats, potions and giant frogs. The mood electrified… The children screamed. Old ladies' false teeth chattered, and old men put their hands on their hearts.

The trees turned red, green, purple and orange. High-pitched shrieks raced across the tops of the trees and pterodactyls flew through the sky. Then the flying dinosaurs changed direction and flew directly towards the crowd. First the audience screamed. Then they fell to the floor, as outstretched talons came in search of ears and scalps. In the frenzy, three children fell out of the trees and half the adults stood up, ready to run away.

Then the silence. Silence the colour of black and the thickness of oil. The sort of silence that precedes the whistle of the witch's broomstick before she lands.

BOOM! BOOM! Came a noise from something unimaginably huge. CLUMP! THUD! CLUMP! THUD! Frightening was gathering pace; inching nearer. Frightening whipped its tail, beat its chest and swivelled its head. Teeth the size of rhinoceros horns snarled and snapped. THUMP! THUD! THUMP! THUD! It pounded nearer. However, it was about to become worse; this was only the vegetarian appetizer – the stegosaurus.

A roar the size of 300 trumpeting elephants bellowed out. The tyrannosaurus had arrived. The villagers covered their ears, too scared to run and fearful that there was not enough time left to say their departing prayers. THUMP! THUD! THUMP! THUD! The direction of the pounding, giant feet quickened; they were heading for the cooking pots and the elders. Within minutes, the gnarling of a feeding frenzy could be heard. The lights came back on. The cooking pots came into view. However, now there were no sacrificial adults to be seen. Only a heap of ripped clothes lay on the floor.

Had the show ended? Should they come down from the trees? Was it safe? Was this a game or had the village elders truly been harmed or sacrificed by these strange people living at the Mustard Garden?

AGH! CRUNCH! Then the mightiest roars yet blew a hole in the tree canopy. The dinosaurs had reappeared; only this time they had cut off the villagers' escape route. They were towering behind them. The audience could feel the sulphurous, hot breaths of the dinosaurs. Pandemonium. The audience screamed, squealed, jumped from the trees and ran in all directions.

It was two minutes before the bright, white lights and dancing music of the forest elves came on. In the meantime, thumping hearts and open mouths lay scattered on the floor. Relief only came when Yutika picked up the microphone and reassured them with her sweetest voice.

Everyone returned to their places. With the forest now all lit up, the pterodactyls slid down their ropes to the floor, the dinosaurs were wheeled to the front and all the actors took a bow. The cheers were so loud that they could be heard in Delhi. What a show, what a night! Now it was just a matter of waiting to see if it worked.

A SURPRISE INVITATION

It arrived in a large, pale-green envelope with a red border, a coat of arms and a wax seal. It wasn't presented on a red velvet cushion, but it was hand delivered by a cream silk glove.

Apolline read it out: "It is an invitation from Parminder, our royal neighbour. There will be afternoon refreshments and entertainment, next Sunday at 3pm.

* * *

The day of the afternoon tea party arrived. They all scrambled into the boat and rowed over to Parminder's palatial home on the lake. However, well before the jetty, the water had dried up. They had to walk the last 30 metres in the squelchy mud, holding their footwear in their hands. Their bare-footed arrival wasn't the one Apolline had anticipated when she had first set eyes on the maharaja's invitation.

After a quick foot-wash, they were encouraged to sit down in sumptuous velvet chairs in an opulent, silk-walled ballroom. Then the entertainment started; a classical dance-drama from Kerala. Onto the stage stepped numerous theatrical characters dressed in multi-coloured Kathakali costumes of a finery that few will have witnessed.

They all fixed their eyes on the central character; it was their host, Parminder. Rice paste and vegetable colours had been used to paint his face a vivid green, whilst the area around his mouth was a brilliant coral red.

Apolline took a photo: "His face makes him look like one of the green frogs that live in the trees by our house."

After the performance came the feast. To begin with, cucumber and salmon sandwiches were passed around on snakeskin platters. Then the plat principal arrived; royal chicken soup, served from giant copper kettles by trained monkeys wearing liveried pillbox hats.

Then their host strode in, now no longer dressed in his Kathakali costume; now merely dressed in the finery of a maharaja. They had expected this; what they hadn't expected was a giant. A monolith with a thick mop of dark hair and a contrasting snow-white beard. A goliath with eyebrows that made him appear badger-like. They all introduced themselves. Then Parminder waved his clapperboard hands and encouraged them to move outside and sample artisan cakes from silver wheelbarrows.

HUNTERS AND GATHERERS

Mindfulness - Diet

Apolline thanked Parminder: "That was a wonderful buffet, sumptuous even."

Parminder took a bow: "I am a gormandizer, and I am passionate about my food."

Then Sollie shuffled his feet, forcing Apolline to the margins: "Perhaps it would be better if you were a provenancer."

"What is a provenancer?"

"Someone who is passionate about the provenance of their food. It converts a person from a hunter to a gatherer."

"Does that mean that you didn't try the royal chicken soup?"

Sollie coughed: "I am sorry, I had to refuse it."

"Why was that?"

Sollie crunched his piece of cucumber before delivering his response: "I am not religious. However, the Bible states that man has been given dominion over the birds, the fish and the other animals. I ask myself, 'What does this mean? Killing and eating them or caring for them?' Tell me, if you were given dominion over all the children, would you shoot and eat them too?"

However, Parminder was not a man to be upset by an opposing view. "Perhaps I can tempt you with some of our exotic cakes instead. They say they taste imperial."

Sollie smiled. However, this time Apolline intervened and stepped on his toe before he could reply.

She quickly changed the subject: "The Kathakali costumes are beyond splendour."

"Thank you Apolline, however, they are more than splendid; they are life savers!"

When Sollie heard this, he immediately twizzled around and looked up at Parminder: "How exactly are they life savers?"

Suddenly, great creases crumpled across Parminder's gigantic forehead, and his boom changed to a hush: "My Kathakali costume maker told me a story that the suit maker to all the American presidents had recounted… 'Ronald Reagan was the most friendly and elegant world leader. He knew that I liked jelly babies, and he always remembered to bring some with him when he came to visit me for a suit fitting. I remember other presidents with less affection; they always seemed preoccupied and revealed none of the pleasantries that the outside world saw.'

"Those words paralysed half of my body and cast a shadow over my brow. For preoccupied, and worse, was probably how the suit maker would have described me. Do you know of India's honey badger?"

"Sorry, I don't."

"Some say that they are the most fearless animal in the world. They will attack the deadly cobra, put their head in a beehive and take whatever they desire. You should watch them on YouTube. I am afraid that I have become like one; unctuous and oily, cunning and conceited, impatient, wanton and sometimes very angry. My appearance has changed; my hair is dark, but my beard and eyebrows are turning white. It seems that I am beginning to look like a honey badger.

"I have become busy with self-importance. I have wrongly concluded that I have so much to do, that there isn't enough time for the things that really matter. However, now I understand that if you permit your vision to emanate from a higher source, you don't become preoccupied with you own plans, because time, light and jelly babies are built into the programme."

Then Parminder signalled for Sollie and Apolline to sit down with him.

LIFE OF A MAHARAJA

Success - Desires - Happiness - Sustainability

Apolline shuffled her chair forward: "I couldn't help but notice that there are no leaves on your lawn. How many leaf sweepers do you employ?"

"About 50."

"Wow. What is it like to be rich enough to buy all your desires?"

"It is an obsession; like catching a disease for which there is no cure. There is no time for anything else. The pursuit of wealth and glamour has stolen my life."

She touched his hands lightly to emphasize her sympathy: "Are you still obsessed?"

He touched her hand in return: "No I am searching for the cure."

This awoke Sollie from his trance: "Are you even remotely happy?"

"No. Not at all. I have found lots of things that make me miserable. However, I have yet to find what makes me happy. I can certainly rule out status and money."

Apolline took over the proceedings once more; "Have you ever been married?"

"Yes. Although the marriage did not last. Now I am alone, and whilst I have no desire for another wife, I would like to be surrounded by children."

"Do you have a plan to change things?"

"Yes. I am going to observe and follow those people who appear to have in their possession what I desire. For I have learnt that this is the quickest and simplest way to be successful. Therefore, I am going to observe you all, if you will permit me to, so that I can elicit your strategy."

Parminder looked towards Sollie and posted a conciliatory look: "Now please tell me, Mr Sollie, what are your plans for the Mustard Garden?"

"I hope that I can find a way to make the Mustard Garden sustainable so that when I leave, it will not fall apart."

* * *

When they returned to the Mustard Garden, another letter was waiting for them. Yutika ran out of the kitchen and waved it in the air: "Shimla, the village head teacher, would like to visit us."

LOVING TENDERNESS

Love - Sensations - Miracles - Nourishment - Being present

> Your interpretation of your challenges will determine your happiness. Your decision to go in search of simple pleasures will give you joy.

Shimla, the headteacher, was due to visit in the afternoon. They planned to discuss the schooling on the lawn. Sollie didn't want Bruno to be seen and asked him to stay in the lodge out of sight. However, he didn't know that Shimla would arrive with her husband, Pravid, and a baby. Yutika met them and, unaware of Sollie's instructions to Bruno, told Pravid to wait inside the lodge with his little girl.

It seemed that the school was particularly keen to learn how the Mustard Garden tackled the teaching of the disabled children in their care. Shimla explained that the school had some deaf and mute children but no qualified teacher to help them. While this was happening on the lawn, a very different type of event was taking place inside.

Shimla's husband, Pravid, placed a baby bag on the table: "Do you mind if I bath her? The water is off where we live." Bruno had just the thing. He returned a few minutes later with a plastic bath from his greenhouse. He washed it out and filled it up with water. Pravid smiled: "Perhaps you would like to bathe my daughter?"

Pravid passed the baby over. Bruno gently lowered her into the water and poured cups of warm water over her head. She laughed and waved her tiny feet. Bruno felt a new emotion… but it wasn't one he was familiar with. Then a little miracle took place; one that stirred Bruno in a way that his carrots, tomatoes and courgettes never had. Pravid gently lowered the baby onto a blanket on the floor. In between little tickles, he patted her dry with a big, fluffy towel: "Now I am going to apply a little soothing cream before you finish things off."

"Me? Are you sure?"

"Of course." Pravid handed him a plastic container: "Just sprinkle her in baby powder. Then watch her gurgle with delight."

Bruno did as he was asked and covered the giggling girl in a puff of baby powder. Its sweetness filled the room and danced around his nostrils: "What do I do next?"

"Put the talcum powder down, then gently rub and stroke her."

Bruno caressed and patted as tenderly as he possibly could: "What does this do?"

"It nourishes the baby's present and future happiness."

Bruno continued with his task in complete silence... The emotion that he was soaking up left no room for words. He sighed and blew on his own face instead. When it was time to pick the baby up and pass her back to Pravid, Bruno attempted to work out what he had just experienced. This, he concluded, must be human tenderness. He put one of his big gardening hands up the back of his shirt because now rivers of perspiration were running down the great canyons of his back.

Pravid gave him a concerned look: "Are you okay?"

There was a long pause... "I don't think that I have witnessed anything like that before. I don't think that anyone ever did that to me."

* * *

When Shimla and Pravid departed, the adults sat down on the lawn to discuss the visit. Except Bruno, he went for a walk. He wasn't going to let such a moment of joy pass by without some more contemplation. He put the back of his hand to his nose. It smelt of baby powder... Some of his grief loosened, and something around his heart began to swirl.

> Sometimes grief, loss and loneliness can make your face crumple. Sometimes joy can make your lines retreat.

INVITATION TO A SAVIOUR

Challenges - Problems - Acceptance

> Life is about a never-ending chain of challenges. It is this that we must accept.

When Apolline did decide to treat Shimla's needs as a challenge instead of a problem, the answer came to her immediately. She went straight to her computer, pressed some keys and then the send button.

Dear Olivia,
I hope that you are well. I am in India. Everything is good but we have a challenge. We need a Special Educational Needs teacher, ideally one who can teach sign language. Would you like to come out and help us for a few weeks?
Love Apolline

PING! The reply came before Apolline had time to make some tea.

Dearest Apolline,
There is nothing that would stop me. Please send me more details.
Yours Olivia.

Later Yutika contacted Shimla and told her about the impending arrival of a sign language teacher. This appeared to change everything. Within two days Shimla outlined a proposal for the teaching exchange that would satisfy the orphanage inspector. 'Thirsty Words' was no longer just a seed; it had begun to flower.

SELF-LOVE

Comparisons - Approval - Relationships - Nature
Mindfulness - Fear - Avoidance - Success - Trust

Selfish actions destroy the world. Selfless actions heal it. Self-love is not being selfish; it is the love that enables us to be selfless.

Imagine two grown men talking about love instead of beer!

Bruno passed Sollie a cup of tea: "Can we talk about love?"

Sollie put his head above his book: "Why?"

Bruno smiled faintly: "I want to make myself more loveable but love is not something that I have ever talked about before. They didn't teach it at my school."

"What exactly is the problem?"

"I like Ling, but she is too beautiful for me. I look like a bowl of boiled rice beside her fried eggs."

"I would not worry about that. Sometimes rice and fried eggs go perfectly well together."

"But I need to know how to love her."

"That's easy. Just tell me how you care for your tomatoes."

"As well as talking to them affectionately every day, I water them, I make sure that they have lots of sunshine and I send them kind thoughts."

"Then that is all you have to do to love another person. If you don't, your relationship will shrivel up and die."

"What else?"

"That will do."

"It can't be that easy."

"It is. Providing that your own petals are open. Which means that you must love yourself, before you attempt a loving relationship. You should also make sure that you understand what love is… before you go and look for it."

"Perhaps you should tell me what love is."

"It is a path. One that we lay ourselves; perfumed and coloured by the flowers that we stop to plant. Love is not a chance meeting. It is a way of being and a state of mind."

"So where will I find it?"

"The love that you are searching for resides within you. However, it is something that you must seed and nourish if you are to make it blossom. What we are searching for is not another person's love; we are searching for the feelings that we think another person's love will give us. In the beginning, do not go looking for it in a partner! The love that another person can give you is a form of love, but it is not the ultimate love. The ultimate love is wider and deeper than that. **Make the search for a loving partner the last thing that you do.**"

"Hmmm. I have heard that you must 'love yourself first'."

"Not true! Our first aim is to practise and master the art of being mindful and the art of being loving. Only then should we study and practise the art of self-love."

"Can we start?"

"Yes. However, please take notes and make headings!"

1. BEING MINDFUL

Lifeforce

"We start being mindful in our home. We 'focus totally' on whatever we are doing, instead of engaging with any thoughts that come to mind. As we become more mindful, that which is manufactured loses its glitter. When we mindfully wash the dishes or chop a courgette, it takes us 'out of our mind', and we connect with our authentic selves. This is one of the key foundation steps towards self-love.

"In addition to practising mindful activities, a new start requires you to break away from any manufactured daily routines that may have trapped you in a world of gloom and inertia. You can do this by, **Increasing your lifeforce; your 'prana'.** It is achieved through activities like mountain walks, sitting by the ocean, watching the stars, walking barefoot, planting in the garden and swimming in the river. **The aim is total immersion; not an occasional experience.** You must also learn how to increase your tempo and your beat.

"When we immerse ourselves in nature, we are able to answer the question 'who am I?' This is because if you spend enough time with nature and develop a relationship with it, eventually it will take you back to your core; to your authenticity. Here you will experience stillness, silence and simplicity. It is here at your core that you can dissolve your conflicts and suffering."

2. BEING LOVING

Nature walks - Gardening

> It is not enough to sit under the tree and listen to the birds sing ... You must want to put a ring upon nature's finger.

"Be loving to who?"

"Everything in the universe; every person, forest, insect, field, sea and river. However, you must go beyond liking and appreciating; you must enter a relationship with the world."

"Where should I start?"

"To start with, I recommend some gardening. Dig carefully with a small garden tool until you discover some wriggling or foraging life, like a beetle or a worm. Ask yourself what its purpose might be. Remind yourself that its role is important; that what it is doing will ultimately affect Mother Earth and you!"

"Then what?"

"Take a trip to the mountains or a forest to meet some animals in the wild. Think of it as going out on a date. Take some nuts to share with the squirrels. As you do with your plants, inquire into their well-being. When you return home from your nature trip, your stomach should be whirling. You should be worrying about whether the wildlife want to meet you again for another date. When you decide that you are in a relationship with the world, know that this is being loving'."

Bruno grinned widely; Sollie did too.

"Yes, I know it sounds crazy, but I am trying to make a point. It is not enough to sit under a tree listening to the birds singing. It is not enough to be an enthusiast. The heart must be stirred. There must be a relationship."

"I think that I understand now… Be mindful, be loving, practise self-love. Finally, search for an intimate human relationship."

"Yes, but don't restrict your intimate or deep love to a few things or a few people... **Know that you can love many things and many people deeply. In fact, the more things that you love, the more practise you will get at being loving'.**"

"However, don't think that this will diminish your love for your family or your main partner; it will enhance it. For it is when your love is limited that you become fearful of loss and rejection."

"Sounds good in theory, but won't people become jealous?"

"The insecure ones may. However, I am confident that there will be no jealousy in paradise. All the people that you have loved will be waiting in a line to dance with you. They will have prepared a loving feast together in your honour."

Create Time and Space

"You, Bruno, are good at 'creating time and space'. This is one of the first steps to being loving'. When you are not chasing desires and ambitions, you have time to stop and say hello or stop and listen."

"What will that do?"

"When you look at your loving thoughts and actions, you will see a loving person. This will give you self-worth. If you increase your loving, you will create good vibrations and energy. Now, those searching for love will be forced to turn their heads before they even see or hear you walk through the door."

> The pinnacle of self-love is seeing yourself as sacred. This can only be acquired when you subscribe to the premise that everything is sacred.

3. SELF-LOVE

How Much Self-Love?

"Now tell me, how much do you need to love yourself?"

"I have heard many people say that we must 'love ourselves more'."

"No. No. No. Please do not say that. Do not attempt to love yourself 'more'!… **You must love yourself 1,000 percent and more.** You must bake and drown yourself in self-love. You must drip it, splash up and down in it and tattoo every single part of your body with it. It must permeate your liver, your lungs and your kidneys. It must be in the books that you choose to read, your thoughts and all your words."

The Order of Self-Love

"The next thing you need to know is the order of self-love. It starts with submerging 'yourself' in self-love; not your lover, not the needy, not your children… Just you."

"Focus on myself."

"Yes. You must love yourself even before loving God."

"Even if other people need my attention?"

"Yes. Trying to help others before you have looked after yourself will exhaust you. Focusing on self-love will make you more loving. Immersion in self-love will give you more energy and bounce… now you will be a better lover to your family, your work colleagues and the wider world.

Sollie stood up, "Wait here for a second. I will explain this in another way." Sollie returned with an empty jar, a jug of water and some washing-up liquid: "The washing-up liquid represents your self-love. Please fill the jar with water and some of the liquid."

Bruno did as he was asked. The soapy bubbles overflowed onto the table.

"That is all you need to do. Focus on filling yourself up with self-love and your soapy bubbles will overflow over everyone and everything that you come into contact with. However, if you focus on others first, your bubbles will dry up and your lips will become thin."

> Love is heavy when it is contained and light when it is free. It is not to be stored in a jar but poured from a jug.

Eat - Pray - Love

"You may be familiar with the concept 'eat-pray-love'. It implies that you do the things that make you happy before you attempt to change your life. For example, eat lots of your favourite food. If you were trying to make changes in your life and you were alone, I might recommend that you follow this advice. However, you are not alone. You have found a support group. Therefore, I am going to do things in a different order."

"So I can't go and fill myself up with my favourite food before I start my transformation?"

"Correct. Here we place the emphasis on nourishment, not pleasure. Remember the body is not yours; it is a gift to look after and to put to good use. Looking after your body gives you the energy to 'find out who you are' and 'carry out your purpose'. These two quests are also important acts of self-love.

Treat Your Body as a Temple

"As well as nourishing your body, you should love it. Everything feels better when it receives a hug and a rub. Now soak your feet in hot, scented water. Bathe your body in scented oils. **When you start cherishing yourself, you become desirable.** However, you need to do more than just luxuriating in the bath. Focus on acquiring positive energy. This is your beauty cream, your blusher, your biceps and your six-pack.

"Also be mindful of your rhythm, beat and pulse. Know that these things also influence your energy, light and vibration. Treat the body like the temple that it is; sometimes it should be a house of prayer, sometimes a house of energy and celebration and sometimes a vessel doing God's work."

Self-Kindness – Fun and Humility – Confidence

"Now let us talk more about how we communicate with ourselves verbally, for this is one of the first acts of 'self-kindness'. Find a favourite quiet place. **Start with a desire to be your own friend. Say 'hello' to yourself… lovingly. Speak softly and slowly**. Practise smiling at yourself. Then dine on a daily diet of verbal affirmation; the continuous calls of 'I love myself and I am beautiful… I am a kind and caring person and I am loving…I am deserving. I 'expect' good things to come my way'.

"Why should I expect good things to come my way?"

"Simple. Self-love changes your fortunes. You start to think that you are more deserving. You build your self-worth. Now opportunities no longer pass you by. You have the confidence to reach out. Now other people change their responses towards you."

"I understand. How often did you say I must do all of this?"

"How often do you water and speak lovingly to your tomatoes?"

"All day!"

"Then you know what you must do. These activities are not about occasional or even day-to-day treats. Think beyond three meals a day, even beyond a call to prayer five times a day. **Repetition and total immersion is the formula for success.**"

> Love is something that you must master; you must know how to give it, ask for it and receive it.

Opening up Your Heart

"Search for activities that will 'open up your heart'. Try painting, pottery and flower arranging. Focus on doing, not competency. Cakes can burn, paintings can suck, pottery can fall apart. It doesn't matter. Add some completely new experiences… Try yoga. Learn about controlling your breathing, stillness, silence and meditation. These are all acts of self-love.

"Then practise other spiritual activities. Know that singing, calligraphy, knitting and sewing will settle peace on you, at the same time that they settle peace and joy on others. After that, decorate your walls with your poetry and art."

Group Activities

"Try group activities. These are the type of activities that you can enjoy on a 'healing retreat'. One reason that they work so well is because your heart comes out to play when it is in a safe, loving environment.

Fears

"Self-love involves frightening yourself. This might sound crazy, but it is true. Fear is a closed heart. When we close our hearts, we turn off our desire for the extreme senses; the shrieks, the shudders, the howls of joy and fear. We close them for safety, to avoid any emotional risks and protect our fragile hearts. Fear equals avoidance. Fear is life without the funfair. Fear turns off the tap of ecstasy and joy.

"So, if you are afraid of heights, we need to dangle you from a cliff edge. If you are scared of werewolves, we need to get you watching horror movies again. If you are afraid of rejection, we need you to receive a thousand rejections a day. Whatever is hiding inside you needs to be brought to the surface. **Open the door of fear and you discover that what lies behind it is joy.**"

Being Childlike

"Loving yourself also involves pursuing adult activities in a childlike manner. Humility equals softness and fires an arrow that brings the ego down. 'Child like' means living with fun and laughter. This is why I asked you to create the idols and mini-shrine. You can also stamp your feet with happiness, jump on the bed and get muddy. **Most importantly, when you are childlike, you can 'expect', because that is what children do.**"

Dressing Up

"Then you need to dress up."

"But most of the time I work alone. Are you suggesting that I dress up just for myself?"

"Yes. **Dressing up, is another act of self-love**. It takes on a different appearance when you do it for yourself. However, don't just dress up at work, dress up at home. Wear different clothes in different parts of your home to bring out your love. Don't think pyjamas in the bedroom, aprons in the kitchen; think love. Dress to reinforce self-love and devotion. If you are a woman, dress up to feel like a Goddess. If you are a man, dress up as a hero."

Forgiveness and Gratitude

"Then I want you to open up a gratitude and forgiveness journal."

"What do I write in there?"

"Before I can forgive others, I must forgive myself."

"Really?"

"Some people might say that you don't even need to forgive your perpetrators, just yourself! **Those that you forgive don't need to be deserving; we are not being forgiving for their sake, we are being forgiving to heal you.**"

"Why do I need to forgive myself?"

"Forgiveness is an act of self-love. We can lose our self-worth when we have been defeated, hurt or abused by others and when we have done things ourselves that we regret. **Inner hurt that deflates our self-worth can be healed with forgiveness.**"

"How do I do that?"

"In the same way that you achieve any other success… You start by imagining forgiving in your mind. In fact, with forgiveness, you might only ever have to do the practise in your mind. You don't need to shake the hands of those that hurt you. You don't have to become their friends. However, you do need to move on."

"What if a person was abandoned, overlooked, hurt or abused by their parents? What if their feelings of hurt and injustice are deep and raw?"

"Then they must remind themselves that, above all things, their parents did something miraculous; they gave them life. This is something to be thankful for, is it not?"

"I think that I understand; gratitude and forgiveness are linked. Gratitude synthesizes pain and leads to forgiveness."

"Exactly. **Gratitude helps you interpret all your difficult experiences as lessons instead of maladies.**"

"Where does one start?"

"Forgiveness is not something that we attempt at the start of our transformation. Moreover, we cannot forgive by ourselves or even with the help of other people!"

"Then who will help us forgive?"

God – Prayer – Closure

With some tragedies, closure is not possible; the answers are out of your reach. However, forgiveness through prayer is always available to you.

"You will get help from the God within you."

"What if someone doubts God?"

"**People doubt God exists because they have not made the effort to find him.** However, I have learnt that it is difficult to heal 'deep injustice and pain' without God. Forgiveness is like compassion; it can be miserly and even dry up when we try and do things alone. It is for this reason that I ask you to love the God 'within you'. When I said 'love yourself before God', it does not mean that you ignore God. It means do not go looking for God first. **We look to find ourselves first, because this is where we find God.** Self-love clears the path of material desires that get in the way of us seeing this. We look to love ourselves because we are the temple that God resides within. As we love ourselves, so we love God.

"**Prayer is a way to forgive ourselves, and we need this to love ourselves**. To pray is to be humble. It is a beautiful admission that recognizes we cannot do our best work alone. Therefore, there is nothing wrong in praying for help. In fact, it shows that we have faith. However, **When you work on your prayers with God, you lift your prayers to another level. Now you can have faith in yourself because you have faith in God**."

"What if a person doesn't believe in God at all?"

"I am not going to answer that question directly. I will simply ask anyone who is alone and without God, 'Are you truly happy? Are you without anxiety? Can you see, feel and hear the sacredness in all things, including yourself?' If the answer to all these questions is yes, then perhaps they do not need God. If the answer is no, perhaps they should ask, 'What have I got to lose by getting to know God?' Remember, I have no religion… other than nature. I am not wishing to convert you to a religious faith. I am just trying to help you find your true, loving nature."

> You can spend a lot of money on bath oils, candles, holidays and desires in an attempt to remove your anxiety. How much money do you think that you need to spend to find the God within you?

Surrender

> Surrender is the big shake of the tree that brings all the rotten fruit falling to the ground.

"Now you have built your faith, you can consider surrender."

"What is surrender?"

"An act of love. Surrender is not something to be fearful of. It is not an icy plunge. It is a release; a lightness; a feeling of being handed over. The desire to surrender bubbles up as you soften, build your faith and desire to get to know God. **Surrender should not be an act of desperation or a cry for help; it should emerge out of self-love.** You do not hand yourself over out of need but because your love has begun to overflow. It takes you to self-worth, confidence and purpose. When you have these gifts, you feel deserving. Now you can graciously accept compliments. Now you feel entitled. Now you can enjoy all pleasure without guilt."

Devotion – Pleasure – Celebration

"I hinted that, **God does not come into your life just by praying. God steps into your life when you get to know him.** The next stage of your spiritual development is pouring yourself into God through devotion. You simply, look to devote the fruits of your labours and your good fortune to God. Devotion is sharing your faith in God with feasting, singing and dancing.

"When you give in this way, there is no fear of rejection – God will not appear and say that he doesn't want your offering. **When you pour your devotion into God, something begins to stir. It is this that brings your emotions, feelings and ecstasy frothing to the surface… it is this that opens up your heart.**"

Sharing – Reaching out – Asking for help

"When you are fortified with self-love, the 'wheels of giving and receiving love' begin to move in both directions. Now you can reach out to others and accept offers of help yourself. When we love ourselves, we can give freely without harming the ego. We can also ask for help without fearing rejection. However, we should start with baby steps."

"Can you give me some examples?"

"Like putting your hand up in the air to ask for help with getting up from the exercise floor. Like asking someone to help you with your bag. From these humble beginnings we can move on to bigger things. Eventually, we can move on to transforming ourselves into 'what others need us to be'.

"Life is about a life of service. However, first you serve yourself and then you serve others. **We can save others, because we have saved ourselves. This is how we find redemption.**"

The Inner Journey

"Finally. I must mention the inner journey, it is the quest to know yourself and the road to self-love. It will also help you settle compassion as you journey through life," then he stood up and stretched himself, "Now, do you have any questions?"

You didn't mention how to find a partner."

"You don't need to know that. When you practise mindfulness, being loving and self-love,' love will come in search of you. Remember these words… **Discover yourself before you look for me."**

> The wise person stays put and yet appears to be contented. They are not outward looking. They go beyond that. Their journey is an inner search. For it is within us that joy is to be found. It is something on the inside that we tune into.

(There is a brief summary of the inner journey in the Epilogue, at the end of this book.)

DOING NOTHING

Stress - Persistence - Patience - Calling - Faith - Visions - Success - Goals

Learn to distinguish between nothing and nothingness. Pursuing personal goals or perfectionism is likely to exhaust you. A more worthwhile pursuit is to empty yourself and practise your skills, whilst you wait for your calling to arrive. It is the art of doing nothing, whilst at the same time doing something. To pursue your own goals requires you to fill yourself with knowledge, logic and experience. To wait for your calling to arrive requires you to fill yourself with faith. To pursue your own goals requires enduring persistence. Waiting for your calling to arrive may require enduring patience. To pursue your own goals requires you to create a vision. To wait for your calling to arrive requires you to shut your eyes.

Apolline was scurrying around. Sollie was quietly reading.

"Sollie, I'm stressed. I have been overthinking again."

"Take a break, sit down. You will miss the good things in life."

"I find it difficult to do nothing."

"Perhaps it would help if you understood the difference between nothing and nothingness!"

However, before he could say anything else, a different type of remedy walked in through the open door; it was Shiva, a friendly neighbour in distress.

"Can anyone fix broken toilets?"

"Apolline, I think that it might be a good idea if you went to fix the toilet. Take Bruno with you."

Despite Sollie's strange request, Apolline went to investigate what was wrong with Shiva's toilet. Bruno diagnosed the fault in a second. Now Apolline knew how to fix a leaking toilet, although she had no idea why she needed to know.

SOARING AND FLAPPING

Being present – Finding God – Happiness

Am I unhappy because I don't believe in God? Perhaps you are unhappy because you have not made the effort to get to know God?

It was a green and yellow afternoon. When Apolline returned from Shiva's, Sollie was busy reading, so she decided to walk around the garden. The first thing to catch her eye was a pigeon strutting around on the spine of the red-tiled roof. Another, possibly its mate, circled high in the sky above, flapping, then soaring.

As her eyes followed the soaring pigeon, her attention was grabbed by the wisps of clouds curdled in the blue sky above. They added colour, she reasoned, without diminishing the warmth of the afternoon sunshine. Suddenly there was a commotion to her left. A large grey squirrel bent a branch and catapulted itself onto the roof to join the pigeon in a manner that would surely have won it a pole-vaulting gold medal at any Olympics. Pale-yellow butterflies darted from tree to tree, whilst turquoise and orange ones chased each other around the garden in pairs. By now the pigeons had started to coo, and tiny birds chirped and chattered in between their to-ing and fro-ing. Right in front of her, ants scurried along the waxy surface of the leaves. She was about to see if they would bite her finger when one of the squirrels came down from the tree to inquire as to why she was visiting. As nature swallowed her, so she became hypnotized.

BOOM! She quickly came out of her trance, as Sollie's big book thudded shut. He stood up.

"What are you thinking?"

"I wasn't thinking. I was watching and observing all the events taking place in the garden. It appears that when you empty yourself of your thoughts and watch and listen, you hear the crunch of your apple, your words are less garbled and everything becomes clearer. I have had such a wonderful afternoon. I feel so happy."

"I am not surprised that you are happy."

"Why are you not surprised?"

"When you listen harder, stand nearer, stare deeper and dare to smell, the mind empties itself. Some people are of the opinion that they need 'to think' to achieve clarity. In truth, all they actually need to do is to spend an afternoon in the garden watching the birds and the bees. This is another way of being present and another form of meditation. More importantly it is another way to get to know God."

"Why do I doubt God exists? Why do I doubt myself? Why am I so unhappy so often?"

"We are unhappy when we doubt God. We doubt God exists because we have not spent enough time in his garden getting to know him. The more time you spend with him, the more you will believe in him. The more you believe in him, the happier you will be. **God is not a praying mantis lying in wait for you. You must go and find him.**"

YOUR DAILY PRACTICE

Spiritual activities - Success - Meditation - Anxiety -Yoga

Apolline and Sollie continued their conversation.

"Sollie, is meditation more important than action?"

"That is a very good question. I am going to say that, **Action is better than meditation. However, if you practise meditation, your decisions and your actions will be more effective.**"

"Can you clarify something else… Is it enough to practise meditation and our other spiritual activities once or twice a week?"

"It depends on what results you want. Do you think that an athlete can be a medal winner if they only train once or twice a week?"

"Probably not."

"Know this … You cannot 'flap and soar' and 'soar and flap' like the pigeons in the garden. **Meditation and other spiritual activities are not hobby classes that you do two or three times a week after a frenetic day at work.**

"If you would like to pursue a spiritual life, you must practise what you learn here every day. I cannot stress how important this is. **Please… do a little, even if it is only 10 minutes a day. It will make you a champion.**"

"I understand. However, there is something that I don't. Can you please tell me why you sent me with Bruno to fix Shiva's toilet?"

"Did you establish what was wrong with it?"

"Yes. The side inlet valve of the cistern had broken. This meant that the water was running constantly and wasting away."

"Well, I thought that it might be helpful for you to compare the leaking toilet with your own challenges."

"Why?"

'If you are troubled and anxious, you cannot be at peace. This is important. If you do not tackle your anxiety, instead of releasing adrenalin occasionally, you will release it constantly. Eventually, this will make you very ill. A mind like this, Apolline, is like the toilet cistern where the water keeps running. It needs to be turned off. The spanner that you need to help you do this is the daily practice that I have just outlined."

SPONTANEITY - REFLECTION - MEDITATION

Thoughtfulness - Thinking - Non-attachment - Belonging to the whole Security - Inspiration - Selfless actions - Lost causes

Apolline thought that she was going to leave with some new learning. However, before she could touch the door handle her precious values were assaulted again.

"Thank you for that, Sollie. From now on, I will concentrate on being thoughtful instead of thinking."

"You can't do that!"

"What do you mean? Are you saying that being thoughtful isn't an admirable quality?"

"Some people think that being thoughtful or reflective is a positive trait. However, in truth it springs from our ego; because it draws on our limited knowledge, personal beliefs and experiences. Therefore, **We should not reflect or be thoughtful when something occurs. We should reflect and be thoughtful before things occur.** Let us call this meditation; it marinates and soothes the mind. Then, when someone treads on your toe, your response will be spontaneous, but it will also be sweet."

"I understand."

Good. For some people a spontaneous life is the only way to live."

"Who?"

"Dominicans and other people who are passionate about non-attachment."

"Oh! What do Dominicans do?"

"They live a spontaneous life. They don't own anything or have anything to keep them in one place. If required, they can go where asked at a moment's notice."

Then Apolline took his arm so that she could show him the pole-vaulting squirrels and the ants dancing on the waxy leaves, "Ahmmm. I am not sure that non-attachment is for me."

That made him disappear. Two minutes later he emerged with a large watering can of water and a magnifying glass. He lifted the glass up to the sun and lined it up with a small ball of dried grass. Within a minute a plume of smoke rose into the air.

"Now watch."

At first she concentrated her gaze on the billowing smoke. Then he pointed the magnifying glass at the tree's branches.

"What do you see?"

She didn't need to tell him. Columns of ants were on the move! Their home and possessions were in danger.

"They are carrying their furniture!"

"Something like that."

Still the smoke plumed. More ants poured out of the ants' nest opening, laden with their household goods. Then the squirrels became frantic with worry and started to chew their tails.

"What's got them into such a flap?"

"They want to rescue their nuts. They are probably hidden near here."

Then one of the pale-yellow butterflies reappeared. It hovered over the smoke before beating its wings as fast as it could. Within a few minutes, a few of the turquoise and orange butterflies appeared and beat their wings too.

"What are they doing?"

"I think that they are trying to blow the smoke away and put the fire out in the only way that they can."

Then Sollie picked up the watering can and poured the water over the smoking grass.

"Enough for today! Let's go back to the table and take a cold drink."

Apolline tried to stop herself laughing: "So what was all that about?"

"Non-attachment and inspiration!"

"Okay, tell me how."

"I don't need to. You saw it all for yourself. The ants charged back into their nest to rescue their possessions. Now half of them will perish from smoke-induced lung cancer. The other half fell off the branches to their death in the scramble to save their belongings. Then there were the squirrels… anxiety and pulsating hearts, caused by fretting over their nuts."

"Oh. I understand now; **The very attachments that were meant to give them security stole or damaged their lives.**"

"Exactly."

"What about the pale-yellow butterfly?"

"It was not attached or pre-occupied. It had the time to help. It didn't see a lost cause. It only saw its brothers in need. It just beat its tiny, delicate wings as fast as it could in the hope it might blow the fire out. This selfless action inspired the other butterflies to come and help."

"Surely by fanning the flames they could have made the fire worse?"

"That's not the point. They did all they could. They transformed themselves into an inspiration that attracted other helpers. It is the humbling inspirations of the tiny that stir the hearts of those with bigger resources. In the end they inspired me – I had a watering can!"

"Oh, I think I understand. When you identify yourself as belonging to the whole, no effort is too small, no beat of your wings is wasted."

"Exactly."

* * *

As Apolline left the garden, Bongo arrived. "Mr Sollie, come with me. I can smell something interesting… lots of buried whisky bottles." Sollie couldn't see anything, so he picked up a spade. It wasn't long before empty bottles began to sparkle in the sun. This discovery made Sollie worry about Tom. Tom was also deeply worried about himself. He had gone far beyond the stage of enjoying his whisky.

TREASURE HUNT

Wants - Acceptance - Compliments - Rejection - Belonging

Apolline liked Tom. He listened to her, he was thoughtful and he could make her laugh… until the evening; then he could become embarrassing. At which point, he annoyed her. Tom also liked Apolline and had been waiting a long time to be alone with her. Tomorrow there was an opportunity; they were going into the forest to lay a treasure hunt for the children.

They laid some of the trail and then sat down for a break. There was a blink of silence. Tom felt the compulsion to fill it.

"Apolline, what do you want while you are here?"

"I want to be noticed. I want someone to put their arms around me. I want someone to say that they love me."

Tom wasn't expecting such frankness and felt unable to respond. Instead, he lifted the large rock lying by her head.

Apolline screamed, "AGH! HELP!"

A green snake with yellow eyes raised its head and spat out its tongue. Apolline grabbed Tom and tried to hold him as a shield. Tom froze and rejected her; unable to accept her embrace.

HISS! HISS! Apolline's heart raced as the snake swivelled and slithered towards her. Then the hissing serpent changed direction and disappeared. Later, they chased each other around the trees and paddled in the shallows of the lake. However, Tom wasn't so happy when he returned to his room and lay on his bed.

He visualised himself rejecting Apolline's hug: 'Idiot. Idiot. Idiot. Will I never learn?' He knew what the problem was; the fear of rejection. He also knew the consequences of rejecting her embrace; Apolline would probably look elsewhere.

Tom consoled himself in the only way that he knew. Then, with some false courage in his belly, he knocked on Apolline's door. He staggered in. She wasn't impressed and told him to get out.

BEING LOVEABLE

Rejection - Relationships - Entitlement - Avoidance

We place our emphasis on examining whether our heart is pumping blood. In truth, we should be examining our heart to see if it is like a plant and growing towards the light.

It was Bruno's birthday and a party had been organised. Ling entered the room carrying a tall package wrapped in shimmering red paper. She placed it in front of Bruno. It was a beguiling-looking plant. The label read 'dieffenbachia seguine'. Bruno looked mystified.

Ling put her hands behind her back: "It is known as the dumb-cane or dumb plant."

"No doubt there is a reason that you have given it to me."

"Yes. Its leaves contain poisonous crystals and if you eat them, it will make you unable to speak. It will make you dumb."

"Why do you want to make me dumb?"

"The plant is not to stop you talking; it is a reason to celebrate. Surely, if there are plants that can stop humans speaking, there must be plants that can hear what people are saying. Therefore, it must make sense to talk to your plants. Which means that you can't be mad." … Then she kissed him on the lips.

After that, there was music and frivolity. Sollie played his shruti box. Yutika handed out tambourines. Apolline danced very closely with all the men, until Tom said something that made her slap his face. Then when Ling went to the toilet, Apolline sat on Bruno's lap and almost received a slap herself.

Bruno went to bed happy but confused. It seemed that he was in a relationship with Ling. He wasn't sure how that had happened but it had. Now he had new worries to contend with: 'Could I really be entitled to the same happiness other people enjoy? Surely she does not think that I am loveable?' Then a strange feeling came over him; he could feel it in his toes and his tummy. He assumed that it was the same one that a ripe tomato experienced before it burst open.

INTERMINGLING

This was not a play that they had observed; this was an act of love.

By now Ling's longing for Bruno was like a fever. She decided to bait her next trap, before Apolline did.

Bruno was in his greenhouse, dressed in a big, blue overall. There was a knock on the glass. Ling walked in wearing a cotton top with spaghetti shoulder straps, a short skirt and wellington boots. She was carrying a large bucket.

"What is in there?"

"Some rose-scented hot water. It's for you."

Then, without saying another word, she knelt-down, unlaced his big, brown boots and took them off. Ling stared at them with disbelief. It seemed that she could almost fit inside them. Then, carefully and slowly, she rolled down his thick, green woolly socks and pulled them off. Before he could protest, she had lifted his feet and placed them into the hot, scented water. Very quickly his blood warmed and a pastoral feeling came about him. Neither spoke. He took her hand, opened her palm and placed one of his tomatoes in her hand. She cupped it. Then, he placed his big, coarse hand around hers. Now he was holding two things that he cherished. Now passion began to move at a pace; coiling out of its box, awakened from its slumber.

Ling gazed into his eyes. Bruno took his spare hand and reached for his greenhouse misting pump; a small, metal instrument that he used to keep his tomatoes moist. He sprayed her face with a fine spray of water that made her close her eyes. It tickled, and she laughed. She pushed her head back, closed her eyes and waited to see what would happen next. Bruno started to trace her neck with his finger and pressed his hands onto her shoulders. Very quickly Ling started to lose sight of land. Then there was a brief pause. Her instincts told her that she needed to help things on their way.

She opened her eyes and began to undo the top buttons of his overall. As the sun shone through the panes of glass, his chest began to glisten. Her thoughts strayed to the day that he had fallen down the well; a time when her tiny hand had found itself entwined in his hairy chest. The same emotions resurfaced, only this time Bruno wasn't lying limp and unconscious. Her heart was jumping, and her lips began to moisten. By now she felt giddy, and when an earthy smell of soil and greenery filled her head, it disarmed all hopes of preservation.

Now Ling knew what she wanted to happen. Bruno had the same thoughts. He effortlessly lifted her up off the floor and sat her on the table amongst the plant pots. Her legs dangled in the air and her wellington boots fell off and bounced on the floor. He contemplated whether he could go through with the next act, given that all his friends were in attendance in the front row seats. However, by now passion and emotion had crushed any feelings of restraint.

When the final act was over and the principal actors eventually stood up, the plants felt compelled to bow, because this was not a play that they had observed; this was an act of love.

IMAGE

Identity

Ling was parading in front of Sollie in a handmade Chinese ceremonial costume.

"Sollie, I wonder who I really am. You hear people say that they have a strong sense of self, however, I have never experienced this. I still live in my mother's shadow. In fact, I have nightmares about her turning up here and cloaking my new life in darkness. Perhaps I need to create a new identity?"

"I suggest that you avoid doing that. Your aim should be to rediscover your authenticity."

"That is what I am trying to do. That is why I have made myself some Chinese robes."

"Your ethnicity might be Chinese but your authenticity is not. You must identify yourself as belonging to the whole and focus on finding your true self. **You need to peel off that which is obscuring your authenticity, not try and paint something over it.**"

"Does this mean that I can't dress creatively?"

"No. Please dress up and have fun as often as you can. However, when it comes to your everyday clothes know that there is an order; one thing comes before the other. Don't pick a wardrobe to express yourself; it will not work in the way that you want it to. Immerse yourself in nature, silence and simplicity and you will be able to see your true nature. Then your clothes and accessories will choose themselves. This way, your wardrobe will reflect you and your habitat. Then, like the colours and textures of nature, they will always look authentic. It is for this reason no leaf is the wrong colour and no squirrel is in the wrong tree."

THE TREE IS NOT ITS BARK

Identity - Your past - Conditioning - Authenticity

> Most masterpieces are not to be found through a new door; they are hidden behind an old one.

Apolline, who was also keen to discover more about herself, joined Ling and Sollie.

"Sollie, can you help me understand who I am?"

"Sometimes a better question than 'who am I?' is 'why am I who I am?' When you were young and defenceless, the people around you passed on their fears, values, experiences and irrational beliefs. This influenced you and painted over your authenticity. In many cases, it stole your free will and left you conditioned.

"The first task is to identify your key beliefs and values. Write them down if you want to. Then identify their source and validate them. If they are not useful or if they imprison you, consign them to the rubbish bin. This will help you make a new start."

"Surely it can't be that easy to start again?"

"Stay here."

A few moments later Sollie returned with a wood plane. He walked over to the white-painted door and started to plane it forwards and backwards. When he had finished, he showed Ling and Apolline the results.

"It is that easy. Your conditioning is like a few coats of paint and varnish on this wooden door. Remove the paint and the varnish and the authentic wood is revealed. You are no different; **Remove your conditioning and your authenticity will appear. Strip yourself down completely and a masterpiece will be revealed.** You must understand that, **The tree is not its bark.**"

You don't need to reinvent yourself or become a different person. You just need to remove what is obscuring your heart, so that you can find the authentic, loving person that lies hidden.

WORTHLESS VALUES

Identity

"Now I know how to discover who I am, how can I find out what I stand for?"

"Examine your values. However, don't put your values on the table so that they are clear. Examine them to illustrate that they can never be clear; that they are susceptible to change."

Apolline folded her arms: "Surely the whole point of values is that they remain constant? That is what I was brought up to believe."

"Really? Please tell me which of your values are fixed?"

"Obviously, I wouldn't kill, and I don't think that I would commit adultery. I definitely wouldn't steal."

"Does that mean that you would not steal a loaf of bread if your children were starving? Does that mean that you would not kill someone who was about to take the life of your child?"

She could only mumble.

"Don't worry, I understand. A moral compass is not worthless; it can guide us through everyday life. However, we should recognise this moral compass can fall into a saucepan of water the minute those things that are precious to us are threatened. Perhaps this means that we don't know who we are. After all, only a few minutes ago you told me that you were brought up with a good set of values, and now we have discovered that you are a potential murderer and thief."

Apolline frowned: "Then what must I do to discover who I am?"

"Meditate and travel on the inner journey. In the meantime, **If you want to do the right thing, don't reach for your values; ask for guidance from your higher self.**"

JOB AND LIFE DESCRIPTIONS

Meaning – Purpose

Apolline surveyed herself in the mirror: "What makes most people glum?"

"Many people who come for healing talk about anxiety, trust, traumas, a lack of human connection and not feeling loved or valued. Few realise that they are unhappy because they have no purpose or meaning in their life.

"Most people who have a job want to know what their job description is. However, most people who have a life don't ask for, **A life description that asks, 'Who am I? What is my purpose?'**

"It is not enough to say that our purpose is to serve others. I say this because I have encountered a lot of exhausted caring people who serve others at the expense of their own health and happiness. We need to find meaning**.** This starts by discovering who we are. It is from this search that something is borne out of us and the meaning of our life is revealed.

"You can read any number of self-help books and attend scores of self-development courses. However, these will not reveal your purpose. **Your purpose will only arrive at your feet when you have mastered self-love and made yourself available to something greater than your own desires**. Writing a life description can help you."

A BRIEF LIFE DESCRIPTION

What is my job title?
To whom do I report?
What exactly am I responsible for?
Why am I here?
Have I aligned my skills and my gifts with my purpose?
How can I be an inspiration for others?
When must I use my experience, and when must I ask for guidance?
Am I the bread maker or am I the dough?
Will my reference say that I was the flower or the bee?

CHESS UNDER A HANGING MOON

Positioning – Relationship with God – Diet – Comparisons – Suffering

The scriptures say that every hair is numbered.

It was a still, blue evening with a hanging moon. Apolline and Sollie sat outside playing chess. In between turns, they stared at the stars.

"Since arriving in India, I have fallen in love with the stars."

"That is good to hear, Apolline. However, you must know that it is not enough to just stargaze. You must look at the stars to plot the position of your well-being, until you twinkle. Have you noticed that there is no hierarchy in the sky; it is horizontal, not vertical. However, on earth, many of us see ourselves at the top, centre or bottom of the universe.

"Have you ever asked yourself where your position is in this world? Are you clear where you have positioned your God? Do you see yourself as equal to the animal and plant kingdom or do you see yourself as superior? For these are important questions."

Apolline did not answer. Sollie lifted up the chessboard and let all the pieces fall to the floor. She laughed nervously. He remained straight-faced and picked up three chess pieces: a queen, a castle and a pawn. They were placed on the table in a vertical line, with the queen at the top, the castle in the middle and the pawn at the bottom.

"Now let us look at your 'personal positioning'. Start by imagining God at the top, yourself in the middle and the animals and the remainder of the universe at the bottom."

"I think I understand that."

"Good," he answered, before swiping the three pieces off the board with the back of his hand.

He replaced them with two pawns, side by side.

"Who did you just kick out, God, me or everything else?"

"I have temporarily removed God and repositioned you. The map has been changed from a vertical landscape to a horizontal one, like the night sky. Now you, the animals and the rest of the universe are standing side by side as equals; like brothers and sisters. Now there is a possibility that you will no longer want the environment and the animal kingdom to suffer. Viewing them as equals and siblings, it is possible that you may even lose your appetite for eating animals."

"Oh."

He handed her a third pawn: "This is God. I want you to decide where God resides."

"What do you suggest?"

"**I recommend that you don't imagine God as someone sitting above you, who you obey or fear. For if you position God above you, it is likely that you will place other things beneath you**. Then you will have created a hierarchy. This results in comparisons. It is comparisons that result in death and suffering. Imagine God to be either at your side or residing within you. Work in partnership with God. When God is this close, you will be compassionate. This way, I cannot imagine you being anything other than kind and loving to all things."

God would not want to hear you say you fear him. God is loving – never say you are God fearing

SEX AND EDEN

Passion – Being moved emotionally – Spiritual love

Sacredness – Purity – Inhibitions

A VIOLIN LOVER

Learn to play every string on her instrument. Practise how to quiver and vibrate. Do not press the bow; focus on gliding across the string. Familiarize yourself with the notes in between one semitone and another. Although to do this you would need to be familiar with the intonation. Know the difference between plucking and bowing. Practise by making fast transitions between the two. Work through the low notes before you attempt to reach the high ones. This way, eventually, her strings will have no choice but to snap.

Sollie was lying down under a coconut tree at the edge of the lake.

Bruno ambled over: "I need some advice. Since my afternoon of passion in the greenhouse with Ling, the bubbles in our love life have gone a bit flat. I don't seem to have many tunes in my repertoire."

Sollie sat up: "Improving your technique is the easy bit! Just ask Apolline to teach you how to play the violin. Dealing with your jealousy and getting your bubbles back requires a bit more explanation… They say that it all started in the Garden of Eden. Why do you think Adam and Eve had to put their clothes back on?"

"I heard that after taking a bite of the apple, Adam and Eve were ashamed of their nakedness and had to cover up."

"You might be right... or you might be wrong. Perhaps it wasn't because they ate the apple but, how they ate the apple!"

"What do you mean?"

"**To be passionate about any activity, including sex, we need to discover and crystallise exactly what 'moves us emotionally'.** This is the source of the fountain of joy. Then we must remove any obstacles that keep it from flowing."

"What are the obstacles?"

"Guilt, fear of rejection, ego, lack of self-love and the absence of devotion can all turn your passion taps off. This will reduce your ecstasy to a phut and a dribble. However, being spiritual will turn your taps on and make them gush. It will also make you more loving and purify your heart. Ironically, this will also dissolve your inhibitions. It will point your passions in the direction of God and shared joy and take you down the path of spiritual ecstasy."

Bruno coughed. He didn't recall any sermons in his church on the subject of spiritual ecstasy.

Sollie continued, "Treat sex like spiritual food; as something sacred, not as something sinful. Be mindful of all your loving acts; the preparation, the activities and all the celebratory feasts afterwards. Your home should be a temple; make your bedroom into a spiritual place for love; not a place for watching television or hanging your clothes. Take your time with your preparations; a sacred feast is not to be hurried but to be meditated over. Prepare a spiritual environment. Usher in some silence before your music. Light some candles, not just for romance but to remind yourself of the sanctity of what is about to take place. Diffuse some fragrant oils before you do your feeling and your tasting. Engage with all your five senses mindfully. Be devotional; consecrate and offer the fruits of your love to God before indulging and taking any yourself. Show your gratitude. Share your joy. It is not just for you; it must be celebrated."

"What does all that mean?"

"Prepare yourself spiritually before taking anything from the tree. Then the fruit is yours to eat. Maybe this is what Adam and Eve neglected to do. Perhaps this was the original sin?"

Bruno's spiritual education didn't extend to devotional offerings; only to harvest festivals and pre-dinner prayers. However, he still felt obliged to defend the sanctity of marriage as it had been taught to him. "Some people say that eating the apple implied that Adam and Eve made love before they were married. This act of passion was the forbidden fruit. After that they awoke to good and evil."

"That is not my understanding! They were told that they could enjoy all the fruits in the garden except those from the Tree of Knowledge. This implies that you can take a bite out of all of the orchard's fruits; you can enjoy the oranges, the plums and the strawberries. You are not denied the sharpness of the damson just because you have savoured the sweetness of the pear. I don't think there was any mention of how many they could sample or take away with them either. Remember the Ten Commandments asks that you do not covet your neighbour's wife. There is no mention of how many women you can covet if they are not married to someone else."

"Whichever ones I want and as many as I want? Really? Is that your interpretation?"

"Not exactly. You can only take the ripe and willing ones; you must be spiritual, which means you would be loving and considerate. If the joy is not a shared joy, it would not be spiritual."

TAKE A THOUSAND WIVES OR HUSBANDS

Awake - Self-love - Self-respect - Anxiety - Sacred

Being awake - Beliefs - Inhibition - Attachment - Jealousy

When you are awake, you will feel compelled to take something off.

A few days after their discussion about the Garden of Eden, Bruno had something else on his mind. He found Sollie by the coconut trees.

"Do you want to talk about guilt or jealousy today?"

Bruno poked him in the ribs: "Actually, I wanted to know why I had to take my shoes off at the temple! You told me you would tell me later. I am still not convinced by your theory about Adam and Eve either."

"I think that the priests or worshippers wanted you to take your shoes off out of respect for God. However, I am sure that God would prefer you to respect yourself. **For you are the temple that God resides in**."

"That makes sense. That was simpler than I expected."

Sollie took in a deep breath and then blew it out.

Bruno laughed, "I feel a 'but' coming."

"When we spoke about Adam and Eve, we concluded that they had to put their clothes back on. Although we didn't necessarily agree why."

"That is correct."

"So now we have a quandary. There are some people that tell us to cover our nakedness. However, there are others who advise us to do the opposite. They say that, 'When you are 'awake' you will be compelled to take something off.' Permit me to explain. **When you 'awaken', it's an epiphany. It's the moment that you wake up and see the sacredness in all things**: yourself, the flowers, the sun, the rain, the rivers and the seas. When you are 'awake', you will also realise that many of the beliefs that were imposed on you are not true... then you will desire to shed them. Some people say that when this happens, you will feel compelled to take something off. You might just want to take off your boots and run barefoot in the dust. However, you might feel that you have no choice but to strip off completely and dance in the rain or stretch out in the sun.

"At the point at which you are awake, conscious and possibly naked, you will feel no shame, no guilt and no inhibition. You will have cleared the devil from your mind. You will have uprooted the Tree of Knowledge. Now there will be no more forbidden fruit. Now you can take a bite and experience the frisson and the thrill. Now you can make love to Ling and Apolline. In fact, you can take a thousand wives if you want!

"However, you can't do any of this without anxiety or guilt, until you embrace non-attachment."

"Non-attachment?"

"Yes. Not just to your home, your work and your personal belongings but to the people you love. It was the Buddha that said, **Attachment is the cause of suffering**."

"Really?"

"Yes. Anyway, surely it is better to have a thousand wives than to invest all your love in one person... a person who might die or leave you?"

"I don't want that. I want a commitment, real love and intimacy."

"If you take a thousand wives and treat them all as sacred, you can have that too."

"Can Ling my partner take a thousand husbands?"

"Of course."

"Then I would be jealous."

"Which is why you must embrace non-attachment."

BOOM! A coconut fell from the tree and broke the silence. It missed Bruno's head by a few centimetres. Sollie picked it up and juggled with it.

"Imagine if that coconut had hit your head and killed you. Now imagine that Ling had a thousand lovers or husbands. Wouldn't you be happy for her if there were lots of arms to comfort her during her period of mourning? Do you think you would be anxious about your wife leaving you if you had a thousand others?"

"Bruno laughed and put his arm around Sollie's shoulder. Perhaps... however, if any man attempts to comfort Ling whilst I am still here, I will chop them up or set fire to them."

A FAITHFUL LOOK AND AN UNOCCUPIED MIND

Transference of love - Fears - Hobbies - Letting go

Happiness - Present - Possessions

> You acquire patience and therefore peace, not because you can wait longer for things but because now you are no longer waiting for things.

Tom had noticed that Apolline had not given him any 'special attention' for a while. It seemed that she had lost interest in him. In fact, Apolline's mind had been occupied by another man. She was discussing him with Sollie.

"I wonder what it would be like to be a maharaja's wife?"

"Perhaps you should find out."

"How might I do that?"

"Invite yourself."

"On what pretense?"

"Tell Parminder that you would like to work alongside his leaf sweepers."

"Then what?"

"Constantly appear astonished. Let him smell the apples in your hair. I will tell you exactly what to say before each of your visits."

* * *

Parminder's thunderous shoulders filled the doorway as he ushered her through the front door: "Apolline, what a delightful, unexpected pleasure."

She curtsied: "I have been thinking nice things about you. I would also like to learn more about your leaf sweepers."

"You jest?"

"I am serious. I have learnt from my master that the important things in life are to be found ensconced in the simplest of things."

However, before he could answer, an unusual, muffled noise made itself known from near her feet.

"What was that?"

She reached down to the floor, lifted a large basket and then placed it on the table. It was made of green reeds.

"Look through the holes in the lid."

Parminder did as he was instructed but failed to see anything.

"Perhaps you should take the lid off."

Whoosh! Something jumped out of the basket and landed on his nose, before falling down and coming to rest on his chest.

"AGH!" he squirmed.

Apolline burst into fits of laughter.

"What is it?"

"It is a gift for you, someone to show you the way."

It was a tiny tree frog, bright green with coral-red lips, about four centimeters long and possessing what appeared to be a faithful look and an unoccupied mind. Parminder carefully picked it up and held it in his hand. It looked straight up at him.

"Her name is Sumati. When you were wearing your Kathakali costume, your face was painted in the same colours as her. It was too much of a coincidence."

"A perfect gift for me!"

"More than perfect! You did say that you were looking for a good wife and many children. Sumati means, 'Of good mind and thought.' However, more importantly, in the Hindi epic Mahabharata, Sumati was King Sagara's second wife. She gave him 60,000 children. I thought that it would be nice for you to have a faithful friend who you could care for. I have learnt that caring for those things that need loving can make you happy... maybe there is a way for you to father 60,000 children too."

"If you come across the answer, please tell me. Now, how can I help?"

"I would like to spend some time with your leaf sweepers."

"I am sure that can be arranged. However, there would be one light condition. You must agree to share with me what you learn."

When Apolline had concluded her leaf sweeping apprenticeship, she sent Parminder a letter to tell him about her findings.

Dear Parminder,
You asked me to share with you any secrets that I uncovered whilst sweeping the leaves at your home. I send them along with heartfelt good wishes.

SWEEPING LEAVES

After sweeping the leaves from the lawn, I worked out how to sweep the weeds from my life.

It seems that after slowing down your movements and stilling the mind, your relationship with the world transforms. You acquire patience and therefore peace. It is not because you can wait longer for things; it is because now you are no longer waiting for things.

More leaves fall, and we sweep them back to the forest from where they came. In the clearing we see where happiness lies; it is not in the hands of those tightly gripping the silver spoons, as I had presumed... It is in the here and now.

Here the simplest and tiniest things become precious, nothing is harmed, everything is helped on its way. This, it seems, is all that we need to know.

Apolline

WHISKERS AND BUSHY TAILS

Self-inquiry - Reflection - Transformation - Success

A week later Parminder stared in the bathroom mirror, grabbed his tweezers and proceeded to pull out a few of the white whiskers that had populated his beard. Then he placed them under his magnifying glass for closer inspection.

'What have I become? In which direction am I heading if I carry on along this path?' he asked himself.

SWISH!

He immediately paled and trembled: "What was that?" He stared again at his reflection in the bathroom mirror. Had he seen a bushy tail springing up from his back and over his head? Surely not, he thought to himself.

Parminder had asked an important question of himself and a direct response had come flying through the window. He might not have liked the answer that flew in; however, he was very happy with his response. He made the decision to transform himself. A committed decision; one which would be proclaimed from the highest tree, and one from which there would be no turning back once it had been heralded.

'What else must I do?' he asked himself.

He was provided with another unequivocal answer: change would not be enough! He needed to transform his life: his goals, his actions and his thinking. A new barber might be able to dye his beard a different colour, but they would be no match for a bushy tail.

* * *

For the next two weeks Parminder joined his leaf sweepers in the grounds. Then he sent a reply.

> Dear Apolline,
>
> Thank you so much. Now I have a new set of goals. Before I depart this earth, I want to take one last look at the sea and remind myself that my contribution made it clearer; look at the grass and the forests and remind myself that my support made them greener. On my final ascent, I want the monkeys and all those in the market place to clap, the tigers to roar and the elephants to trumpet. This will hopefully mean that I have made a difference.

THE THINGS THAT MAKE YOU RICH

Activities - Happiness - Senses - Possessions

Forget possessions. Store the vibrant senses of a summer's day and they will stay with you for all time.

Sollie had organised some children's activities. He bellowed the instructions for the first children's activity through his megaphone: "I want each of you to go away into the forest for one hour and 'collect as many experiences' as you can. Each one of you can also take one of these small boxes. Be gentle. Do not harm anything!"

The children returned at lunchtime. Feeling very pleased with their achievements, they proudly emptied the boxes onto a blanket. Buttons, insects, leaves, etc tumbled out. The children waited for some praise from Sollie. They were to be disappointed!

"IS THAT IT?" he thundered. "How many fragrances have you captured? Show me the mud under your fingernails, let me see the marks that you have from rubbing your backs on the trees. Why are your ears not red from putting them to the ground to listen to the scurrying of the beetles? Why aren't your lips chapped by blowing on the grass? Have you only collected those things that you could pick up and store as a possession in your box? Sniffing is not something that you only do when you have a runny nose; it is an art and a vocation! Have you forgotten our lesson on happiness already?"

There was only silence.

"You have missed the fun. These things in the boxes will soon weigh you down, fade and decompose. When you are in the countryside, store the vibrant senses of a summer's day. When you are in the city, bury your head in bookshops, florists and fish markets. These memories will stay with you for all time. These are the things that will make you rich. Now go away again, and don't return until you are muddy and green from head to foot. Don't come back until you understand that joy is under every rock and inside and outside every tree."

When they did return, Sollie was his normal self. Stromboli knelt down before him: "Are we forgiven?"

"Of course. Just tell me, how did you manage to find so many insects in such a short space of time?"

"We found a pile of dead, rotting leaves. We kicked them in the air and lots of bugs and insects ran for cover."

Sollie's face turned scarlet, and all those in attendance saw the full vista of his teeth. "Come here!"

They all sprang forward.

"Take me to where you found the leaves and bugs," he demanded.

Stromboli led the way. The others marched behind him, knowing that they had done something wrong, without knowing exactly what it was.

LIFE AFTER DEATH

Purpose - Immortality - Sacrifices - Fear

The roosters were still dreaming, the stars were still lighting up the sky. Sollie marched towards the children's sleeping accommodation and blew his conch. There was yawning, disorientation and bewilderment.

"What is happening?" came the cry from the dormitory.

"I want you to understand the grave crime that you committed when you kicked the bugs into the air and disrespected the fallen leaves. Now follow me."

He marched them to the location of the rotten leaves, where they had disturbed the insects. Here he instructed them to sit down in a line, so that they faced a wall of tall trees.

"Do not speak, only watch."

An hour went past, and although they enjoyed the silence of the early morning forest, they were unsure of the reason for the exercise. Another hour went past. Eventually Phi Phi plucked up the courage to speak: "Can I ask what we are trying to see or hear?"

"Shush. You can only speak when you have seen a leaf fall from the tree."

However, the air was still, there was no wind and no falling leaves. Komodo put his hands together and said a little prayer for something that he had always taken for granted: the wind. However, nothing was forthcoming.

Two hours later there was some noise up above: several birds landed in the tree, and a single leaf started to fall from the sky. The eyelashes of 14 children fluttered; they watched it every step of the way as it threatened to stay airborne. To the relief of everyone, it eventually fell softly to the ground.

Sollie coughed and motioned for the children to stand up: "Tell me again how you found the insects."

Phi Phi opened her palms in an attempt to profess her innocence: "We just kicked some rotten, old leaves. The leaves were of no use, they were all dead. I don't think we harmed any insects either."

"It is not how you say it is, Phi Phi. You must know that every leaf and every insect is part of the grand plan. Like you, each one has a unique purpose and is to be cared for and protected. They are givers and preservers of life."

"Oh."

"Now, who can tell me if the leaves are of any use when they fall to the ground?"

Bongo put his hand up: "They are! Even as a rotten leaf, each one continues their good work. They provide homes and shelter for the beetles, ants and mites that we found. They produce food, they shelter the insects from the sun and protect them from predators, so that every insect can play its part in the grand plan."

"Thank you, Bongo. Now we will sit under the tree in silence for one more hour. I want you to work out how you will emulate the work of the 'fallen leaves' in your own life; now and after you have stopped breathing. **When you understand the important role that you can play when you have stopped breathing, you will no longer fear death.** For death is just like a leaf that falls from the tree to the ground; it gives rise to another opportunity. When you understand this, you will realise that you are immortal and that there are no sacrifices; only falling leaves."

PLANTING SEEDS

Patience – Discipline – Consequences – Giving life

> Tree planting is not just about planting trees that blossom long after we have gone. It is about laying down acts of instruction and acts of love that might not be understood until we have long gone too.

To complement his talk on leaves, the next day Sollie delivered a lesson about planting seeds.

"We call our home the Mustard Garden; however, we should not forget the name's true origin… The name, 'The Mustard Seed Garden', is based on Li Yu's manual of instruction for discipline and patience. Therefore Bruno and I are going to tell you about seed planting."

The children looked towards Bruno: "Can we help plant some of your tomato seeds?"

Bruno immediately stood up. His huge stature stretched itself to its full height and width. Smoke and lava plumed and spewed from every orifice … but not one word came from his mouth.

'Was he about to turn into a tomato plant monster?' the children asked themselves.

Such was their trepidation that they all scurried back several metres. They knew that there was something wrong with their request. Bruno turned towards them and stepped forward. Again, they shuffled backwards.

"Planting seeds is not a game, you know! It is not something that you 'try out' to see if you like it!"

Then Sollie walked Bongo to the other side of the garden where Tom was working on the hedges. He helped Bongo to feel the outline of a hedge with his hands. It didn't take Bongo long to work out what it was: "That is amazing. You have made the hedge into the shape of a sarus crane."

Sollie placed a packet of seeds in Bongo's hand and spoke to him in a deep, serious voice: "One day I want you to plant these seeds and grow some hedges. When they have grown, Tom will teach you how to shape them into birds. I am not going to tell you when to plant your seeds. I want you to decide when to do that yourself. However, it should only be after you have thought through all the responsibilities that come with planting seeds and giving life.

"Be careful; plant your seeds before you have acquired the disciplines of your art and mediocrity will follow you around for the rest of your life. Fail to question the consequences of what you plant and you may inflict great misery on yourself and those that you love. Fail to plant your seeds at all and life will pass you by."

Bongo put his packet of hedge seeds in his trouser pocket. Morning, noon and night he would tap that pocket just to reassure himself that they were safe. After school, he practised his drawing and painting, so that one day he too could sculpt the hedges into birds.

PUDDLES OF TEARS

It seems that joy and sadness are like the sunshine and the rain.

One morning Yutika's sleep was broken by a gentle knocking on her bedroom door. Bongo walked into the room with tears in his eyes and his lips stuck together. He sat down on the floor in the corner of the room and bowed his head.

"Whatever is the matter?"

Bongo stayed tight-lipped. Yutika brought him a beaker of orange juice, which he tried to drink through a straw. However, he only succeeded in blowing bubbles into the cup.

"My life is over before it has started."

"Why do you say that?"

He sniffed, "I will never reach my potential. I will always remain a seed."

"Whatever do you mean?"

"Sollie gave me a packet of seeds and told me that I should not plant them until I had acquired certain disciplines. He told me that I would remain a seed for the rest of my life if I planted them too early or not at all."

"What is stopping you doing that?"

"I left my packet of seeds in my trouser pocket and someone washed my trousers, now they have disappeared."

"What will happen now?"

"Nothing. Everything I have dreamed about is over before it has started. My life is doomed. I am destined to never soar like an eagle. Instead I will be confined to a life in the hedgerows."

"Surely there is a possibility that someone else will find them. They might even plant them for you."

"That is not going to help. Sollie made it quite clear that I am responsible for planting my own seeds."

"Why didn't you plant them straight away?"

"Sollie said that we must consider all the implications and consequences of our actions before we plant anything… I was still thinking it all through."

Yutika opened a drawer and rummaged around inside: "Wipe your tears with this."

He fingered the embroidered edge: "This is my handkerchief. Where did you find it?"

"It was in your pocket. I took it out before I washed your trousers."

Then he carefully opened the handkerchief. Sitting in the middle was a little brown packet. He pressed the bottom with his thumb and finger: "It's my packet of seeds. Oh Yutika … Now I know why I love you."

THE WHEELS OF LOVE

Giving and receiving love - Self-love - Trust
Broken hearts - Compliments - Rejection - Belonging

> Love is not a layer of thin ice on the lake; it is not something that you should be fearful of stepping on in case it breaks. Don't let the fact that the ice may melt in the future stop you from dancing on it now.

Sollie was carving a wheel out of a piece of wood when Tom approached him.

"What are you doing, Sollie?"

"I am making some 'wheels of love' in preparation for one of my lectures!"

"Why?"

"One of the most important things in a person's life is being able to give and receive love freely. Unfortunately, some people have been deprived of love or their wheels of love have been damaged.

"The wheels of our love need to be moving freely in two directions; they need to be able to give and receive love. Some people are able to give love but they are not able to receive love. Others cannot give or receive love at all."

"Why?"

"Some people cannot give love because they are fearful of becoming a receiver of it. They might not feel worthy, deserving or entitled. They might feel that they don't 'belong' in a certain group or loving relationship. Therefore, they have no expectation of finding love. Often, when people try to give them compliments or show signs of affection, they are unable to receive the love coming their way and reject it.

"Know this… many of the people who say nice things to you are either trying to be kind or they are in need of some comfort themselves. **If you struggle**

to accept compliments, know that you don't have to accept other people's kindness or love and wound your ego; you can just accept their compliments or gifts in order to be kind to the giver." Then Sollie stopped talking for a moment and rolled one of his wheels towards Tom.

Tom put his hand out: "That wheel is a bit wobbly, like mine."

"That is understandable. Lots of people have 'no trust' in loving relationships; they may have witnessed heart-crushing experiences at home with their parents or partners. Those that were rejected when they were young, or when they were in a relationship, might also be fearful of love. For these people the thought of rejection or a broken heart further down the line is too much to contemplate. Consequently, those with fragile hearts often keep potential lovers at arm's length. Alternatively, they tear up friendships and relationships when they start to become too close. Others close the door on relationships and close friendships altogether."

"I think that I might be one of those people who can't receive love easily. I usually bat back any compliments or expressions of affection and avoid getting too close. What should I do?"

"You should accept that damaged and broken hearts are not repaired by protecting them. **Broken hearts are repaired by standing in the very queue where they might be broken or damaged again.**"

"Ouch! I feel a dagger through my heart just thinking about that. Are you sure?"

"Very sure. Anything that you love can leave you or die. **You must be prepared to love again and again and again.** Additionally, **You must not seek permanency; you must live in the moment of love.** You can still mourn the passing of a lover for a week or two! However, you must see the death of one damaged heart as the signal to give birth to a new one. Similarly, if you have 'trust issues' with love, because of your past experiences, know that only a loving relationship will heal you."

"So should I join the queue for another broken heart?"

"No. Before you do that, you should attend a self-love course! Self-love is your inoculation against emotional suffering. Start by chatting with Bruno."

THE PAIN THAT CANNOT SAY ITS NAME

Hugging - Order of love - Rejection - Emotional risk -Inner child
Unexplained feelings - Giving and receiving love - Self-love

Sollie and Tom continued their talk.

"Sollie, what should I do in the meantime?"

"Hug a tree! This will help you become a giver and receiver of love."

"Really?"

"Some people suffering emotional pain can't find the words to express their hurt, confusion or anger. A loving hug could be the answer. Unfortunately, some people worry that they might be rejected. However, if you hug a tree there is no chance of being rejected."

Tom stared at Sollie as his childhood escaped from its box and took him back to the age of six: "It isn't always easy to reach out to people, Sollie."

"Tell me why?"

By now, Tom was pale and his voice was trembling: "When I was a little boy, I had a teddy bear. I saw the other children hugging theirs; however, for some reason I couldn't hug mine. I wanted to love it, but I did not know how to. I can remember a hollow feeling and despair. I knew that something was wrong, but I did not understand what it was. In the end, I stabbed my teddy bear with some scissors and cut its heart out."

Sollie answered in a hushed voice: "You are not meant to understand it, which is why the mathematics of the most important things rarely add up. Not all feelings make sense either; however, there are certain ones that can redeem you."

Sollie stood up and outstretched his arms: "Now come here a moment." Then he wrapped his arms around Tom and gave him a bear hug. Tom had never experienced anything like it.

HUGGING

There are some holes that you need to fill by pouring something in or picking up a spade.
There are some holes that can only be filled by wrapping something around.
There are some people that you need to wrap a present for.
There are others that you just need to wrap your arms around.

Some people go in search of the words that will help them express their deep emotions. Perhaps this is why Shakespeare and Confucius wrote as they did; turning the world upside down for the words that would redeem them. In truth, all that they needed to do was to find a tree or someone to hug.

GARDENS, PONDS AND BRIDGES

Joy v excitement – Problems – Visions – Goals

The true cause of unhappiness is not the presence of unhappy events in your life. It's the absence of happiness. Attempting to remove what makes you unhappy will not bring you happiness. Removing the weeds and pests from your garden will not make the birds sing.

Sollie handed Apolline a pair of gardening shears: "Apolline, I have a very special task for you. Our house does not have a palatial roof to attract the auspicious cranes. However, if we create some beautiful grounds with ponds, bridges and fish, the cranes might still visit us."

"Can you tell me what your vision is for the rest of the gardens?"

"There can be a frisson of excitement, but the aim must be joy. Sit down next to me, and I will explain what I mean."

JOY AND EXCITEMENT

If you pursue joy, excitement is included in the package, for excitement is contained within joy. Pursue excitement without joy and it can agitate the soul. Joy does not flicker. Joy is not a buzz. Joy is an inner swirl; it flutters and fills you with spirit. Joy can still take your breath away. Joy is a heartfelt moment shared. Excitement is for you; joy is for you and them. Joy is empathy. Joy is love. Joy is passion from compassion. Excitement is tribal. Joy is inclusive. Excitement wants to win. Joy does not want anyone to lose. Excitement can be thoughtless. Joy is always mindful. Pleasure is something that you seek. Joy is giving. Excitement wants things to finish. Joy never wants things to end. Excitement often turns its back on you when it is done; joy puts its loving arms around you. Exhilaration is fear turned into joy. Ecstasy is love achieved through devotion. Joy takes you to bliss. Joy is a union with God. Excitement can take you to the devil.

Apolline paused to write down a few of the things that he had said. Sollie peered over her shoulder: "Where are you going to start with your garden?"

"I think that I will concentrate on weeding the garden. That will make everyone happy."

"Are you sure? **The removal of the things that make you sad will not make you happy. Happiness arises when you spend your day planting flowers. It is this that makes the fish jump.**"

With that, he disappeared.

SAFARI IN THE FOREST OF THE EMERALD-EYED TIGERS

Weighed down with tents and provisions but light with excitement, the children arrived at the forest, put up their tents and made a campfire.

Over the next few days they carried on trekking, blissfully unaware of the tigers, wild dogs and snakes that were silently weaving in and out of their tents as they moved deeper into the forest. They catalogued as many birds as they could. They took pictures, recorded each bird's call and where possible its eating habits, preferred habitat and movement. They had no idea that they were recording a phenomenon. No one seemed to appreciate that as fast as they catalogued one species of bird, another was arriving. However, more importantly, they immersed themselves in nature and began to understand what it is like to identify yourself as a universal soul.

REALISATIONS

Change – Stillness – Intuition

> When your principal intention is a good one, you do not have to work out what you must do... Just ask your higher self for clear guidance... then the answers that you need will arrive.

Apolline decided to visit the big lakes by herself. Her desire was to sit under a tree by the waterside and watch the falling leaves. She also hoped that the answers needed to create the ponds, fishing and bridges for her garden would be forthcoming. However, she wanted to try out an experiment; there would be no working things out: 'I am going to ask a higher source for some help!'

She arrived by the lakeside, unfolded a flowery blanket and made herself comfortable. She took out a small writing book and pencil and watched some storks walk through the lake. Her next action was to stare at the water. As she did, the sun dropped and the height of the water rose in front of her. It brought with it debris, which it deposited onto the bank. Out of that washed-up debris emerged some of her garden.

MEETING RISHI

Becoming available

> Do nothing more than make yourself available and your teacher will come to you.

Apolline packed up and decided to walk home a different way. For 30 minutes there was only silent water and whispering yellow fields. Then, in the distance, the outline of a solitary figure appeared. They seemed to be walking on the water. Her footsteps quickened. A few steps later, the figure saw her too. He waved and splashed through the water towards her. He was naked except for a white cotton lungi; a type of male sarong that stopped just below his knees. Then he stepped nearer. He had taut, light-tanned skin and a head of thick, wavy hair that most women would want to trim. Apolline just wanted to touch.

SARUS CRANES

"Hi, my name is Rishi."

"Hello, I am Apolline. I thought that you were Jesus walking on the water for a moment."

He gave her a melon-slice smile: "I think that it just looked like that because there is so little water left in the lakes." However, she wasn't listening… She was staring at his soft lashes and boyish eyes, polished like dark brown beach pebbles and marbled with mystery.

Apolline quickly gathered herself: "Can I ask what you have been doing?"

"I have been observing and recording the behaviour of the sarus cranes. There is one behind you in that nest."

Before he could answer, a majestic, giant, grey bird with a red head and long, skinny legs hopped out of the reeds… Apolline screamed and ran as fast as she could.

Rishi ran after her: "What's the matter?"

She trembled, "Feathers scare me. Birds scare me too."

"It is the tallest flying bird in India; six feet high with an eight-feet wing-span. I am not surprised that you are frightened. However, they will not harm you; they are loving."

"Do you live near here?"

"I used to, but now I live near Darwin, Australia."

"Why are you interested in sarus cranes?"

"That could be a very long story, and I fear it is becoming dark. However, if you are interested, I could tell you tomorrow when I return to do some fishing."

Apolline took her sunhat off: "You fish?"

"Not too seriously but yes."

"Then I would love to join you?"

"Okay. Same place… tomorrow at sunrise."

Apolline skipped home, brimming with excitement. Ling met her at the gates: "Do you have a story to tell?"

"I think that I probably do… I witnessed a man walking on the water…" Then she recounted her story, before taking a few precious hours sleep.

FISHING WITH RISHI

Present - Meditation - Nature

Apolline approached the lake just as an orange ball of fire walked on stage. When she arrived, Rishi was meditating by the water's edge.

"Good morning Apolline. What have you brought with you?"

"Some sandwiches."

"Good, because I forgot mine."

"Maybe we could cook some fish."

"I doubt that."

"Why do you doubt that?"

"I don't expect to catch any fish, I never do."

"How do you explain that?"

"That is not the purpose of fishing," he said, as if that was obvious.

"Obviously I have a lot to learn. Perhaps before you tell me how to fish, you should tell me why it is not necessary to catch any."

"Fishing is just an excuse to go away by yourself and spend some time with nature. It's a can opener that opens up your senses. It is a time when you can meditate and restore yourself without any effort. No navel gazing is required."

"How does it do all that?"

"I have no idea. All I can tell you is that it works best if you don't actually attempt to catch any fish. Just look in the water and ask yourself where your current actions are leading you. If you look for long enough, you will see consequences floating to the top and your legacy at the bottom."

"I understand; the purpose of fishing has nothing to do with catching fish."

DELEGATING YOUR IMPORTANT DECISIONS

Marriage vows - Fears

I like the idea of passing over my very important decisions to something that I love.

"Can you tell me more about the sarus cranes?"

Rishi stood up and craned his neck: "The cranes play their own trumpets using their long necks. They also dance. It's truly stupendous. They live peacefully alongside the villagers here because they are venerated. It is traditional to take newly-married couples to see the cranes, because they are a symbol for being faithful in a partnership. When cranes mate, they stay with their partner for life. If their partner dies, they often pine and die of starvation."

"Are you trying to tell me that they have loving hearts?"

"Yes. If they can have broken wings, surely they can have broken hearts too?"

"Have you just married?"

"No, but I will soon."

"Where is your wife to be?"

"I don't know. I haven't met her yet."

"Then why are you coming to see the cranes?"

"I want to do all that I can to make my marriage work. I think that the more effort I put into thinking it through before it happens, the more chance I have of having a successful marriage like the sarus crane."

Apolline gulped, "How do you think you will meet your wife?"

"My mother has already chosen one for me."

There was a quiet period, not because Apolline didn't agree. It was because she was thinking about her own failed marriage. One based on looks and shared interests, a formula that is meant to bring happiness.

Rishi seemed to read her thoughts and lightly touched her hand: "To be honest, I like the idea of passing over something so important to my mother. I cannot think of a more appropriate way of thanking her for all her love."

Apolline gulped again. For a minute, she wished that she could have been Rishi's chosen woman: "Can we sit in the sun for a little longer, now I know there is no big hurry to catch a fish?"

At some point, everyone's love is tested. While Rishi took a drink to quench his thirst, he noticed that the water was still. He was thankful for this, because his mind wasn't.

Still water stills the mind. The presence of a beautiful woman can make it choppy.

BHOPAL AND KAKADU CAVES

True facts

Kakadu National Park is a nature reserve in the Northern territories of Australia near Darwin. Like Bhopal in India and Lascaux in France, it boasts amazing prehistoric rock art in its ancient caves.

Rishi offered Apolline one of her own sandwiches: "Have you been to the Bhimbetka rock shelters just south of Bhopal?"

"No. Should I?"

"Like the Kakadu caves near Darwin, they are also a UNESCO World Heritage Site. Some of the caves display paintings of birds and dancing that are 30,000 years old."

"Are there any cranes there?"

"Until recently there were only a few. However, there are now too many to count. Something strange is happening. It is for this reason that I am here."

"Do you think we should check the bait on our fishing lines?" They brought their fishing lines in, but nothing had changed. "I think that I could begin to like fishing, particularly if I don't find anything slimy on the end."

He laughed loudly. Now she felt confident enough to tease him: "Now tell me: how many wives can you have in your religion?"

"I have no religion, just fishing, which teaches me the virtues of patience, observance and acceptance."

That answer silenced her for a moment. She began to wonder if Sollie had planted this man here to help her with her garden project: "When do you return to Australia?"

"I am here for another five weeks or until I have solved the mystery of the crane movements."

"Then you must meet my friends and help me with some of my other challenges?"

Rishi helped himself to another of her sandwiches: "Do you know anything about the lakes of Bhopal?"

"I know that Bhopal is known as the city of lakes and hills, but that is about it."

"Upper lake was commissioned by King Bhoj in the 11th century to secure his borders. The big and small lake together form the Bhoj wetland. The story of how the lakes were formed is one of legend and mystery; like the lake's much sought-after fishing permits. I will tell you more about King Bhoj another day."

"How are the permits administered?"

"My father issues them. He is an elected local sarpanch. In the eyes of the local fishermen, that makes our family fishing Gods."

HOW TO WALK ON WATER

Identity - Surrender - Attachment - Ego - Miracles - Resentments
Desires - Logic - Spiritual activities - Present - Sacrifice - God

"Rishi, tell me truthfully, are you able to walk on water because you are a God?"

"Anyone can walk on water. Look in front of you. As we speak, an insect is walking on the surface."

"How does it do that?"

"There is a membrane on the surface that is too fragile for those laden with heavy goods to walk on without sinking. However, it is strong enough to allow those who travel lightly to skip across it."

"What must I do to be light enough to walk on the water?"

"It is a long list. You must be prepared to empty yourself and be free of your ego, resentments, logic, experiences, knowledge, beliefs and desires."

"Where do I start?"

"Start with some self-inquiry. Ask yourself, 'Do my desires, attachments and ambition give me anxiety? Is my pursuit of security and a better future stealing my present life?' Then start to arouse your curiosity; ask yourself, 'Who am I? What is my purpose in life? How can I find my higher self?'"

"Then what?"

"You must review your working hours and leisure time. Pursue a spiritual life. **Create spiritual and hobby time. Practising activities like: prayer, poetry, calligraphy, painting, singing, silence and meditation will result in your spiritual thoughts overflowing into your everyday life.** This will build your faith and move you towards God. **Place your emphasis on the development of your spiritual being. Then your material desires will begin to melt away.** This will take you another step towards 'surrendering and merging'. Now you can bob up and down in the water."

"I don't want to bob up and down in the water. I want to walk on it!"

"Then the ego must be removed!"

"How do I drop my ego?"

"You don't 'drop' the ego. When the time is right, the ego will 'fall away' effortlessly, like autumn leaves."

It seemed that Rishi understood the importance of falling leaves. Now she wanted to touch him. She managed to restrain herself and spoke in a manner that she hoped would not betray her thoughts: "When I have completed my self-inquiry questions, and created more spiritual time in my life, can you suggest an order?"

"Learn the art of being loving. Be mindful; pursue activities that help you enjoy the present. Immerse yourself in self-love. Practise the spiritual activities that I mentioned, and build your faith. Search for your higher self; practise gratitude, forgiveness and devotion. Then you can look to simplify your life and move away from self-concern and comforts. After this, you can prepare yourself for joy, sharing and turning your attention to the needs of others."

"Then?"

"Things will begin to loosen; like the desire for approval and recognition."

"How might that be possible?"

"By appreciating that much of what you have done was actually built on the sacrifices of others. After that, you must appreciate that the amazing work that you are really capable of requires a partnership to ignite it."

"What type of partnership?"

"A meaningful partnership with God; one where you allow yourself to become a vessel. Entering a relationship with God is another way to help you stop imagining yourself to be an individual. This will transform your life."

DOWNSIZING

Success - Intuition - Positioning - Surrender - Ambition

The fruit will fall naturally when it is ripe. Likewise, your desire to hold on to your possessions will fall naturally when you are ripe. You can hold your possessions; you don't have to drop them. However, you must not be attached to them.

"Rishi, what about my possessions and comforts? Do I need to give them away?"

"No! This is not the way. It is important that you understand this. Your possessions are not obscuring your happiness; your ego and attachments are. **Our material desires drop naturally and lose their hold over us when we are truly happy. We don't drop our desires… to become happy.**"

"So I can keep my possessions?"

"**You can keep your possessions if you want. However, you must not be attached to them.** Non-attachment requires you to be able to let go of all your possessions in a heartbeat."

"That is what Sollie told me, but how do I do that?"

"Imagine yourself being happy with a downsized, simpler life before you experience one for real."

"What is a downsized, simpler life?"

"A life free of extravagance, ambition and status."

"How do you imagine such a life?"

"Everyone has their own different method. For me it was easy. I just meditated on the consumerism that had ensnarled me. I asked what the true cost of my house, promotions, car, wealth and social standing was…I didn't like the answer. Then I asked myself what my real needs were. I looked into the future and imagined myself living in a small, plain room with a few good books and a small vase of flowers by my bedside."

"Does downsizing not leave you feeling insecure?"

"No. Not at all. **At the point that you let go of those things that are weighing you down in the material world, you feel a greater sense of belonging in the wider world.**"

"Then?"

"Then the only desire that will remain will be the one to surrender and merge. It is this that will make your steps saintly and light enough to walk on the water."

"Are you sure that I won't sink?"

"If you surrender and merge, you become the water. How can you sink in the water if you are the water?"

"What exactly must I surrender?"

"You must surrender everything; your mind, body, gifts and personal plans."

"Surrender does not sound easy."

"No one is asking you to surrender all that you know and all that you possess on a whim. No one is asking you to have total faith in something that you cannot see or feel. **You build your faith gradually. It's not a dive from a high board into a bottomless sea.** You start out in the shallows. You wade out slowly. With each step the water becomes warmer and clearer. When the time comes to surrender, merge and put your head under the water; no blind faith is required."

They didn't catch any fish. They did, however, enjoy the most fantastic day. Apolline went to bed visualising the mysterious lakes, the dancing cranes and walking on the water. Her final act before she fell asleep was one of gratitude: 'Thank you Sollie. You delivered the miracle that you promised me and the God of fishing too.'

ADMISSION

Habits - Giving up - Success - Drinking - Secrets
Denial - Confessions - Control

> Redemption arrives when we shift our focus away from ourselves and on to others. Becoming the pourer instead of the drinker.

The following evening, the safari team arrived home from the forest of the emerald-eyed tigers. Tom immediately looked for Sollie. He had something that he wanted to discuss.

"On safari, I told Bruno that I had been drinking too much whisky. I would imagine that it will not be long before everyone knows."

"Why are you telling me this?"

"I am 'interested' in knowing what I must do to stop drinking."

"When your intentions change from 'being interested' to 'being totally committed', come and see me again. I cannot help those that are merely interested."

There was a silent pause: "I suppose that I doubt my own commitment."

"Why is that?"

"I don't believe that what happened to me when I was younger can be repaired. Therefore, I cannot imagine a brighter future."

"I think that you are telling me that your thoughts are broken."

"Yes, exactly."

Sollie tutted: "I thought that I had already demonstrated to you that you are not a piece of smashed glass; you are simply a piece of clay that can be rolled out and reshaped without any blemishes. Or do I need to hit you over the head with that rolling pin? Out of curiosity, can you tell me what type of better life you want?"

"No, I haven't got that far yet. All I know is that my life lacks meaning."

"You need to do something about that. **If you haven't mapped out a compelling future, there will not be any incentive to give up your limiting habits.**"

"Then I suppose I should think of something."

"You don't need to. There is a plan for you… if you make yourself available."

"You said that with great certainty!"

"Tom, someone you know must carry out a very important task; a prophecy that was painted onto cave walls many thousands of years ago. Once they know what it is, they might become fearful and feel overwhelmed. They will need someone to support them. Do you think you could be that person?"

"Yes."

"Then we will do whatever it takes to stop you drinking whisky so that you can."

AGITATING THE WITCH'S BREW

Past problems – Timing – Bright futures

The whys of the world are not important; in fact, they are an obstacle to your release.

Apolline wanted to understand her problems and difficult past. She hadn't grasped that the 'whys of the world' are not important. Sollie had an alternative remedy in mind.

"You will not cure your difficult past by trying to understand it. All this will do is stir and agitate the witch's brew."

Apolline ruffled her skirt, crossed her legs and sat upright.

"The answer is in two parts. **First we must validate your past.** You must ask, 'Are my past difficult experiences still taking place?' If they are still occurring, they need to be dealt with. However, if they are no longer happening but you are just suffering from their effects, you must adopt new thinking.

"A better alternative than trying to make sense of your past problems is to say, **My difficult past happened for a reason.** Now instead of raking over your past, you can ask how you can use it as a force for good? Raking over and looking back was the mistake of Lot's wife. She pined for the past, which was not good for her. Deemed unworthy for doing so, she was turned into a pillar of salt. The same will happen to you if you keep looking into your rearview mirror. You should, instead, follow the example set by Muhammad. It is said that he was always so immersed in the present that he would never look behind, 'even if his cloak was caught on a thorny bush'.

"Look at your positive attributes. Ask yourself if you would still have these if you hadn't experienced your difficult past? If you can accept that difficult pasts contain invaluable lessons and gifts, your past can propel you forward, instead of turning you into a statue or a pillar of salt."

KARMA AND ACCEPTANCE

Pain and joy - Ego - Humility - Problems

"Maybe I deserve to suffer? Maybe it is karma? Perhaps I did terrible things in a previous life and now it is payback time?"

"Thinking like that won't help you. **Use the concept of karma to help you embrace acceptance... then karma will help you.**"

"Accept what?"

"Accept that the world moves in mysterious ways. Accept that there are some things that we should not try and work out."

"Why not?"

"If we are to work everything out, it would mean that ego is higher than humility; that acceptance has no role in enlightenment. Acceptance is not about doing nothing either; acceptance can still be a call to action."

"What does that mean?"

"That we still fight injustice. Remember the pale-yellow butterfly...never see your small contribution as futile. Remember Martin Luther's message ... Plant a tree even if you think the world is about to end.

"**Karma is about taking action, whilst accepting that it is not possible to understand why everything happens.** If you can do this, you have discovered the answer to everything that does not make sense … from now until eternity. This is the true meaning of good karma."

"How exactly?"

"Ask yourself, 'Is it possible that my past difficulties are the platform on which my future greatness will be built? Is it possible that in life we need pain as much as we need pleasure? Is it possible that life is meant to be full of challenges and joy simultaneously?' If you can answer yes, you have found another way to synthesise your problems." Then he paused to clear his throat: "**Whenever something does not make sense, simply say to yourself…**

Everything is as it should be.

"Don't try and work anything out. Just say this mantra. If you can't remember it, tattoo it on your body."

"Can you give me an example?"

"No. It is something that you should go away and meditate on. It needs to be percolated."

MISSING KEYS

The unexplained past - Justice - Closure - Healing

So Apolline went away and meditated on the mantra, **Everything is as it should be.**

Was it helpful? Wow, it certainly was! Did she get any sleep? No, she did not. She was up at dawn knocking on Sollie's window.

"It is unfathomable."

"Wonderful. Now nothing ever need worry you again!"

"What a wonderful thought. However, can you give me one good reason why I am not allowed to work things out?"

"I told you. Acceptance equals humility. Humility melts the ego. Without humility there will be no enlightenment."

"I am not on that path yet. Can't I have another explanation?"

"Personal problems are not to be solved or understood; they are to be healed. Explanations rarely explain horror, and problems often defy logic. Sometimes, there may be no explanation because the key to the missing answers may have been lost or thrown away. However, that does not mean that you can't still be set free."

"What do you mean?"

"The people who did harmful things in the past are not always there to provide answers or explain themselves… They may be dead, or they may not be contactable. If you pursue answers or justice, you may endure a life of suffering. It is for this reason that you must view difficult pasts as something that can give you a better future."

"Really?"

"Yes. However, if that fails, I will give you another cure…I will show you how to change the past instead!"

WORRIES AND UPSET

Problems - Responsibility - Control

Apolline returned a few days later.

"Sollie, I owe you an apology. I doubted you!"

"What happened?"

"Tom and I had lunch in a café. It was terrible. The waiter was rude, and the food was awful. At first I was upset."

"And then?"

"I put my frown away. I stopped trying to work out why it was all so bad. I repeated your mantra… **Everything is as it should be!** This helped me synthesize my hurt into a lesson. I have no idea why my meal did not match my expectations. Perhaps the waiter had received some terrible news. Perhaps the chef was about to lose his job. I don't need to know."

"Very good."

"Now you need to explain to me how I can change the past."

CHANGING THE PAST

Miracles - Friends and lovers - Despair

All the miracles that you need to perform are within you.

"Okay Apolline, come with me."

On the way, Sollie took a detour to the main house and grabbed some candles, incense, cushions and a portable music player. Then they followed the winding path to where the tree frogs lived. He scattered the cushions, placed the candles in a circle and told her to sit down in the middle. When the music mirrored the moon and persuaded the candles to dance, he sat down opposite her… Now their bare knees were almost touching. Very quickly her body began to wake up. He said nothing and just stared at her. It was enough; Apolline could feel him swimming in the watery pools of her eyes. Her legs began to tingle, and her mind wondered, 'Is he going to reach out and touch my bare leg? Is this magnetic force pulling him towards me too?'

It was…the blood in his veins was on the move, his soup was beginning to thicken… but he tried to not let on: "Close your eyes. Silence your thoughts for a minute. Absorb the music and the fragrance… Now, think about someone that you used to love, who is no longer here. Imagine holding a memory or a photograph of them. Bring them nearer to you. Imagine giving them your deepest love."

Her grandmother came to mind. Tiny, frail but still strong. Hand-knitted shawls, baked apples, kind words, patience. Apolline twirled her grandmother's snowy-white, curly hair around one of her fingers. The candles began to flicker, Apolline's heart began to flicker too. The love that they had once shared was shining brightly.

"Now I want you to think of someone that needs some love who is living. Someone overlooked or down on their luck. A person that occasionally flutters into your thoughts. Step a little nearer than you normally would. Offer your hand. Offer the love that they need."

Apolline instantly knew who that was. Eloise, a friend in need. Someone that could become a best friend if she stepped a little nearer. Normally they would only exchange pleasantries, but not today; this time Apolline went below the surface and dared to ask in a heartfelt manner, 'Are you really okay?'

Eloise was sitting on the floor… forlorn, heart barely beating. Apolline offered an outstretched hand. Eloise put her hand out too. They entwined their fingers and gripped each other with their thumbs. For a few minutes they shared each other's feelings; they also shared some love.

The next time Apolline heard a voice, it was that of the moon.

"Now I want you to imagine yourself when you were very young. When you were innocent of all things. This can be a photograph or a memory. When you have that image, I want you to know something… You have just shown yourself how loving you really are. How deep and wide your love really is. Now that you know how loving you really are, I want you to give that little girl all the love that you are capable of… all the love that she needs… all the love that is deserved… all the love that the little girl never felt as a child."

Apolline imagined a photograph of herself at school when she was six years old. One that told a tale of a little, lost girl. The flames of the candle lit up the photograph. It warmed the little girl's cheeks and brought the photograph's colour to life. This time Apolline repeated the moon's words to herself: 'I am indeed a loving person. Someone capable of giving and deserving love.'

Then a miracle did indeed happen. A boulder that could not be moved did more than just roll away. The immoveable boulder that says, **We can't give love until we can receive love, but we can't receive love until we can give love,** turned into dust. Apolline put her arms around the little girl. They hugged each other. Then they kissed each other, held hands and danced in a circle with abandon. An abandon that Apolline had never experienced before. This was not the unloved little girl that Apolline knew. The overlooked and unhappy girl was now smiling in a way that she never had before… The past had been changed. Now there would be a bright future.

The music stopped. Apolline felt Sollie's hand gently brush her cheek.

"Oh my God. What did you just do? You performed another miracle. You really did change the past."

"No, Apolline. You did it. Never forget, **All the miracles that you need to perform are within you.**"

* * *

After that, they should have gone their separate ways. Unfortunately, Apolline's mastery of seduction breached the defences of Sollie's weakness. However, nothing was said the next morning. Sollie was, after all, their teacher, and Apolline had some other seeds to harvest.

CREATING MINDFUL ART GARDENS

Silence - Stillness - Finding God - Pilgrimages - Spirit and soul - Mindful Propriety - Beyond peace - Purity - Art - Discipline - Self-love

Gardening is another way to purify your heart and take you away from your mind.

When Hubert returned to conduct more studies on the migrating birds, Apolline met him at the airport.

"Hubert, do you know anything about sarus cranes?"

"A little, but I don't profess to be an expert."

"My friend Rishi would like to meet you. He is curious about some unusual crane migrations in Australia. I think that you might have a lot in common. He is coming to dinner tomorrow night."

However, today Apolline was meeting Rishi herself. She was keen to hear what other gardening advice he could offer. After a tour of the Mustard Garden grounds, they sat on the grass in front of the house... Tom watched his crumbling love through envious eyes at the window.

"Rishi, can you now advise me on ponds and bridges? I thought at least one large pond with some fish to attract some Manchurian cranes."

"Good idea, providing there is still some water!"

"What about a bridge over the pond?"

"What about a bridge to God?"

"How do I do that?"

"**We have it within ourselves to reveal God; to lay a path that God will be at the end of...** That could be your bridge?"

"Are you serious?"

"Yes. However, if the people visiting your garden are going to meet God, you will need to create an area where they can prepare themselves."

"How?"

"A Muslim friend of mine recently went to Mecca for the Umrah pilgrimage. He said, 'Before the pilgrims set out on their journey, they had to wash and purify themselves in preparation for meeting God.' This, it seems, helps pilgrims be mindful about the purpose of their journey."

"So I need to fashion a mindful garden where people can prepare themselves for a meeting with God?"

"Not exactly! You need to create a mindful garden that will help people discover their higher selves; the God within. This could be a quiet preparatory area, outside of the main gardens. It would school people in the art of propriety and reverence; encouraging visitors to be respectful in their dress code, refrain from folding their arms and to walk slowly through the grounds. However, this would not be out of respect for God; it would be because, **Propriety and reverence is part of self-love.**"

"So visiting a garden is an act of self-love?"

"Yes… if the garden has been designed mindfully. You should also know that the starting points for self-love are mindful breathing and silence. When we are silent and present, we silence our thoughts. This filters the mind and helps purify the heart… Think about this when you watch the lilies filtering and purifying the pond water."

"Sollie didn't explain any of this. I had no idea that I had to design a garden that would facilitate self-love and help people discover the God within. Do you think that this is why Sollie delegated this task to me?"

"Yes. Gardening also helps you understand that you are a universal soul. Now, what else did Sollie ask you to do?"

"Something that would rekindle Emperor Huizong's life."

"What type of life?"

"A life full of tea-making competitions and art."

"Then perhaps you need to incorporate those disciplines into your gardens."

"How?"

"In ancient times, in some art schools, there was a procession of different gardens laid out in front of the main house of learning. The first garden would be furthest away from the main house. It would be simple and austere with no flowers; only hedges, trees and lawns. Here, the students would practise observation and master the disciplines of basic calligraphy.

"As one moved nearer to the main house of learning, the gardens progressively became more elaborate. As the students became more advanced, they were permitted to paint in the more ornate gardens. Here they could use more free-flowing brush strokes."

"Is that it?"

"Obviously you need somewhere for tea-making competitions. You will also need to set aside an area in the garden where people can bring their ancestors' work to life!"

DANCING WIDOWS

Visions – Needs – Losing ourselves – Dance – Recognition – Music

> First we must find ourselves again, in order that we can lose ourselves. This is the way, the right order.

Sollie finally found time to discuss his Varanasi and Vrindavan adventure with Yutika. Someone or something decided to make it indelible; waving in a cool breeze and softening the light.

"What did you find?"

"It was as you said. Although, I had not imagined the magnitude of the widows' misery."

"Tell me about your hopes."

"I would like it if all the widows had their lights turned back on, like the desert sky. I want to see them dancing in a ring of light. Maslow's 'Hierarchy of Human Needs' must be turned upside down. I don't want us to prioritize food and shelter for the widows. We must go beyond giving care and making them feel valued. Time is not on their side. They must go direct to dance.

"The trees will sway in the breeze before the music plays. The widows' backs will straighten, their heads will rise and they will acquire poise. Then they will dance, whatever their age, whatever their infirmity. I want them to vibrate with rhythm and energy, for life to flow through them, until they are one with this world again. For this is the pinnacle of life. Self-actualisation is further down the totem pole."

"You have thought about this, haven't you? Do you also know the detail of this dance?"

"Oh yes. I want the music to be arranged like the forest. When I listen, I want to be able to distinguish the violin from the viola. I want to know that the harp has been plucked and the cello has been bowed so that they vibrate, like the bees loosening the pollen from the flower. I want the woodwind's flute, clarinet and oboe to enter like the saintly steps of the young deer. Then the horn will call the stag, and the widows will begin their dance. I hope that my little speech does not sound too serious, but it is what I hope for. It is a dream that I would like to come true."

THE COCONUT TREE CLIMBING OLYMPICS

Sport - Winning - Personal best - Fears - Training
Joy - Disappointment - Pain and suffering

The children had learnt how to shimmy up trees in preparation for the dinosaur show. Now they could put their skills to use in the Coconut Tree Climbing Olympics. There were several categories, including team relay, sprint and the Coconutathalon. As far as Stromboli were concerned, the one that mattered was the coconut sprint: this involved climbing up and down the coconut tree four times, as fast as possible. Sollie addressed all the children soon after the announcement.

"You have one month to train and improve your fitness. Prepare yourself mentally in equal measure for disappointment or victory. The most important thing is to have fun."

Stromboli's hand shot up: "Won't preparing ourselves for disappointment make us less likely to win?"

"There are 14 of you and only one of you can win, so preparing for all outcomes seems sensible to me."

"Doesn't that make it meaningless?"

"No. Not at all. We are all of different ages and abilities. Therefore, we need a different way of measuring a winning performance; one that keeps everyone interested and motivated. It is for this reason that we measure each individual's starting point and their improvements. This way everyone can win. Of course, there will be some straightforward races too. This will give most of you the opportunity to experience injustice and defeat."

Despite this explanation, Stromboli remained dissatisfied: "I understand the concept of improving on my personal best performance. However, if I did want to make sure that I was the fastest, what would I have to do?"

"In that case you would have to train every day and every night: before lessons, at lunch time and after lessons."

"That much?"

"Yes. That much. **You would have to do 'whatever it takes'.**

"If you only train in the morning, you might find that Ascension also trains in the afternoon. If you both train all day, you might find that Ascension starts training in the night, and therefore, you would need to do so as well. When you speak to Olympic champions, they will tell you that all their success is built out of suffering. They interpret pain as gain. In fact, they go searching for pain because they believe it leads to gold medals."

Batiki's hand went up: "I have a different challenge. I am terrified of heights."

"Good. **Know that if you can conquer your fears, you can find joy and exhilaration that you didn't realise existed.** In many cases, what you once feared will not only bring you happiness, it will be the making of you. It might even make you more loving."

* * *

Finally, the time for the great coconut-tree sprint arrived.

The starting gun cracked and the race began. Stromboli flew up the tree, closely followed by Ascension. After two tree climbs Stromboli still led, but his lead had shortened. By the third climb Ascension had caught him up, but surprisingly so had Batiki.

"Where had she come from?" they all asked. No one had even seen her practise. No one had ever heard her mutter a word about looking forward to the big day. Suddenly there was a scream. Phi Phi fell out of the tree and on to the ground… but she would be alright. Sollie blew a whistle and stopped the race.

Now they had time to think. Stromboli looked at his hands. They were cut open and bleeding so much that the blood was dripping. He winced. His first thought was that he couldn't carry on. Then he recalled what Sollie had said about imagining his success and moving through different levels of pain. That persuaded him to exchange his worries for something more empowering; an image of himself standing on the winners' podium and Bruno putting a winner's medal around his neck.

The gun went off again, and they shimmied up and down the tree for the last time. Stromboli's feet touched the ground in first place. However, so did Batiki's!

"What happens next?" an out-of-breath Stromboli asked.

"We must ask Tom. It appears that it is a photo finish."

After a five-minute wait, Sollie blew his conch and read out each child's personal best improvements. They all received a rousing round of applause for this. However, Stromboli was too preoccupied to enjoy that adulation. He was busy pacing nervously whilst he waited for the supreme winner to be announced.

'If medals are fashioned out of pain and blisters, then surely I deserve one,' he muttered to himself.

Eventually, Bruno prepared to read out the winner of the Olympic coconut sprint.

"Third place is awarded to Curacao. First and second place could only be decided by the heel of a shoe." Everyone held their breath for a few moments. "In second place is Stromboli. Therefore, our amazing champion is Batiki."

Later, they all made merriment and enjoyed a celebration dinner; everyone, that is, except Stromboli. He sat in silence. To him the night tasted like the burnt edges on his pizza crust.

FAITH IN THE IMPROBABLE AND THE IMPOSSIBLE

Beyond winning – Higher self - Sport

Sollie found Stromboli sitting all alone by the tree frogs, tearful and inconsolable. He sat at his side and gently ruffled his hair.

"What happened Mr Sollie? How did that happen? It was not possible."

"It clearly was possible, because it happened. However, now it is over. Now we must learn from it. This is what makes true champions. Only because you have experienced this defeat can I now ask you to help me with something more important."

"More important than winning the Coconut Tree Climbing Olympics?"

"Yes. Helping some other people achieve something that at the moment appears to be an impossible dream."

"How would I do that?"

"**You would have to become interested in building your faith in your higher self, instead of just your mind and body.** Then you would understand the difference between the improbable and the impossible.

"Many people have faith in the improbable. Sport provides us with wonderful examples of this... comebacks that seem 'beyond belief'. Many of these 'amazing results' occur because individuals and teams believe that the highly improbable is possible. However, the highly unlikely and the highly improbable are measurable. They can happen because it is possible that they can happen, even if it is unlikely.

"This is not the same as having faith in the God within us. Now the possible outcomes change. Now we can go beyond the highly improbable and what is mathematically possible; we can achieve the impossible. **The impossible is what is not possible when we work alone, without God.** It may be difficult to measure, but it represents the feelings that many of us are searching for. I can't find all the words to describe it, but it includes a feeling of belonging, peace from anxiety, of being loved, of being loving, of shared joy and of compassion. It is these feelings that will give us the faith to travel further than our feet could ever wander and to pursue the good things that our eyes can never see."

Then Sollie drew a smiley face in the dust: "Stromboli, perhaps you could help me with an impossible dream… one that would make you feel as if you had a world champion's medal around your neck."

"Me?"

"Yes, you."

EMPATHY AND THE COLLECTIVE WILL

Tribal teaching

However, a few days later Stromboli was caught cremating live beetles with the sun and his magnifying glass. Sollie decided something needed to be done. By sheer good fortune, an opportunity arrived almost immediately. Apolline made it come about.

"Sollie, do you think that it would be a good idea to divide the children between us, so that each one has a specific mentor or principal teacher?"

Sollie twitched his nose before replying, "In some schools and workplaces, teachers and managers often concentrate their efforts around those people that they are directly responsible for. However, I would like to suggest another way. After normal classes, we will all come together and discuss the specific needs of each child. This way our 'collective will' may straighten things out that at first glance appeared beyond correction."

Apolline nodded her agreement: "Will we tell the children of our plans?"

"Probably not. However, if we did, can you imagine how they might feel if they knew that a 'collective will' cared enough to work specifically for their benefit?"

During the group's second 'collective will' session, Stromboli happened to be passing the room where they were all gathered. He had been warned that it was dangerous to listen at keyholes. However, on hearing what he thought were whispers, he decided to stay and listen anyway. He was in for a shock.

First, he heard them say that he lacked compassion. They said that this was not because he was a bad child but because he was hurting from his loss. He thought about this for a while and guessed that they were referring to his cruelty of the insects and his compatriots. After this, he expected them to start discussing how they might punish him. However, every word they spoke dumbfounded him. Every sentence that they uttered appeared to be a sermon of love. 'They all seem to want to help me!' Stromboli said to himself, in utter amazement.

Their voices were very faint, and so he pressed his ears even harder to the keyhole. By now his heart was pounding and his tears were dripping. This, it appeared, was love. A love that, until then, he had thought only grew on trees. It seemed that a group of people had come together to use their 'collective will' to overcome the insurmountable; himself. Eventually he could take no more; he wiped his tears and walked away.

THE DEVIL COMES TO DINNER

Security - Meeting fears

Unaware that Stromboli had been listening, the adults began to look for ways to help him. Apolline was the first to come up with an idea: "I will tell the children a satanic tale that I heard when I was a little girl."

Her story was told at a time and a place where the devil was more likely to be in attendance; in the forest, one hour before midnight and accompanied by the crackle of a campfire. The children sat cross-legged in a circle. Then Apolline began.

"A young family lived in the wood chopper's cottage, just a few miles from here. One day they were informed that the devil wanted to visit them for dinner. The parents had a predicament to wrestle with. Would an invitation for dinner change the devil into an angel or result in their children being eaten and their house burnt down? After a thoughtful night wrestling with their dilemma, they decided that there would be no invitation. Furthermore, they would do all that they could to prevent the devil from inviting themselves.

"The chimney was blocked off with cement, and the door and windows were all boarded up. The flower gardens were dug up and replaced with a pond of muddy sludge. Snarling and cantankerous dogs were chained to the fence posts. When they were finished, they were confident that the devil wouldn't be paying their house a visit. Within a week, cawing crows had commandeered all the surrounding trees, and plagues of qwarking toads had moved into the swampy garden. It wasn't long before summer felt like winter. The natterjacks had frightened off the nightingales, and the hiss of snakes had replaced all the bird song."

Batiki trembled, "What happened next?"

"That question is too terrifying to answer. You must use your imagination. However, I can tell you that when the missing-children inspector arrived, they found that the window frames were swinging in the wind and all of the family were missing. Toads, black crows and rabid dogs had all occupied the house. From this little tale springs an important question, **If we don't invite the devil to dinner, will the devil invite themselves?**"

Very quickly the children decided what they needed to do. Over the next three weeks they organised a lot of parties. One particular child's name was written on every invitation list. Would this bother him, or would this change him?

NEW LEAVES

Bees

Stromboli approached Sollie on the lawn: "I really enjoyed the forest safari. Can you teach me more about trees?"

"Of course. We can go for a forest walk as soon as I have finished my work."

Whilst Sollie worked at his desk, he could see that Stromboli was prodding something on the window ledge. Sollie stood up and walked over to see what he was doing: "What is that?"

"I think it is a dead honey bee."

"What were you doing to it?"

"It is only a useless, dead bee, so I was poking it."

Sollie's mouth opened wide: "Only a bee! Do you know how important bees are?"

"They make honey, don't they?"

"They do far more than that." Then Sollie handed Stromboli his magnifying glass: "Take another look at that dead bee, and tell me what you see."

Stromboli picked up the glass and studied the bee. He watched it for a while, and then stared at Sollie: "I think it moved a bit."

"Take another look then."

"It definitely moved, a tiny bit. I think that it could be alive."

"Are you sure? You told me it was dead and useless a few minutes ago."

"No, it is alive. I can see it better now."

"Go and find Yutika and ask her for a spoonful of honey and a tiny pot of water."

A few minutes later Stromboli returned with Sollie's requests.

"I want you to put the bee on the saucer next to a drop of the water and honey. Then we will go for our walk into the forest."

TREE GROWING AND FELLING

Winning - Soul - Spirit - Confidence - Empathy
Thoughts v actions - Looking inwards

A wise tree would look to avoid ending up as firewood. It would surrender before it dies.

Stromboli and Sollie walked deeper and deeper into the forest until its cold darkness whipped up the mist. Eventually, its softness enveloped them and its secret sounds were all around. Stromboli had never been into the forest at night before. The creaks and the sighs of sleeping timber were all new to him. Never before had he felt watching eyes that he could not see.

"Stromboli, why are you squeezing my hand so tightly?"

"It feels as if the trees are watching us."

"I am sure that they are. Did you not know that the trees have eyes and the woods have ears?"

Stromboli tightened his grip: "How could that be? I never saw a tree with eyes or ears."

"You must know that it's not just here in the forest that you are being watched. Wherever you go there is always something watching you. **All your thoughts can be seen by someone.** If this were not true, bad thoughts would not be any worse than bad actions. However, you know that this is not true."

"Why did you bring me at night?"

"I wanted you to see that the darkness isn't frightening; it's enchanting."

"But it's so very dark in here."

"Not for everyone. Some of the tall, fast-growing trees are hogging the sunlight, just like some people hog the limelight. That can make it difficult for those left in the shade to prosper."

"Do the trees left in the dark die?"

"Not necessarily. Sometimes it can be beneficial. When a tree grows at a slower pace, its crowns thicken; some say this makes it more surefooted and knowledgeable than the faster runners. It appears that if you are not in a hurry to climb to the top, you notice more of the amazing things that take place on the journey. Many of these other trees still reach the sky, it just takes a little longer."

They carried on walking deeper and deeper into the forest. All they encountered was darkness, the eerie calls of the owls and the crunching of leaves.

CRACK! A twig snapped. As it did, they saw some movement ahead.

"Look. Look, I can see a deer."

The deer sensed them but did not run away. Sollie motioned Stromboli to sit down with him on the leaves of the forest floor. Then, to their surprise, the deer walked over to them. It brushed against Stromboli's legs and then stopped to stare. Only when it was sure it had their full attention did it bound away into the thickness of the forest.

"Now, tell me, what is your favourite forest animal?"

"Chameleons. I wish that I could change colour like them."

"You can become a chameleon, but you don't have to stop at changing your colour! If you continue to develop your empathy, you can also learn how to turn your eyes into ears and your ears into eyes."

"How?"

"It's all about direction. Some philosophers tell us that, to find ourselves, we must first go inwards. Other say that to find meaning in our life, we must reach outwards."

"Which way is right?"

"I think that we should try and do both at the same time. If you watch the chameleon, you will discover that its eyes move independently. It can turn one eye on one thing and the other on something else, simultaneously. This is what we must do, **We must look in and observe our own behaviour, at the same time that we reach out to the outside world.**"

"If I become a chameleon, will my eyes move somewhere else on my head?"

"No. It doesn't work like that. Just refer to yourself as a universal soul, then whichever way you look, you will be coming from the right direction."

MAKING HONEY

Lost causes - Kind thoughts - Transference of love

The morning after the forest walk, Stromboli was standing outside the main house at 7am waiting for Sollie.

"Good morning, Stromboli. You are up bright and early."

"I have come to see the bee."

"Oh, I forgot about that poor little fellow."

He invited Stromboli in and they went over to the table. The bee was still there, although it remained still. Stromboli picked up the magnifying glass. He looked despondent.

"How is it?"

Stromboli puckered his lips: "It does not look good, but I would still like to wait at the bee's side."

Thirty minutes later, Stromboli jumped up in the air. "HELP - COME QUICKLY! The bee is still moving! It is still alive!"

Sollie inspected the bee with the magnifying glass: "I do believe that it is still alive. Top up the water and the honey. Then go to school. You can return again tonight. In the meantime, send the bee your kindest thoughts and wishes."

For the next three days Stromboli cared for the bee as much as he could. When he wasn't watching over it, he continued to develop his awareness and empathy by reading about insects. On the third evening, there was a sudden noise. "Buzzzzzzz."

Stromboli jumped in the air: "Mr Sollie, quick! It buzzed!"

Sollie walked over to verify Stromboli's discovery. Then the bee found its feet. Sollie and Stromboli stared at each other with smiles that could have bridged the river Ganges. They both knew what they needed to do next; together they opened the window and watched the bee fly out. Then Stromboli went to his bed. Some of the mud that had been obscuring his loving heart was left behind on the windowsill.

A COMING TOGETHER

Identity - Character - Suffering - Anger - Sadness - Meditation - Success

> We are not a duality. We are not good and bad. However, our actions might be until we find our true nature.

Stromboli sat in front of Sollie with his lips gummed together.

"Why are you so quiet, Stromboli?"

"I was having second thoughts. Perhaps I should become a lion instead of a chameleon?"

"Who do you think that you currently are?"

"I don't think that it is possible to say who I am. I have many personalities. I am fun with my friends, serious with adults and angry with my enemies. Isn't that normal?"

"It probably is. However, that doesn't make it right. It represents a fracture; one could call it 'a split personality'. Even the lion makes this mistake; it speaks softly to its cubs whilst roaring at its dinner. However, there is a way to make you whole."

Then Sollie went off to the storeroom at the back of the art studio. He returned a few minutes later with something in his hand and placed it carefully on the table.

It was a gold-painted, wooden head. The head had four sides, and on each side there was a different facial expression. Stromboli picked it up: "What is it?"

"It is a four-headed Buddha."

"What is its purpose?"

"Its many faces demonstrate that one person can act thoughtfully, happily, sadly, angrily etc."

"That is what I said."

"I know. The problem is that when your lion escapes from its cage, it is likely to terrify or eat people. You might not like yourself when that happens."

"What should I do?"

"You should recognize that certain stimuli can give rise to certain responses. You should also know that whilst there are many different puppet characters wanting to play on your stage, it must be you who pulls the strings and decides who enters."

"How?"

"Identify your 'many faces'. Then get to know the principal players a little bit better; particularly the happy, sad and angry ones."

"Then what?"

"Make them into puppets, and give each character a name. Identify their habits and behaviour. Establish what makes them come out to play. Then you can start to tame them and remove their elements of surprise."

"I think that I am going to enjoy this game."

"It is not a game. Your Mr Angry Lion and Mr Sadness characters can cause you and others great suffering."

"How do I remove my sadness?"

"Sad things happen in our lives. It is not always healthy to suppress feelings. However, we can make sure that we do not become embalmed in our pain and sadness, for this might ruin our lives. Remember what it says on the toilet door sign:

'PAIN IS UNAVOIDABLE, BUT SUFFERING IS A CHOICE.'

"What does that mean?"

"It means that you will surely experience sadness in your life, this is unavoidable. However, if you do not move on from the sad episodes in your life, you will experience great suffering. Fortunately, this is avoidable; it is a choice."

"How do I tame anger?"

"Meditation is a good place to start. It will change you on the inside. If your inside changes, so will your external actions."

"What else?"

"Practise other spiritual activities. Look inwards; this will lead you to your true nature. Here you will discover that at your core, the authentic you, is a loving, beating heart. **You are not good and bad, you are only loving."**

"Then what?"

"You might want to give yourself 'a handle' that sums up the new you."

"You mean like, Stromboli the Magnificent."

"I was thinking more like, Stromboli the Caring."

When you choose to let go of the ego, you do not just free yourself from approval and the anxiety of maintaining a mask; you discover your true, loving nature

APOLLINE'S INNER CHILD

Present – Mindful provenance – Stillness – Silence
Happiness – Control – Rejection – Admonishment

Stromboli's chair was still warm when Apolline gently tapped on the window.

"I have just been chatting with Stromboli."

"And…?"

"I think that I understand why I am both hell fire and holy water."

"Very good. What is it that you do not understand?"

"I don't understand why a few innocent words can change my happiness into sadness in a heartbeat."

"Can you give me an example?"

"Yesterday, Bruno asked me to join him for lunch. I started talking to him, then without warning, he told me to shut up! My heart sank, and then I had to run to the bedroom to sob."

"Why do you think that he told you to shut up?"

"He said that I was not being mindful of my food's provenance and the sacrifices made to deliver it to my plate. That I was being disrespectful to all those who were hungry and less fortunate."

"I understand. However, perhaps it would have been better if he had told you that you were taking yourself away from your happiness."

"What do you mean?"

"Silence, slowing our breathing and meditation are actions that change our state to one of being present. When we are in the present state, we are in the state of happiness. **We are happy because we are not projecting any negative thoughts on the past or the future – we are in a 'thoughtless state'.**"

"Oh. I should have known that. I am, after all, creating a garden for that very purpose."

"Now tell me, if Bruno was only trying to make you happier, is it possible that you were the problem? Is it possible that you asked the wrong question?"

"I don't know?"

"**Next time someone upsets you, don't become disturbed and ask why they reacted as they did. Ask yourself, 'Why am I so upset? Why are my responses so inappropriate?'** By framing your questions this way, you wrestle back control."

"Okay."

"Now tell me, why you think that you responded as you did?"

There was a period of silence and reflection: "I think that I respond like that whenever I feel rejected and feel unloved."

"Why?"

"Because of my father. He was never interested in what I did unless it was an accomplishment. No matter what I did, it was never good enough, and my requests for affection were always ignored."

"How did you respond to your father's behaviour?"

"I would feel worthless, not valued and unloved. I would cry."

"I understand. Do you think that as an adult, you respond to rejection or admonishment as if you were still a child?"

There was a further period of silence: "I suppose that I do."

"Then you must remind yourself that you are now an adult, not a child. As an adult, child-like responses can be unhelpful and inappropriate. **Know that what other people say is unimportant. Only your interpretation of what other people say matters.** Your interpretation will determine how you feel and how you respond."

"Then what must I do?"

"Exactly what Stromboli told you to do. You must become familiar with all the characters in your personality and identify what brings them out to play. Some people call the character that you are describing their 'inner child'. You must become familiar with this character's behaviour. **If your inner child dares to speak to you in an unhelpful way, you must put it back in its box.**"

SHARING OUR STORY

Emotional stimulation - Listening - Salvation

Each one of us has a story to tell, by all let this be heard.

Yutika had been baking the sort of bread that changed moods and loosened tongues.

"Sollie, I would like to know more about your trip to Varanasi and Vrindavan. You said that you filmed the widows talking of their sorrows and joy. Where did you show the film that you made?"

"In the market squares, the cow sheds and in the fields."

"Did many people come to watch?"

"Of course. People always want to know what is going on in their neighbours' lives. They came in their thousands. Every vantage point was taken; they watched from the balconies, rooftops and trees."

"What happened then?"

"The villagers watched the people that they thought they knew and then they realised that they didn't know them at all. They had to put their hands over their mouths, they were silenced, they cried and then they clapped ferociously."

"What happened when you had finished showing the film to the villagers?"

"I talked with the widows about their next role… to be the principal actress in their own salvation as well as the salvation of others. Allow me to explain."

WRITING YOUR OWN COMPELLING ENDING

Sisterhood - Widows - Art - Connecting hearts - Seed planting - Discipline Patience - Suffering - Souls - Spirits - Faith - Inspiration

"One of the greatest trials of human suffering took place in the Second World War during the 900-day blockade of Leningrad in Russia. The people starved when Germany surrounded Leningrad and cut off supplies. Such was their plight that the women dissolved buttons to make soup and used leather and tree bark to make stew. By 1944 three quarters of a million people had been deliberately starved to death.

"The women in certain towns of Scotland wanted to express their solidarity with the surviving women of Russia. They were desperately anxious to show how much they cared. In a heart-warming act of sisterhood, they held meetings and gathered thousands of signatures so that they could send a message conveying their support and admiration. However, they did something else; they produced a book, 'To the heroic women of Leningrad from the women of Airdrie and Coatbridge.' Then a delegation of housewives took it to London to ensure it was dispatched to Russia.

"It was a book of love. It still is. A book of art wrapped up in silk with heartfelt messages. A story of true friendship, hope and inspiration. A tale of the heart by some women from a distant country, deeply troubled by some people they would never meet. When it was received, it swept a tide of joy through the city.

"The unexpected gift helped the women of Leningrad understand that although their bodies were starving, they could still satisfy the hunger of the human soul. Later the women of Leningrad, along with some of their city's most accomplished artists, reciprocated. They too, created a book of love; a collection of art and gratitude with lithographs, engravings, beautiful watercolours and letters. They sent this to Scotland. It still sits in The Mitchell Library in Glasgow, each letter and brushstroke a testimony to how hearts are connected.

"Eventually, I would like the widows to do something similar. To produce a noble book of their stories and art to show the power of the human spirit. I think that this will stir consciences. I hope that it will inspire all the women in the world to come together and do what they can to change things. I hope that men will reach out too."

"Is that the only reason?"

"It is what Emperor Huizong would have wanted: for the widows to win their freedom through art instead of war and to paint their pain on silk. He planted the seed a long time ago. The time has come to sow it."

"Wasn't that centuries ago?"

"It was; however, understand this and you will understand the difference between patience and discipline. Discipline is something that you do or something that you practise. Patience is something that you have. Patience is not waiting for what you want. Patience is planting seeds that you may never see flower. Faith is handing the caring over to someone that you have never met. Together they describe our role in this world."

There was a period of solemn quiet before Yutika spoke again: "What happens then?"

"Then, realisations will launch themselves like rockets and crisscross the sky. Bitterness will be tempered, hearts will be reignited, sacrifices will receive their acknowledgements and dark clouds will pass. Then there will be a dawning. The widows will realise that they themselves hold the pen that can write the final chapter and a new ending to their own book. In the same way that we all can. Our role is to give the widows a helping hand. Do you think that you could help? For such a broth of wizardry will still need the hand of sisterhood and an alchemist to stir it."

She nodded.

"I thought that you would."

SILENCE AND BUTTERFLIES

Identity - Not fitting in - Excitement - Responsibility - Happiness
Lost for words - Recruitment - Being missed

Wherever he goes, he passes through silently, and yet people are always pleased to see him.

Bruno had been out of sorts for a few days. Therefore, Sollie was not surprised when Bruno asked to see him. They agreed to meet in the greenhouse after breakfast.

"I am thinking about leaving."

"Why do you want to leave?"

"I think that I am spoiling everyone's fun. Everyone else is cheery, and I am boring. I have no idea how to become more fun and useful. And, I don't deserve Ling; I have no idea how to make sure that she is always happy."

"I don't think that it is your responsibility to make sure Ling is always happy. However, remember: she is not a cactus in the desert who can survive by being watered just once a year. If you want to make her heart race, she needs to feel that you are going to chase her round the garden occasionally. However, on the more important matter about being boring etc, what you say is just not true. You were recruited because you have a magic factor. You are not here by chance… you are here because our project needed someone exactly like you." Then Sollie stepped back: "Look around, tell me what you see and what you hear?"

"I see tomatoes and I hear silence."

"Look and listen again."

"There are lots of butterflies flapping around. Apart from that, there does not seem to be much."

"When you came here there were no butterflies. Then you built a greenhouse, planted seeds and now it is alive with butterflies and tomatoes. In addition to that, the children here love you, all the adults care about you. One of them even adores you. Please tell me where you don't fit in?"

"I never know what to say."

"**You don't need to say anything**. It is your slow movements and your quietness that is attractive to others. Being present but not saying anything is an endearing quality. It brings some of those that don't feel so sure about themselves into play."

Before Sollie could continue, a plain, green butterfly landed on his head. Bruno carefully picked it up and placed it on the bench. Sollie studied it for a minute: "I think that we should call it Bruno. Someone who does not try to impress or put on a performance. He says little and so creates calm. Wherever he goes, he passes through silently, and yet people are always pleased to see him. He would be sadly missed if he went away."

"Do you really mean that?"

"I sincerely do."

SPECIAL RELATIONSHIPS

Approval - Love - Rejection

"Tom, can you describe to me what has troubled you most in your life?"

"It's my cord, Sollie. I have the wrong type. As a child, my school friends appeared to be attached to their parents by a powerful, elastic cord. They could test their parents' love with bad behaviour, but their cord would never snap… it would always spring back. It seems that it was bonded with unconditional love. However, I didn't have a cord… The relationship with my adoptive parents was just like my frayed shoelaces."

"How did that play out?"

"I was always afraid of my adoptive parents' disapproval. I was worried that if I misbehaved, I would be sent back to the orphanage."

"Does that mean that you were well behaved all the time?"

"No, I was usually bad. I felt compelled to put my adoptive parents' love to the test. I tried to prove that their love for me was conditional and that eventually they would cut the cord."

"What happened?"

"I overstepped the mark. The cord was cut… I was sent to live with my grandmother in Scotland."

BECOMING UMBILICAL

Being alone - Rites of passage - Trapped in childhood - Connections

Sollie squatted down: "Tom, would you show me your shoelaces?"

"If you insist."

"Do you remember the first time that you managed to tie your own shoelaces?"

"I do. It felt like a great achievement."

"It is. Progressing from our parents' tying our shoelaces to tying them ourselves is a great transitional period in our lives. We 'come of age'. It is a sayonara to one stage of our childhood and the start of another."

"I understand. However, that does not apply to me. I had no parents to tie my shoelaces for me. I was not adopted until I was eight. I was alone with my shoelaces when I was young."

"Then there is something that we should resolve or you might find yourself alone for the rest of your life!"

"What?"

"You may know how to tie your shoelaces now, but it does not follow that you have 'come of age'. For it is little acts of love, like having our shoelaces tied for us, that enable us to safely progress from childhood to adulthood. If we miss out on these little acts of love when we are young, we can find ourselves forever trapped in our childhood.

"Now kneel down please, and give me your shoelaces." Then Sollie placed them on the ground and straightened them out: "You say that the love in your relationship with your parents was like your frayed shoelaces... ready to snap at any minute. I like that analogy… however, your thinking is wrong! The condition of your cord or shoelace is not important. Only what you do with the two ends of your cord matters. Now read these words out for me."

BECOMING UMBILICAL

It was an umbilical cord that connected you to your mother, carried oxygen, brought you food and gave you life. However, in many cases this cord was discarded in a surgical waste bin, thrown away and forgotten. To find your purpose and give your life meaning, you must retrieve the two ends of your umbilical cord and ask a life-changing question: 'What must I connect my cord to, so that the two ends disappear?'

"So what must I do?"

"Master the arts of being-loving' and 'self-love'. Then, and only then, look to be umbilical… **Pick your cord or shoelaces up again. Take the two ends. Look to reach out and make circles for others. If you do, your own loose ends will disappear.**"

You will hear people say that they are at a loose end or that they cannot make ends meet. They always will be, until they become umbilical.

AN ARRESTING BREAKFAST

Worries - Cause - Security - Purpose - Preparation
Faith - Projects - Success - Direction

Purpose is a woodpecker's hole in a tree. It's a ship in a bottle. Unlike possessions, no one can steal it.

Gabriel was arriving in the afternoon, so plans and entertainment were being discussed. Then a police car came hurtling through the entrance gates.

"We are looking for Sollie St-Martin."

"I am Sollie. How can I help you?"

They didn't say anything; they just put some handcuffs around his wrists, lifted him off his feet and took him to their car.

Yutika followed them and stood next to the driver's door: "What has he done?"

"The children's Sunday protests have upset local politicians and religious leaders."

The next morning, Gabriel went off to obtain some legal assistance. The lawyer outlined his thoughts to him: "I will secure a bail hearing and a complete discharge for your friend. Don't worry. This happens all the time."

The bail hearing was carried out in private. Gabriel and Yutika sat outside the court room on the corridor floor. The lawyer appeared... His face was glum: "I am sorry, there is no bail. The judge is concerned that if Sollie is released too early, there will be riots in the villages."

"Oh my God, when will the case be heard?"

The reply was stern: "No date has been set yet."

Yutika paled; she had a better understanding of how quickly the wheels of justice rolled in this country, and it was not downhill.

* * *

Gabriel was allowed to see Sollie for 10 minutes before he was locked away again. Sollie practised his juggling skills with some metal ashtrays before speaking: "Don't look so worried, Gabriel."

"Have you considered that you could lose your entire investment?"

"What do you mean?"

"That with a questionable lease, there is no guarantee that Durga couldn't find a way to take everything back off you."

Sollie grinned, and his eyes sparkled: "That's why it's not a financial investment... Our aim is simply for something purposeful to be borne out of our work. Unlike possessions, our purpose can't be lost, stolen or set on fire because it's a ship in a bottle; no one else can get it out, unless they share the cause. It also means that Durga, and people like him, can never disturb my peace of mind."

Sollie laughed again, only this time Gabriel laughed with him. However, Sollie's mind wasn't completely still. He was worried that he was about to let everyone down. That thought pained him greatly.

"Sollie, can I do anything for you, before I go?"

"Just give this short letter to the others."

Remember, I prepared for the difficult times before I planned for success. Therefore, please do not worry about me. I also ask you to remember that it is not resources, money or logic which delivers the greatest projects. It is faith and momentum. Please continue to build your faith.

Some of you know what you are passionate about, but you are not sure what your purpose is. Remember what I said: 'The greatest discipline is to sharpen your arrows and practise your aim when the target has not yet come into view.' This means that the direction that you must move in is forward, even though your movement may be still.

Should we continue pursuing the student gap year programme and other activities? Possibly. These may all be worthwhile pursuits. However, let us not be in any doubt that these are all side dishes. We cannot decide or create our purpose, we can only exercise patience and make ourselves available.

Sollie

THE SECRETS OF SUCCESS

Purpose - Gifts - Ambition -Total commitment
Doing nothing - Ordinary lives

When your purpose is correct you will not need to write reminders down. You will feel and see the things that must be done when you hear the birds sing.

Ling, Tom, Yutika and Apolline were all visiting Sollie at the same time. As usual, he was in high spirits.

Ling was decked out in a sunny yellow headband and in an exceedingly good mood too. "Sollie, I have given birth to something new."

"What is that?"

"A quiet ambition, although I am not sure that those are the right words to describe it."

"Tell me more about it."

"It is a feeling that is burning the inside of my cheeks and ribs. It is telling me that I can do something wonderful with all the gifts that have been bestowed on me. Now I just need to know what to do with it."

"Well, if you want, **The Formula for success and wealth**, the recipe is quite simple… **Just commit to doing 'whatever it takes'.** All the additional information that you require is readily available in lots of books."

"I don't want anything material for myself. I just want to feel that I have made the most of my capabilities."

"In that case, **You must learn the distinction between 'whatever it takes' and 'total commitment'.** The former is what you need to do to achieve personal success. The latter, 'total commitment', is what you must do if you want to devote yourself to serving Mother Earth. If you want personal success and are prepared to do 'whatever it takes', you can't just be 'interested'. You can't miss work or training because there is a furniture delivery. You can't take the day off to watch your child's sports day. Your goals must take precedent.

"However, 'total commitment', unlike 'whatever it takes', isn't something that you swim towards; it is something that you immerse yourself in. It is still a commitment, but it has stopping off points for rest, family, pleasure, reaching out and the unexpected built into it. Of course, this type of life is not for everyone. If you only want to 'get by' and live an ordinary life, you will find that there are many mundane things to consume your day. By the time you eat, go to work, take a run, and make a few calls, the day can be done. You will not move forward, you will not even be facing in the right direction, but you will have killed off another day of your life."

NOMADIC PATHS

Families - Commitment - Downsizing - Relationships

Wider love - Being loving - Non-attachment

Whilst Tom, Ling and Apolline thought about this, Yutika shuffled on her seat. She had another question for Sollie: "If someone did want to make a 'commitment' to a God, what would they need to do?"

"Surrender. We have talked about this before. However, some people follow other paths."

"Like what?"

"There are some religious sects who make a total commitment to 'non-attachment'. This does not just include material things; it includes refraining from 'being attached' to their families. They will not stay in one house for more than three nights; they are perpetually on the road."

"That is a considerable commitment!"

"It is. However, they test themselves before they set out. This is to establish if they have the mental endurance to stick things out. For example, they will pull their hair out with their hands. Afterwards they will take a ceremonial bath in butter, milk and saffron."

Ling and Apolline's mouths opened together: "Ouch."

Yutika appeared less circumspect. "What do you think about that?" she asked.

"I think that it is radical. However, I do understand their goal. They are committed to being one with the world. They do not want to be limited by living within the confines of their own families."

Sollie bit his lip. Apolline noted his concern: "Is something worrying you, Sollie?"

"I was just reminding myself that those who are totally committed are capable of acts of great joy. Unfortunately, if people feel disconnected or if they have lost hope, they are also capable of horrific acts of sorrow."

The ladies stood up to leave. Tom waited until the room was clear and walked towards Sollie.

AN UNUSUAL FAMILY LIFE

Feeling unsafe - Rejection - Attachment - Desensitized

"Sollie, how do you give up all your material attachments and your family?"

"You just mentally rehearse not being attached to them. Then you commence your journey."

"So you don't give away all your attachments or throw them out before you set off?"

"Correct. You just set out. Leave your possessions in their boxes and your family in their house. Later, as your faith builds, your possessions and attachments will lose their hold over you; they will fall away like ripe fruit from a tree."

"If I did have a family, I am not sure that I would want to give them up."

"You wouldn't be giving them up. The goal is not to diminish your love for them. The goal is to love them even more. You would just seek to drop your attachment to them."

"What are the consequences of that?"

"You would need to go out and love the wider world even more! If you succeed, everything, including your family, will appear more precious and loveable, and you will become more loving too."

"I will give that some more thought."

"I would like you to do more than that."

"Go ahead, tell me."

"Some of the children staying with us here have been abandoned by their parents. This might leave them feeling powerless, alone, scared, desensitized and isolated. They might also find it difficult to connect with other people or be intimate… They might have a fear of rejection. Tragically, they might find themselves alone forever, unless they confront their challenges."

After that, there was a long silent pause: "I can relate to some of that."

"Good, because I have something for you to meditate on… If abandonment and a lack of 'loving attachment' can cause so much suffering in an infant child, why do you think that some people think that 'non-attachment' will end suffering?"

A SOOTHING HOUSE

Gardens - Heaven

The next time Apolline saw Sollie in prison she was keen to share her new gardening knowledge.

"Rishi has unlocked the secrets of fishing and bridges for me. Now I can design a garden that the emperor would be proud of. The entrance area will be minimalistic and school people in propriety and self-love. There will be archways to pass through to reach several further gardens. Each one will set new challenges for the meditator and calligrapher. When the students have mastered their art, they can thicken their brushstrokes in the flower gardens and approach the bridge to heaven."

"Really?! What do you think that this heaven might look like?"

She pulled a piece of paper out of her pocket written in his unmistakable scrawl: "Maybe something like this. I found it in a box along with your original outline sketches for our home."

She read it out in a hushed voice, soft enough to draw a golden light through the prison bars:

WINDOW BOXES

My vision is for a simple place; more a window box than a garden. More a hostel than a hotel. A house and a garden of serenity with a fragrance and a soothing shop. One where people of all ages can find a sense of belonging. Somewhere that the wind can pass through. A place that makes the birds want to chatter. A guesthouse where you feel a valued guest. A place where you can find yourself, write your story, add a ribbon and leave your mark.

OLIVIA AND MEDITATING BEARS

Patience - Risk

Apolline took Phi Phi with her to meet Olivia at the train station. Whilst Phi Phi put Olivia's luggage in the hold of the truck, Olivia and Apolline embraced and asked the same question: "How did this happen?"

At the Mustard Garden, Apolline took Olivia straight into one of the classrooms where Ling had asked the children to paint their favourite forest animals.

Ling showed Olivia a painting of a stalking tiger: "It seems that Tom and Bruno have turned my beautiful children into monsters. I have never seen so much ferocious wildlife."

"Katakua. Why a fearsome bear?"

"Bears meditate, although Bruno said that bear meditation is called hibernation."

Phi Phi giggled, "Miss, I was going to be a squirrel, and they are cuddly."

"Please tell me what changed you from a furry squirrel into a charging rhinoceros?"

"On safari, we learnt that when squirrels travel from one place to another, they stay close to the hedgerows, Miss. They avoid crossing the open field. However, to be alive we must take risks and venture into the unknown. **Every day of our life must be full of doing things for the first time.**"

Then there was a knock on the classroom door. It was Komodo. He had his painting rolled up and was carrying it under his arm.

Ling sighed, "I think that I can guess what animal you have chosen?"

Komodo didn't disappoint; he had painted a huge, fire-breathing Komodo dragon. Hoots of laughter rang out.

"Couldn't you find anything less fearsome?"

"We did find lots of praying mantis, Miss Ling."

"Why didn't you paint one of those, they look quite cute?"

"They spend most of their life hiding in the wet leaves on the forest floor, waiting and hoping that their lunch will walk past. **Wasting your life waiting for someone or something that may never turn up is no way to spend your life.**"

* * *

As well as teaching at the village school, Olivia continued to implant her wisdom and play the role of older sister to Apolline. When reflecting on why Olivia might be investing so much of her time in her, she concluded that Olivia was preparing her for something.

PLANNING FOR RETIREMENT

Spiritual life - Resurrection - Immortality - Ancestors - Gratitude
Pensions - Family trees - The present v future - Time management
Happiness - Sacrifices - Savings – Fears

"Dig your well before you are thirsty."
Chinese proverb

Instead of bribery, Sollie had found an alternative way to acquire his daily bread in prison; he had befriended Gringe, his jailer. A man with grey stubble on his chin, suffering brown eyes and a shirt long overdue a good wash. Sollie had been drip-feeding him a cocktail of possibility, hope and expectation, until Gringe could see a future that he had previously dared not imagine. Sollie also asked Gringe a set of carefully-crafted questions to establish what made him tick. He learnt that Gringe's greatest desire was to be rich. That his greatest fear was staying poor and that only his pet made him happy.

Gringe arrived at Sollie's cell door with some bread and water: "Why is it, Mr Sollie, that you look as if you are on holiday, rather than in prison? Are you not aware that this is a house full of murderers, scoundrels and thieves?"

"If you want a life of purpose and joy, you can't just float around with the butterflies. You must visit the wet markets and the back alleys of the postcodes that you might normally avoid. The body must go to the places that the mind fears.

"I am also happy because I am not pinning my hopes on the future, I am enjoying living now in the present."

"How can you possibly do that? You are surrounded by cockroaches and the dark heart of India?"

"I value my time here. That is because I value all my time, wherever I am. Some people think that the future will be better. They say, 'I will be sitting on a beach or moving into my new house soon, I can't wait.' However, until that moment, they want the present time to pass as quickly as possible. They yawn or do puzzles to count the clock down. They toss great chunks of their precious life away, as if they were throwing crusts of perfectly good bread into the river."

Gringe scratched his stubbly chin: "I think that I spend most of my life trying to survive and preparing for a better future. I work ten hours a day, six days a week. Do you think that I am right to make these sacrifices today, so that I can enjoy a better future?"

"Let me clarify something; **A true sacrifice will not reduce your present happiness. If it does, then it is the wrong type of sacrifice.** With regards to the 'better future' that you mentioned, were you referring to your retirement or your afterlife?"

Gringe stopped cleaning the floor and rested his chin on the end of his mop handle: "I was thinking about my retirement."

"Can I ask if you are religious?"

"No. Why do you ask?"

"If life is hard, at least the religious believe that they have salvation and a place in heaven or paradise to look forward to. What do you and other non-believers have to look forward to after death?"

"We rely on hope!"

"Tell me again what you are doing in preparation for your retirement?"

"Working hard. In order that I have some savings put aside."

"I think that I understand. You are doing what many other people do. They don't rely on hope; they study and work very hard during their working life to save for their retirement."

"What's wrong with that?"

"Can you explain to me why you are prepared to sacrifice the best part of your working life to save up for your retirement but leave the comfort of your afterlife, which might last for eternity, to 'hope'?"

"What do you recommend?"

"**I recommend that you don't make your principal investments in religion, a retirement savings plan or hope. I suggest that you plan for immortality instead.** This way there is no need for salvation from death; only salvation from an unfulfilled or bad life."

"Why are you telling me this?"

"I have responsibilities. The first is to help you enjoy a spiritual life during your time on earth. The second is to help you plan for your 'retirement', without sacrificing the best years of your life. The third is to ensure that you carry on living after your death."

"How exactly?"

"Dig your well before you are thirsty!"

"What does that mean?"

"Dig a well and fill it with a purposeful life that your spirit can drink from. Do not confuse your well with your will. Your well needs to go beyond being something that you are remembered for; it must continue to live and flow for eternity. All those following in your footsteps must be able to draw from it too, not just your close family."

Gringe dragged his mop and bucket back across the cell floor: "Are you suggesting that I shouldn't save for my future?"

"No. I understand that you need to provide for yourself when you are no longer working. I am just saying that it is your well that will make you wealthy and give you a rich mind, not your savings account."

Gringe wrung his mop out before mopping Sollie's bare feet: "I hadn't thought of it like that."

"Why do you think that I am here?"

"I think that possibly you are filling up a well. Which would explain why you are still singing like a songbird."

Sollie smiled and handed Gringe a bookmarker inscribed with his last words of wisdom.

> I have lost all that I had, except that which I have given away.

CURIOSITY

Living v surviving

> When you have found your purpose, you will know exactly what you need to do to live, instead of what you must do to survive.

Immediately afterwards, Gringe made a vow to himself; he vowed to start living and to stop trying to survive. Very quickly he learnt that curiosity leads to awareness and awareness leads to empathy. That resulted in Gringe taking an interest in the conditions of the prison and the lives and challenges of the prisoners. After that, he changed his thinking; he stopped worrying about the weeds and began to plant some flowers.

"Mr Sollie, you have helped me a great deal. I was wondering if I can help you?"

"You could. I would like you to find out who has the power to release me, and then I want you to find out what they desire, what they fear and what makes them sad."

"Your fate is in the hands of Dabeet, the senior superintendent of the prison."

Then Gringe collected a dossier of information about Dabeet. From this, Sollie learnt that Dabeet was an ambitious but God-fearing man, who was used to getting his way. Sollie also discovered that Dabeet had something in common with Apolline; he wanted to be a storyteller. He yearned for an audience that would appreciate his tales of the Hindu Gods.

SECOND CHANCES

Giving up habits

You must know that it is never too late to right a wrong or make an apology.

It wasn't long before Dabeet noticed all the positive changes in the prison. He was curious what had woken up Gringe from his slumber. When he discovered that it was Sollie, he arranged to meet him.

Sollie pulled a chair out for Dabeet: "Tell me, Dabeet, what is the most important thing in your life?"

"My son. Unfortunately, he is very ill. He has a heart condition, and I fear that he will not live long. He fears the same for me."

"Why is that?"

"He knows that I am a heavy smoker. Someone has told him that this will kill me. Unfortunately, I can't stop. I am addicted."

"What would you be prepared to sacrifice in order to make your son happy?"

"Anything, whatever it takes."

After that little exchange, Sollie took Dabeet's mind on a journey into the unknown; a crawl through a waterless desert. A walk on a perilous rope ladder over a bottomless gorge. Just as Dabeet thought that he had scrambled to safety, Sollie kicked him into the lake below. Dabeet's body went numb in the cold, black water… now all he could feel was a joyless future. Sollie could have thrown him a rope; instead he pushed Dabeet's head under the water again: "Tell me more about your son…What is your fondest memory of him? Tell me about the day that you learnt of his illness? When your son does die, what regrets will you have?"

Dabeet came to the surface breathless and spitting water: "Enough! Enough! Let me be." He shook the perspiration from his brow. "I will do whatever you want. Just tell me what I need to do?"

"I want you to shift your focus. Every time you light a cigarette, I want you to stare at it until it burns away. However, as you stare, I want you to understand that what is really burning away is not the tobacco… it is the happy times that you can spend with your son."

"When do we start?"

"Right now. I would like to hear you tell me about your smoking in the past tense."

"What do you mean?"

"Something like… I used to smoke. I can't believe that I was so stupid. I didn't respect the body that I had been gifted. I was heartless and ignored my son's cries for me to stop."

Dabeet did as instructed: "I used to smoke. I can't believe… etc."

Sollie clapped at the end: "Perfect. I can't believe that you were so stupid either."

At which point Dabeet called for a jailer to lock Sollie back up in his cell.

NOT YOUR BODY

Diet - Body maintenance - Self-love - Appearance

Senses - Pleasure - Vessels - Karma - Afterlife

> Have we been gifted a body to do things with or a vessel that amazing things can happen through?

Before the prisoners were fed, Sollie had noticed that Gringe took a stainless-steel platter towards the courtyard each day. One day, Gringe placed the platter down on the floor in front of Sollie's cell bars. Without thinking, Sollie put his fingers through the bars and dipped his finger into the contents of the platter. There was a lightly-spiced lentil puree, some fried corn, diced carrots and a mango dessert topped with slithers of orange. A few days later, when he was alone with Gringe, Sollie made an inquiry: "I could not help but notice your wonderful platters of food. Is it for the governor or a high-security prisoner?"

"Oh no. That's for Nee-Noor, my donkey."

"Are you fond of your donkey?"

Gringe's eyes sparkled with affection, and his nostril hairs twitched: "I love her like a daughter."

"Tell me Gringe, when Dabeet smoked did you ever give him any cigarettes?"

"Yes. We gave each other cigarettes all the time."

"Do you ever give Nee-Noor a cigarette?"

Gringe took a step back and stared at Sollie in amazement: "Why would I damage her health? Why would I hurt the thing that I love?"

"Well, you smoke yourself and you also give cigarettes to your friends."

"I know that, but I wouldn't give them to the things that I love."

"Oh. I understand now. You smoke cigarettes because you don't love yourself, and you give them to Dabeet because you don't really care about him either."

* * *

When Sollie woke up the next morning, Gringe was waiting for him with a vegetarian donkey platter. Then he spoke of the things that had been curdling his mind: "What you said is true, Mr Sollie. I don't love myself. You have made me realise that I care for my donkey's health more than my own. Why would I do this?"

"Perhaps you imagine food to be about pleasure and nutrition instead of something that purifies the mind. Perhaps you haven't properly questioned the ownership of your body! Please tell me, is it possible that you think that you are your body? Is it possible that you think that your body is yours to do with as you wish? Do you think that you own it?"

Gringe looked at him as if he was stuffed with madness.

"I accept that you may doubt me. However, please tell me how you would treat your body if you believed that it was merely a receptacle that had been lent to you, in order to carry out a purposeful life and mission? A friend who lends you their tools hopes that you will use them for a good cause and not return them damaged or dirty. Your body is no different. It should be put to good use and looked after, so that it is wholesome when it is time to hand it back and enter the soil."

"Now, imagine for a moment that your body is merely a vessel. Something that enables something higher to work through you."

"Like God?"

"Something like that, yes. If this was true, would you still ply your body with fats, smoke cigarettes and consume excess alcohol? All that I ask is that you consider that you may not be your body! You have access to a body so that you can function and carry out your mission. However, fail to soak it in peace, marinate it in forgiveness and stretch it like a nan bread and it will not be in a state of readiness when your calling arrives. Then you would have to ask if you feel your creator could forgive such a crime.

"Of course, this might not become apparent until the day arrives for you to be lent another body because the old body you have been using has finally collapsed. Then you must ask yourself, 'If I have not cared for the first body, what sort of replacement am I going to be offered for my next adventure?'"

Just on cue, a huge, greasy brown rat ran over Gringe's bare foot. Gringe shuddered; he didn't like rats, and he certainly didn't want to become one. His suffering brown eyes stared at Sollie for a moment whilst he contemplated all that had been said: "The thing is, Sollie, as you said, I don't love myself; and if I don't love myself, how will I summon the strength to look after my body?"

"You have not been listening, Gringe. It is not your body; you are just its custodian. It is a gift that you have been entrusted with. Look after it and this will make you loving. Do loving things with it and this will make you lovable. The body is not your pleasure vehicle; it is a vehicle to help you carry out your purpose."

BEING LIGHT AND LOVEABLE

Diet - Fasting - The past - Life duration - Second coming
Anger - Impatience - Self-love - Devotion - Mindful

Ling was a vegetarian. When Sollie told her about his discussions with Gringe, it made her think about her own diet.

"Sollie, I have a silly question. How would you describe me?"

"You are light and loveable."

"Thank you. However, I'm serious. I want to make sure that I look after my body, and I am not sure if my vegetarian diet is making a difference."

"It won't make a difference, if all you do is eat vegetables and avoid meat. You must also focus on 'how you eat' and re-examine why you need to look after the body. You can also change how you monitor your progress. Many people record their weight, fat ratio and cholesterol levels. However, what they should measure is their peace of mind and the sweetness and lightness of their mood and thinking."

"How do you become a light thinker?"

"As I told you before: imagine your body as a temple that God resides in."

"How might I do that?"

"Use your body as an extension of your heart."

Ling stared at her outstretched arms and hands, "I suppose that if God is residing in my temple, I must make sure that my channels are not silted up, the water is clear and the skies are blue."

"Beautifully illustrated! You might also want to consider fasting; it complements a mindful and purer diet."

"Why?"

"Fasting helps your body slow down."

"Why is that important?"

"It might help you live longer."

"Surely it is more important to live well and die younger?"

"Mmm. I'm not sure."

"Why?"

"It might be that your younger life was full of troubles or misery. However, if you look after yourself, you will still be healthy enough to do incredible things when you are older – you will give yourself a second chance."

"Why do I need to eat a mindful and purer diet?"

"It is another act of self-love."

"How exactly?"

Some people say that 'you are what you eat'. I prefer to say that, **Your character is shaped by what you eat and how you eat it**. Eat mindfully and you will act mindfully, eat devotionally and you will be loving. Conversely, if you don't eat mindfully, your food will surface in unpleasant characteristics, like impatience and anger."

"But I am rarely angry."

"I know. This is the reason that you are so light and loveable."

HEART BYPASS

Purpose - Vibration - Spiritual energy - Lifeforce
Creativity - Spirit - Art - Ego

"Apolline was visiting Sollie. She looked down at her shoes.

"Is there something wrong?"

"Sometimes I don't feel that I am developing as well as Ling. Everything that she does seems so effortless, so wonderful. She is always bubbly and full of energy, whilst I often feel flat. We are both supposed to be artists; however, her classroom is blooming and my garden isn't. What am I doing wrong?"

"**If your life feels flat, it won't just be because your life lacks purpose. It is also likely to be because there is an absence of spiritual energy.** This means that your vibrations will be low. This is life-threatening!"

"Really?"

"Yes. If your vibrations are low, good things can't flow through you."

"You mean like a dried-up river trying to transport logs of timber?"

"Beyond that... love, happiness, creativity and everything else that makes your eyes sparkle will get stuck. Now, can you remember what I told you about creativity?"

"**You told us that true creativity does not belong to us. You said that it is something that 'flows through us' when we make ourselves available to a higher source**. Perhaps this is where I have failed; I have not allowed the real creator to hold my spade, like Ling has with her brush."

"What particular art has Ling done that has so impressed you?"

Apolline paused: "I can't think of anything in particular, it's just the feeling that comes over you as you walk along the corridor to her studio."

"I understand. It is the spirit that impresses you, not her work."

"What does that mean?"

"When an artist uses their ego, they bypass their heart. When the heart remains closed, the spirit in their work remains locked away."

"What happens if I open my heart?"

"The spirit will flow through whatever you are holding: brushes, spades, violins, etc. You must know that, **The heart is not an organ to be maintained, it is an instrument to be played.** When the heart speaks, creativity flows. This is the spirit that you feel."

MIGRATION AND PARADISE

I am a nature watcher. Paradise is not somewhere that I hope to find when I die; paradise is something that I discovered when I entered a relationship with nature.

On the night of the dinner, Tom had to pass two tests: controlling his emotions while Apolline canoodled with Rishi and getting through the evening without any whisky.

Fortunately, Rishi directed most of his communication towards Hubert. "How did you enjoy your trip around Bhopal?"

Hubert's reply left no one in any doubt of his joy: "It was absolutely incredible. I saw a paradise flycatcher, a purple sunbird and a black-shouldered kite. If I am told that I must die tomorrow, I will go contentedly."

Rishi wiped his mouth: "What else did you see and learn?"

"I have concluded that something worrying is about to happen."

"What makes you say that?"

"There is an extraordinary movement of birds all around the world. They all appear to be heading for Bhopal. I fear that it will not be long before there is a famine here."

Knives and forks clattered on china as his words sunk home.

Rishi seemed more alarmed than the others: "I think that we need to alert the Bhopal authorities to what you are telling us. Their concern is a lack of water and food for the people, because of the drought. No one has mentioned an invasion of birds. That will only compound the human tragedy."

"You are right. However, we should wait a few days. I have friends coming from France and Italy to give updates on bird movements in mainland Europe."

TOO MANY PRISONERS

Bhopal was no longer the city of the lakes. There was hardly any water to drink and no crops to harvest. Soon the people would be dying. Crime was also increasing. This resulted in overcrowded jails.

As well as the prison board, Dabeet sat on the municipal corporation board along with Ajeet, the chief minister. The municipal board believed that the drought was in the hands of the Gods. Unfortunately, the people of Bhopal believed the drought was in the hands of the municipal board. That included Dabeet and Ajeet. Dabeet believed that his reputation was at stake. An emergency meeting of the prison board was held to deal with the prison overcrowding. The obvious solution was to authorise some early releases. The board gave Dabeet the delegated authority to decide which prisoners to let out.

* * *

Yutika informed Sollie of Hubert's fears on her next prison visit. "Hubert said that we are experiencing an invasion of migrating birds. This will compound the drought and cause a famine."

As Yutika turned to leave, Sollie stopped her heart at the door: "I hear you. Perhaps it is time to leave the prison."

In the meantime, Dabeet had made a list of the prisoners whom he thought should be released. Sollie's name was not on the list. The reason for that was simple. Sollie had offended the politicians' and the people's religion. Despite this, when Yutika asked to speak to Dabeet personally, he felt a debt of gratitude to Sollie and agreed to meet her.

* * *

"My name is Yutika. I am a friend of Sollie St-Martin, an innocent man waiting in your prison for his trial. I think that Sollie might be able to help Bhopal. He offers some hope at a time when there doesn't seem to be any."

"I have already compiled my list. Besides, if he was released it would not be a popular choice."

"Then you must know that it is never too late to right a wrong or make an apology. I would like you to visit our home and see his work."

Dabeet went to consult Ajeet, the chief minister, and told him of Yutika's invitation. They both knew that they needed something like a miracle. Ajeet simply asked if he could accompany him.

GARUDA

Yutika met Ajeet and Dabeet at the entrance to the Mustard Garden. They were still hoping that Sollie might offer some miraculous solution to the city's dilemma.

As she toured them around the gardens, they felt the tranquillity and spirit that comes from a mission of good endeavour.

However, Yutika's first question took them by surprise: "Do you like children?"

They replied in unison, "Very much so."

"Come with me, let me introduce you to the children who live here. I think that they are all in the classroom." Yutika took them to the studio. The children were sitting in a circle, singing. They stopped as soon as the door opened.

Yutika announced them: "This is Dabeet and Ajeet. They are important visitors."

The children called out together, "Welcome to The Mustard Garden."

Then, without any prompting, Komodo walked over to the visitors, grabbed their hands and persuaded them to sit down in the singing circle: "Please sing with us."

For five transformative minutes, Dabeet and Ajeet became light; they also experienced real joy at work for the first time in many years. After the singing, the children showed their guests their bird paintings and the stegosaurus and tyrannosaurs now guarding the back door.

Then Komodo clapped his hands: "What story are you going to tell us? Our visitors always tell us a story. It is a custom."

Dabeet could not believe his luck, and something that had been dormant for many years moved through him. "Do you know the story about Garuda?" he asked in the voice of a pantomime villain.

There was silence.

"If you like dinosaurs and birds, you might like Garuda. He is even bigger than a dinosaur, a creature that is half bird and half man. Would you like to hear about him?"

Every hand went up. Komodo banged Bongo's drum. This was the cue for the rest of the class to join in and ratchet up the noise. Apolline and Yutika put their hands over their mouths, but they need not have worried. Dabeet had the sort of audience that he had spent his life dreaming about. Apolline asked all the children to calm down and listen. In an instant, a hush brushed across the room.

REASON AND SWEETEN

Approval - Leadership – Decision-making - Unlearning

Sacred partnerships - Intuition - Trusting self - Vessels - The God within

Ajeet and Dabeet left the classroom unable to conceal their lightness and glee. Yutika led them towards the garden for some tea and her final plea.

"If it helps, I can tell you what Sollie would say to you?"

Ajeet nodded: "Please tell us."

"When he has important decisions to make, he puts his personal experiences aside and asks a higher authority to guide him."

Dabeet tutted: "Ajeet and I are leaders. It is our job to make decisions. Are you suggesting that we delegate our responsibilities?"

"It is common for leaders to make decisions without seeking approval. However, this does not necessarily make them good leaders. For important decisions, a leader must go beyond self-approval and the approval of others."

"Then how do they arrive at a decision?"

"They must have the courage to put aside their authority, knowledge and experience and seek out their higher self."

Ajeet moved closer: "Can you explain yourself further?"

"Logic has its place. It is not to be discounted entirely. It is for this reason that we have a mind. A leader still needs to check facts, legalities and procedures, etc – this we call 'reason'. However, when it comes to the judgement, an enlightened person will put their own experience and knowledge aside. They know that they must leave their mind and beliefs outside the door. Instead, they must delegate important decisions to their higher self. This second part we call 'sweeten'. When a decision maker does this, something magical happens. A beautiful, pure, unadulterated response arises through the person. Now we have 'reason and sweeten'.

"Surely this means handing the decision-making over to God?"

"I prefer to think of it as handing it over to the heart. This is who you should consult with about Sollie's release."

LIBERATION AND COMPROMISE

Injustice - Influence - Faith and effort

After his visit to the Mustard Garden, Ajeet arranged a one-to-one meeting with Sollie. Then the day arrived for Dabeet to announce which prisoners would be released. This wasn't going to be like the day that Barabbas was set free. Today, there were going to be at least a hundred releases.

One by one, Dabeet announced the names of the lucky prisoners. Eventually, there was only one more name to read out. Dabeet paused and sought out his higher self, asking for the right name to come from his lips. There was a period of silence, fat enough to generate great expectation... "I have also chosen to free a man called Sollie St-Martin."

There was a forest of raised eyebrows at the board table. Dabeet looked his audience in the eye and waited for the first angry stone to be thrown. However, his fears never materialised. Dabeet felt something else that he had never experienced before. He sensed that when you pass over important decisions to something higher than yourself, purity swirls in the air. The board sensed this too. His decision to drop his ego had disarmed any would-be dissenters in a way that logic never could. Tomorrow the lock on cell door number eight would turn and Sollie would be a free man.

FREEDOM AND DISAPPOINTMENT

Pain – Entitlement – Happiness – Unrequited love – Success

We must learn how to ask for what we want and imagine our requests being granted.

The night before Sollie's release, Yutika didn't bother undressing. She knew that this would be a sleepless night. Then Sollie rang to discuss his first night of freedom.

Her stomach quaked: "As you requested, I have arranged a quiet night away from the Mustard Garden with a picnic on the Shyamla hills. Hubert will join us so that he can update you on the bird migrations. I have also reserved some rooms at the Bhopal Grande Hotel overlooking the lake."

Yutika spent the rest of the evening lying on her bed wondering where her head might lie the following evening.

* * *

Yutika unwrapped platters of sandwiches and heated up Sollie's woodland soup. Then, as they rolled out the tablecloth and lit the candles, the stars seasoned their picnic in a way that no ordinary condiment could. For the rest of the evening, they watched the stars and listened to Hubert's update on the birds. Then Sollie stared into Yutika's eyes: "The perfect end to the evening would be a tuk-tuk back to the hotel. Can we arrange that?"

"Of course."

Hubert decided to stay behind and look a little longer at the stars. In the back of the tuk-tuk, Sollie sucked in the night air while Yutika closed her eyes. She recalled what Sollie had once said to her: 'We are all entitled to life's chocolate flakes. However, **We cannot be happy until we first imagine ourselves being happy. We must also learn how to ask for what we want.**'

However, before they reached the accommodation, they hit a bump in the road: "Yutika, is your hotel room on the same floor as mine?"

There was an uncomfortable interlude of silence: "What about me? What do you think of me?"

"You are my moon-cheese."

"Then you should know that I am not a cheese to be nibbled at."

Sollie stayed quiet whilst he questioned his own rationale. He certainly found Yutika seductive… and tempting. However, now he had a question mark over her true character. This was enough for her to be barred from his love chamber.

WHAT SHOULD I DO?

Self-reflection - Anger - Lost - Desire to change

The next morning there was a queue of people waiting to see Sollie. At its head was Stromboli.

"I have missed you, Mr Sollie."

"I have missed you too, Stromboli. What did you do whilst I was away?"

"I spent time in the forest observing the trees and seeking their advice."

"Were they able to help you?"

Stromboli slid a piece of paper across the table. Sollie read it aloud.

THE TREE

What should I do?
I am here with these hands, I am here with this heart, I am here with these feet.
What should I do?
It's here with its branches, it's here with its roots, it's here with its hollow.
What does it do?
I am busy collecting, comparing, rushing and winning.
It's full of fragrance, flowering and standing still.
I stand alone with my sadness, my horror, my fears and my rejections.
What does it do?
I am full of desires, myself, my needs, my habits, my guilt, my shame and my anger.
What does it do?
I seek to harm it with my axe, my saw, my knife and my fire.
What does it do?
Who is this, that despite all that I have done, bows down before me and lets me pick its fruit?
What should I do?

Sollie put his large hand over the top of Stromboli's small one: "Oh my, what has happened to you?"

COINCIDENCES

Hubert was looking forward to meeting his birdwatching friends: Dominique, who was taking a flight from Paris in France and Umberto from Rome in Italy. Sollie had invited them to stay at the Mustard Garden. They were going to provide updates on the European bird migrations. However, before that, Hubert accompanied Rishi on a sightseeing tour of Bhopal's wetland. It was here that Rishi told Hubert about the unusual migration of the sarus cranes from Queensland to Darwin in Australia.

Hubert listened in silence. Then he asked Rishi a question, delivered in a manner that guarantees a response. It was the sort of question a Dominican's superior would have asked a Dominican. "Will you delay your wedding

LASCAUX CAVE ART

plans and return to Australia to provide updates on the movement of the cranes?"

* * *

In the early evening there was a welcome party for Umberto and Dominique. As the party was in full swing, a tuk-tuk pulled up; Olivia had arrived from the village school. Apolline went to fetch her a drink.

Whilst Apolline was away, Umberto approached Olivia like a long-lost friend: "I think that we have met before."

Apolline returned with the drinks: "Have you two introduced yourselves?"

"I was just saying that I think that we have met before."

Apolline stood back in surprise: "Where was that?"

"I believe I helped Olivia with her luggage on the train from Naples to Rome airport."

Apolline interrupted, she could see that Olivia was distressed: "I think that you might be mistaken. Olivia flew here from Paris, not Rome. I collected her from Bhopal airport myself."

"Oh, sorry, I must be mistaken."

At which point Umberto walked away and joined Dominique and Rishi. Dominique had some pictures at hand. He showed them the similarities between the ancient cave paintings in Kakadu, Lascaux and Bhopal.

"The Lascaux cave paintings were not discovered until 1940; however, they have been dated at more than 17,000 years old. Amongst the cave paintings is a picture of a mysterious large bird's head on a stick, called the *Birdman of Lascaux*.

Rishi looked startled: "Do you think that Bhopal, Kakadu and Lascaux could be linked by the birds and the rock art?"

In the Lascaux caves, France, there is a cave painting of a mysterious bird's head on a stick.

THE ALBATROSS

THE ALBATROSS

Fidelity – Fitness – Intuition – Hearts

The next day, Umberto and Dominique gave everyone an update on the crane migrations from Europe. "The autumn migration route normally takes the cranes from their breeding grounds in Scandinavia and Eastern Europe to Spain. However, this year 150,000 cranes disappeared. They were found a few days later digging up the tomato plants and seeds on the lower slopes of Vesuvius in southern Italy. From here the cranes flew directly to Bhopal. It appears that they have brought their own food with them."

Bruno was beyond intrigued. However, he simply asked, "What happens next?"

"My next task is to find out why thousands of albatross have also come to Bhopal. Dominique will return to the caves at Lascaux. Rishi has informed us that he will return to Australia at the end of the week to monitor the sarus cranes there."

Apolline looked down. She was hurt that Rishi hadn't told her he was leaving so soon.

* * *

Yutika passed Umberto a cake: "Could you tell us a little bit about the albatross? I have never seen one."

Umberto flapped his long arms like a soaring bird: "I would be delighted to. Once you see one of these birds, you will never forget them." He paused to put some pictures up onto the screen: "They are extraordinary. In the southern hemisphere albatross fly north and take a clockwise route, whilst in the northern hemisphere they fly south and travel in a counter-clockwise direction. Perhaps we should ask what would happen if they decide to fly the other way?

"They also dance… Wow, do they dance. They practise their dancing over many years in large dance groups. Once a bird has found their mate, they never repeat that dance again. In common with the sarus crane, they never split or divorce from their partner unless they fail to produce eggs.

Know this: the pendulum of life states that whatever can go one way, can also go the other.

ACTS OF SURRENDER

Merging - Diversity - Perfectionism

Nothing is either one thing or the other. Everything is like the estuary, where the river meets the sea.

After a noisy dinner, Hubert suggested an evening walk outside. Sensing an opportunity to show off her new garden, now that it was illuminated, Apolline jumped at the opportunity to accompany him.

Hubert's eyes sparkled: "It is wonderful: perfectly imbalanced, full of surprises and very welcoming to wildlife."

She took her straw hat off and laughed, "I am not sure that is a compliment."

"Trust me, it is."

"I didn't do it alone. I had lots of advice from Rishi and Sollie. However, the truth is that I still crave order. I don't like surprises. I like things to be as they should. I like things to be black and white and just right."

Apolline expected him to laugh. However, he didn't. He touched her hand in a friendly way and gestured for her to sit down on the grass. He loosened his neck scarf: "It truly is splendid. How on earth did you create it?"

She laughed, "I didn't. I had to resist creating it. It is someone else's work. If it was my work, the topiary would be in line, the pond would be spherical and the lawn would be square."

"Would that make you happier?"

"Maybe not."

"I agree. The Wash estuary near my home has four different rivers flowing into its bay. It cannot be defined or made orderly because it is never the same two days running. Despite this, it is loved by people, animals and birds. If it were uniform and perfect, I am not sure that it would be as welcoming. For the estuary symbolises the splendour of diversity and the joys of merging.

"It seems that life is like the estuary, where the river meets the sea. The water is brackish, with salt water and fresh water meeting and mixing. Consequently, the plant and animal life found there are unique. It is living proof that nothing is black or white; nothing is either one thing or the other. It was at the estuary that I surrendered my own goals and offered my services."

She gazed up at him: "Tell me more."

ACTS OF SURRENDER

When the river reaches the sea at the estuary, it does not always simply disappear. Watch enough times and you will be rewarded with an act of submission, an assembly where the sea opens its mouth and puts its top lip, in the form of a wave, over the last vestiges of the river's current. Its waves glide and ghost over the river before it swallows it up, like a whale opening its mouth to take in some plankton.

The waters at the estuary are not just an act of merging; of acceptance, submission and belonging. They also signify the end of a journey that has run its course and the beginning of a new one. There are also nights that the moon shines a silvery light on the proceedings, and the meeting and merging of the two waters becomes an act of benediction.

When I made the decision to merge and surrender myself, I took my lead from the merging of the river and the sea at the estuary. Now, whenever I can, I visit the estuary in the early evening under the gaze of the silvery moon. I witness the river offering itself to the sea, and the sea receiving the river. I believe that this holy communion takes place, not because everything is orderly and the same but because it is not.

When Hubert had finished speaking, Apolline kissed him on the forehead and gestured for him to stand up. Then she closed her eyes and held his hand in a way that she was never able to do with her own father. They walked slowly back to the main house. Suddenly, the garden began to feel sacred and sparks flew from her feet. Now she could smell the true glory of the flowers that are at their most fragrant during the dark; the ones that attract the humming birds and the pollinators of the night.

* * *

Later Tom and Apolline laughed and flirted. He may have let Apolline slip into the arms of Rishi, however, he had not let that affect their friendship. "Are you going to tell me about your fishing trip?"

Apolline put her hands behind her back: "It was so enjoyable that I was hoping that you would take me fishing one day."

This wasn't the reply Tom had expected. He paused to gather himself: "You surprise me. I can't imagine you with a slimy fish on the end of a pole."

"Fortunately, fishing has got nothing to do with catching fish."

Making sense of what she had just said wasn't easy. Should he feel flattered or disappointed that he was second choice? In the end Tom decided that he wouldn't try and work it out. He would just accept the priceless gift of a second chance.

BEETLE MANIA

Security

"There is nothing either good or bad, but thinking makes it so."
William Shakespeare

Stromboli gripped Sollie's hand tightly as they entered the magical kingdom of the trees: "Will spending time in the forest make me wise?"

"It is true that the trees soak up knowledge, like their roots soak up water. However, acquiring knowledge will not make you wise."

"What knowledge have the trees soaked up that would be useful for me to know?"

"To begin with, they know how to survive as a group. A tree knows that it thrives as part of the forest, not as an individual. Fungi under the ground distribute sugars and nutrients amongst all the trees to ensure an even share of resources. However, at some time in their life, even the strongest trees are attacked or fall ill and need help."

Then Sollie stooped down and moved some of the soil at the base of a tree.

Something scurried away. Stromboli stepped back quickly: "What is that?"

"That is a beetle. The tree's friend and nemesis."

"What do you mean?"

"When a beetle attacks a tree and opens the tree's protective bark, the tree becomes vulnerable to all manner of maladies."

"If I was a forest ranger, I would order all the beetles to be crushed. That way all the trees would be safe."

Sollie picked up a small weevil: "I am not sure that would be wise. The forest's relationship with its adversaries is not as simple as it appears. Take this little fellow. It is not interested in travelling. It is quite content to hang around and break down the old fallen trees to enrich the soil."

Stromboli scratched his head: "So are the beetles good or are they bad? Should we kill them or endure them?"

“They are neither good or bad. Nothing is. **Only your thoughts make things good or bad.** That is how it is. We should not ask whether we should kill them or endure them, for they are neither a force for good or bad; they are simply nature.”

BECOMING A SYNTHESISER

Play your part in making the world beautiful and there is no need to go and search for beauty somewhere else. Now other amazing things will come and visit you.

Another disturbed beetle scurried past. Stromboli tried to poke it before Sollie pulled his finger away.

“That one is a stag beetle. It also likes to break down dead trees. They spend most of their life as larvae, preparing to live, in the same way that some people waste their life whilst they save for their retirement.”

“I hope that I don’t live my life like a stag beetle.”

“Some people would say that a hermit beetle’s life is even worse. They live inside an old tree at the base. Can you imagine living all alone in a damp room full of darkness?”

“It sounds a bit like Bruno’s life. He keeps himself hidden away.”

After that, Stromboli was quiet for a few minutes and Sollie had to tap his shoulder: “What are you thinking about?”

“I was wondering why the woodchoppers don’t remove the old trees and then the hermit beetles wouldn’t have to live in misery? Why don’t we just dismantle Bruno’s greenhouse, then he will have nowhere to hide?”

“Because life is full of difficulties, and how we approach these difficulties determines our happiness. **Problems are not to be solved, avoided or killed off.** If you remove the beetles’ natural habitat in the old wood, they will simply ruin the new trees. If we take away Bruno’s greenhouse, who knows where he might disappear to?

“Why are problems like that?”

“Problems are an energy, and energy cannot be killed. Energy can only be converted or synthesised.”

“How do I convert bad energy into something good?”

“Look to convert weeds into flowers.”

ASSUME BEETLES ARE HAPPY

Identity - Thoughts - Pleasure - Meditation - Mantra

However, it wasn't long before Stromboli was scratching his head again: "I can't work out if the beetle is happy or miserable."

"Assume that it is happy! Look closely and you will see that the beetle does not stray far. It does not appear to pursue pleasure or be outward looking. It does not look to express its views, personality or identity. It seems that it only seeks to serve."

Stromboli continued to scratch his head. Sollie continued with his lecture: "The beetle is not concerned with personal goals or visions; only its role in the grand plan. **It goes about its business calmly and unhurriedly. It is not disturbed by any activity taking place around it.** You can do something similar, if you drop your mind. Then your body will move independently from your thoughts. You can write a book in a nightclub or meditate in Tiananmen Square and your performance will not be affected by the activity all around you. You live in the world without being swept along by it. You move and yet your mind remains still."

"Is that important?"

"It is beyond important! If we can go through life without being disturbed by the activity around us, i.e. remain in the 'present state', we will be happy all the time."

"How do we remain in the present state?"

"We do not attach ourselves to any thoughts passing through. We do not engage our emotions with them. We do not project thoughts on the past or the future. If we do attach ourself to any thoughts that arise, we risk putting our happy state in danger."

"That sounds difficult!"

"It is difficult if you do not train the mind. It is for this reason that we meditate and sing our mantras."

BIRD ATTACK

As predicted, both of Bhopal's big lakes eventually became dry. Tom and Apolline decided to take a look. Tom held her hand as they stepped over the lake's perimeter wall. He put his foot onto the muddy lakebed to make sure it was safe and prodded the bottom with a stick.

"The lakebed looks firm enough to walk on."

When they were halfway across, a large group of cranes came into view. As they approached, the birds raised their huge wings and started to squeal. They stopped walking, and Tom zoomed in with his binoculars: "The cranes are standing by some large rocks. They seem to be trying to pull something out of the mud."

They were about to take some more steps when they heard noises in the sky. They looked up. Large white storks and bar-headed geese were circling them.

Apolline's face paled. She placed both of her hands on her head: "What are they doing?"

However, before Tom could answer, like a squadron of tornado fighter jets, the birds dive-bombed them. They missed their heads by a centimetre. Tom instinctively held his stick in the air. Apolline dropped to the ground, lay on her stomach and screamed. Tom lay over her and protected her head with his arms. Then he grabbed her feet and dragged her through the mud and away from the birds. Now she couldn't scream; her mouth was full of mud.

When they were 20 metres away, Tom whispered gently in her ear: "Stand up, don't look in the direction of the birds and we will calmy walk away."

Apolline gingerly stood up and grabbed his hand tightly. She closed her eyes, put all her trust in him and let him guide her. This time Tom did not pull away.

Later, when they arrived home, Ling and Yutika comforted Apolline while Tom explained to the men what had happened: "I think that the birds were just trying to protect their food, but I can't be sure."

Sollie spoke calmly to Tom: "We should return tomorrow. Bruno can make us some protective wire suits."

Bruno stood up. He had the very thing that they needed. The very thing that he used to stop the birds stealing his tomatoes.

LIGHT FROM THE DARKNESS

Worries - Focus

At bedtime, Apolline could not sleep. All she could think about was the bird attack. Her stomach was knotted. She lay on the bed and reminded herself what Sollie had told her: **'To disarm worries, change your focus immediately… move away from your dark thoughts and worries ... focus on light thoughts, where the darkness can't exist.'**

Immediately she cooked up some light; the perfect plan to take her mind off her worries. First she took a short walk outside. Then she knocked on Tom's door and walked straight into his room: "Tom, it's such a hot night, do you want to take a walk?" However, she didn't wait for an answer. She just grabbed his hand and pulled him up off the bed.

They walked along the forest edge; she held his hand, he looked up at the moon. After 30 minutes they headed back. He wondered what might happen when they returned. Apolline knew exactly what was going to happen. It would not take place in Tom's room, either. She yanked his arm and led him to the Tree of Frogs. Tom's back was soon pushed against the tree trunk. Within a second their lips were pressed together. Whilst he was disorientated, a push put him on his knees. Another saw him lying on his back. Before he could get up, Apolline sat on his legs.

Tom should have remained quiet and enjoyed the moment. However, he felt compelled to protest. Apolline sighed. Her left hand disappeared into her dress pocket. It reappeared with a handkerchief. She knelt over him and ruffled his hair with her free hand. He laughed. She pulled his shirt down to reveal his bare shoulder. Her teeth sunk in.

"Ouch."

Apolline ignored his cry and lifted his head up by his hair. While he endured his discomfort, she kissed and softly bit his lips. After a few minutes he came up for air and tried to speak again. This time Apolline stuffed the handkerchief in his mouth. That was the last of his protestations.

A SECOND ATTEMPT

Non-violence – Nurturing

Violence and innocence are seeds planted and cultivated by parents. So I say, take away your little boy's plastic guns. Point your children away from all words, films, books and games of violence. Spoon-feed them a diet of gentle words and actions, until love is the only response that they know.

After his explorations with Apolline, Tom didn't get much sleep. At dawn, Sollie was knocking on his door. They took the truck and parked it by the lakeside. When they had wriggled into their beekeeper-like wire suits, Sollie picked up a spade, some flares and a torch.

Tom wondered if that was enough: "Don't you think that we need some weapons to defend ourselves?"

"I think that if we take a weapon to defend ourselves and fear gets the better of us, we might just use it. However, if we stay quiet and calm, our philosophy of non-violence will be rewarded."

"You have faith. However, you didn't experience the bird attack yesterday."

Sollie gazed at the floor for a second before looking Tom in the eyes: "Let me just say this Tom, **Non-violence is a philosophy**. Read about violence, think about violence, watch films about violence and when put to the test, violence is what you may draw upon to confront your fear. Correspondingly, if you marinate yourself in spiritual books, films and activities, then this is what your gun will be loaded with when you feel aggrieved or threatened. Know that all this has a beginning."

Then they made their way across the muddy lakebed. When they were 50 metres from the cranes, Tom passed his binoculars to Sollie: "The cranes are digging in the mud again by the rocks."

However, there was no time for Sollie to reply. THUD! A bird almost took Sollie's head off. They both dropped to their knees. Now the storks and geese were attacking them like kamikaze pilots. The cranes joined the assault too; they formed a circle and started to walk towards them.

Sollie calmly put his hand inside his pocket: "I am going to light this flare. Bring a spade and walk behind me. As soon as we reach the rocks, start digging." The smoke from the bright red flare worked. The birds stopped attacking from the air and the cranes stepped back. “Dig there, where the birds were pulling at the rocks. Hurry. This flare won’t last forever.”

After five minutes of digging, a hole appeared. Tom dug furiously until the full extent of his discovery became obvious: “It appears to be a cave! Although there is a huge boulder wedged in the entrance.”

They quickly realised that they would not move the rock with spades; a vehicle was needed to pull it away. They decided to return home. The birds stood in a line and watched them. Only when they were 100 metres away did Tom feel able to take a deep breath: “Phew. That was close. I thought that we were going to die.”

Sollie put his arm around Tom’s shoulder and smiled: “Which is precisely why we didn’t take any weapons.”

KING BHOJ

Past problems

At dinner that night there was no need for Yutika to season the soup; mystery swirled around the table and strange birds could be heard pitter-pattering on the roof. Apolline found the perfect way to spice up the evening and thicken the broth at the same time. She banged the ladle: “Rishi should tell us all about King Bhoj. I think that his tale might be important.”

All eyes turned on Rishi. There was complete silence. It seemed that even the birds on the roof were listening in.

True Legend

"Raja Bhoj, or King Bhoj, ruled this land from 1005 to 1045. You can see his statue on the lake. Legend says that he was told by a saint to build the Bhopal lakes and then bathe in them, to rid him of a skin disease. The lakes had to be made from the sources of 365 rivers and dammed with rock from the Bhimbetka caves. This might sound far-fetched; however, clearly something compelling drove King Bhoj to order an engineering feat that resulted in the largest artificial lake in Asia. Perhaps we should ask, was it really his health that compelled him or were the lakes created to conceal a secret?"

Sollie cleared his throat: "What do you think that we should do next, Rishi?"

"I think that we should remove the boulder and explore the cave under the lake before the rains return. It might be thousands of years before the lakes dry up again."

Apolline shook her head; she didn't agree: "I am not so sure. If there is a secret lying at the bottom of the lake, we should let it stay there. Didn't Sollie say that digging up the past and trying to make sense of it is not the way to sort out problems?"

Everyone looked at Sollie, to see how he would reply.

"If this was a personal issue, then Apolline's advice would be absolutely right. However, this is about unravelling the mysteries of the universe; the very essence of life. We should not be fearful; we should put our greeting clothes on. There is a very good chance that something that has been lying dormant for a very long time is about to reveal itself."

"Dominique nodded his head: "I don't believe the skin disease tale either. I think that someone wanted to hide something of the utmost importance."

SADHUS

The next morning Sollie asked Ling to accompany him to Bhopal's Bhimbetka caves. They arrived early and walked towards the entrance.

Sollie spoke to the guide: "Are these all the caves?"

"There is another one, but it is guarded by an important sadhu called Sudarshan. Unfortunately, it is not open to visitors."

Sollie made a call to Ajeet: "I am at Bhimbetka. What can you tell me about a sadhu called Sudarshan guarding a cave here?"

"It has been said that since time began, one family in Bhopal must bring its eldest son up as a sadhu. They guard the caves and act as personal confidants to the Raja or Prime Minister [PM] of the day. In return their families are always given food and charas."

"What are they guarding?"

"I have no idea. The sadhus are forbidden to speak to anyone but the PM."

After the call, they headed away into the undergrowth. An hour later they found what they were looking for. The sadhu was standing by the entrance of a

STATUE OF RAJA BHOJ

cave. Sollie motioned for Ling to keep quiet and watch him from a distance. He was easy to watch; he filled her eyes with a blur of bright orange and yellow silk from his turban and Ali-Baba trousers. Intrigue dripped from his long, matted beard. Green and red glass stones and beads adorned his bare, ash-covered chest. A gold bracelet, with a many-pointed gold star and the other charms, adorned his wrist. Never before had she seen such a colourful and strange-looking character.

"What exactly is a sadhu?"

"The genuine ones are India's wandering holy men. They have renounced worldly goods and their families. They are revered because they have placed themselves next to the Gods. You heard what Ajeet said: 'The Prime Minister might not listen to his parliament, but he will listen to his sadhu.'"

Then Sudarshan saw and approached them. However, he wasn't friendly; he shook his arms and beat his spear into the ground and gestured for them to leave. As he turned away, he revealed a bare back. It was tattooed with caves, diamond-marked snakes, warriors on horses and soaring birds. However, he left something behind. His bracelet had come off and lay gleaming in the sun. Sollie took a photo of it, then they headed for the truck.

EFFORT VERSUS LIGHT

Persistence - Vibration

"Sollie, do you think that the sadhu stands outside that cave all day doing nothing?"

"I doubt it. However, if he does, it is quite an accomplishment."

"What do you mean?"

"You told me that on the way to Bhopal you stopped off at Delhi. Did you enjoy it there?"

"No. I could not wait to leave."

"That is possibly because in the market places of this great city, the wretched and the meek have to scratch out a living. It is not always easy. People often have to work incredibly hard just to survive. Many choose effort and persistence as their weapons of choice. They shout, they haggle, they harass, they draw on all their connivance. Some might even try and cheat you! The negative energy that they create is surely no worse than Delhi's toxic smog."

"That is why I couldn't wait to leave Delhi."

"Then ask yourself if their method of earning a living is justifiable, even though they are poor."

Ling thought about that: "It's a hard one, because many are genuinely desperate."

"The majority of sadhus are materially poor too. However, most are not like Sudarshan; they are friendly, colourful and peaceful. They create good energy around you. They may take a few of your coins if you offer them. However, they are just as likely to give you a cup of tea as take one from you... Consider this when you are looking back at the success of your working day. Know that, **If you seek to put out light and good vibrations wherever you go, you will change the direction of the wind that blows in other peoples' faces.**"

FAMINE AND DROUGHT

Control - Fate - Destiny

I must permit the horses of destiny to decide where to go, whilst I hold the reins and do my best to steer.

Sollie sat opposite Ajeet and Dabeet. He looked straight into Ajeet's eyes: "Please tell me what the key concerns of the municipal board are?"

"Famine, drought, a breakdown in law and order, disease and death. The migrating birds have drunk the remainder of the lake water. Now they are laying siege to the cornfields. The birds have become the new enemy of the people. Ajeet tapped his pen on the table: "What do you think that we should do?"

"Let us start by separating out those things that we have control over, from those that we do not. I find that this can be a helpful place to start."

"We don't appear to have control over anything!"

"We do. We have control over our interpretations, our responses, our peace of mind and our happiness."

Dabeet put his hands over his ears: "I think that we should let the Gods decide. Are we not powerless to alter the path of fate?"

"Is that how you live your life? Do you lie back and hope that you will be lucky? Surely it is better to work alongside God and make a contribution."

CROCODILES AND LIZARDS

Gloomy moods – Intervention

> Gloomy thoughts are like vampires: put the light on and they have no choice but to run away.

Apolline was in a good mood, which was probably a good time to talk constructively about her bad moods.

"Sollie, my gloomy moods have diminished. I put it down to leaf sweeping and planting more flowers. Do you have any remedies to reduce them further?"

"One way is to develop an early intervention strategy that deals with gloomy moods before they take hold. Something that allows you to monitor what happens immediately before your worries grow. Let me tell you a story. In the early days of Egyptian civilization, villagers would bathe and wash their clothes in the river Nile. Lurking nearby were deadly Nile crocodiles. To protect themselves, the villagers tied monitor lizards to large boulders on the edge of the river. If the lizard lay still and warmed itself in the sun, the villagers knew that there was no danger. If the lizard became agitated and started to thrash its tail, they knew that it was time to run to safety.

"The lesson says, **Don't try and record how bad you feel when the crocodile has you in its jaws**, as by then it is too late. Next time your mood starts to darken and your lizard starts to thrash its tail… stop! Record exactly what triggered your mood change. Was it a smell, a taste or a sound? Something someone said? A memory? A fantasy? A worry about the future? It is good to identify what triggers your mood changes, before your crocodile has you in its jaws. Then you can introduce an intervention strategy to help you in the future."

Apolline smiled: "I like that story. Will that cure all my worries?"

"Of course not. It won't deal with the new worries that you will have tomorrow, caused by the new events that happened today."

"Oh. Then what must I do?"

"You must understand that it is not really the crocodile that is dangerous; it is the river. The river is your mind's negative thoughts. We must change this river's course."

MIND TRAINING

Chanting - Worries - Personal development - Positive mantras
Daily practice - Meditation

Know this... The conversations that you have with yourself determine your mood. Personal development is about managing the conversations that you have with yourself. Practising positive mantras will help you do this.

"How do we change the course of the river?"

"We stop negative worries through meditation and training our thoughts. Call this mind training.

"Most people live their waking hours in their thoughts. They are in a dream-like state, without any control or awareness. They have no idea what they are doing. To compound matters, people believe whatever they say to themselves during their bouts of negative thinking. This has an adverse effect on their lives."

"What should I do to avoid that?"

"Inject concentration into your mind through meditation. This will ensure that you are awake and conscious. Complement this with a daily diet of positive mantras."

"How exactly?"

"At the Mustard Garden, we share our music and we sing and chant together... You play your beautiful cello music to sweeten our ears. While you play, we chant to deepen our awareness of what is underneath our thoughts and emotions. **When we chant, we air and share our worries and darkness. Chanting also takes us away from our thoughts and brings us back to the present.**"

"How does it work?"

"Regardless of how much you try and focus on something, the mind will always wander. However, the chants are a form of mind training. They help bring your mind back to the present. **The more often you chant, the more you train the mind. The more you train your mind, the more you weaken your negative thinking and emotions.**"

"Now I understand why we do so much chanting; it's not just to share our worries, it is also to train our mind."

"Exactly. It is for this reason that it is part of our daily routine."

IMMORTAL TREES

Fear - Death

Remove the fear of death and you don't have to worry about salvation or resurrection.

Just as Sollie was about to put his music on, Ling knocked on his door. She was shaking.

"Come in, whatever is the matter?"

"I need your help Sollie. My mother has written to me saying that she is coming here."

"Surely that is a good thing?"

"A good thing! Are you mad? She will destroy everything. I will turn back into a pumpkin; I will feel worthless, lose my confidence and everything that I have gained."

He grinned wildly and tickled her chin: "No you won't."

"Yes I will. You don't know her. She will humiliate and suffocate me."

"Tell me, how often do you worry about that?"

"It is always at the back of my mind."

"That is why it is a good thing that she is coming. You must know that you cannot banish fear to the back of your mind or hope to face it with a different-coloured headband. You must meet it head on. In fact, I should have invited her myself… just to prove to you how much you have changed."

"What should I do?"

"Tell her to buy an open return ticket. I would be surprised if she stays for long, when she sees that the old Ling is dead."

Ling sniffed: "Don't say that. I am scared of dying. Aren't you?"

He laughed insanely: "Of course not. Why do you think that I am a Tree Mystic?"

"I don't know. Why are you a Tree Mystic?"

He put on a straight face: "Trees are immortal, and I figured that if I could become more like a tree, I might become immortal too."

"You don't mean that, do you?"

"Of course I do. It's not easy to kill a tree off forever you know. For death is just another way to blossom. Like the tree, we should all be thinking about how we can be useful after our first passing, in preparation for our next flowering. Some dead trees stay in the forest so that people can rest on their trunks or take respite in their hollows. Others move into our homes where they become domesticated and watch over us."

"You are playing with me."

"Doubt that the moon is made of cheese, but be assured I speak the truth. If you bring a door or a piece of wooden furniture into your house, it will adjust its shape until it feels at home. Two hundred years later you can paint it or give it a new use, and it will still be there for you. The tree does not crumble with age or death; it mellows like a grandparent."

"I understand, but you do accept that you are going to die, don't you?"

"My body will. However, I was just pointing out how useful trees are, even when they are uprooted. We should be preparing for this day too."

The tree is never on the move; reaching out is as far as it needs to go.

BIRD TABLES AND SPIDERWEBS

Becoming available - Empathy - Reaching out

Apolline tapped a super-sized calligraphy brush on the table to grab Sollie's attention: "I wonder what would happen to me if I was a piece of wood? Would I become a source of enjoyment like a child's swing, useful like a wardrobe or as useless as a door that is never opened?"

"What would you like to be?"

"Useful. I want to become more available to people."

"Just make yourself into a bird table."

"What if I am in a shopping mall?"

"You can still be a bird table. Just look for an empty bench and take a seat."

"Is that it?"

"Well, you have to understand and practise the art, for even such things as this can take a lifetime to master. It is not just sitting. You must be sitting and making it clear that you are not preoccupied. This tells everyone that you have put your own desires aside and that you are available to them." He moved to the bench in the kitchen and slid from one end to the other to make his next point: "First you move to one end of the bench. Then you clear the bench of any articles and clutter, placing any bags or items neatly on the floor. If there is a table, do likewise. This should make it obvious that you are not preoccupied. If you can find a spare chair, always place one nearby. Then you arrange your focus and your surroundings so that they become an invitation card; like a bird table offering bird seed or nuts.

"Now just look outwardly. There is no need to kidnap anyone. Be assured that the lonely, the lost, the confused and anyone else in need of help or a kind word will come to you. They will see your light. They will know that you have pushed your own desires and worries to the corners of your mind and made yourself available."

Then she realised why everyone had wanted to sit next to Olivia on the train; Olivia had turned her carriage into a bird table.

He tapped her on the head to wake her up: "However, be warned: the same method works for those spinning a spider's web."

BECOMING MIGHTY

Identity - Capabilities - Go beyond yourself

Surrender - Ego – Transformation

MITE ON THE TREE

Some people will tell you not to 'stretch yourself too thinly'. They are wrong. You need to imagine yourself as a mite settling on a tree. A mite so small that eventually you become part of the mighty tree itself. Now you have no limits. Now you can go beyond yourself.

Apolline now understood a way to make herself available to other people. Her next task was to work out 'how to make herself available to something higher than her own desires'.

Needing some inspiration, she opened the cleaning cupboard and picked up a broom. As she did this, her father's advice came to mind: 'Don't spread yourself too thinly.' She laughed as she thought about that now. Sollie had told her to do something different.

She recalled their conversation: 'I don't agree. Not fanning yourself out too thinly is not the answer. Such thinking will limit your true capabilities. You need to do the opposite. **You need to become mighty! You need to think that you can save the world.** However, to begin with, you need to make yourself small… Imagine yourself as a mite settling on the bark of a tree. This will help you go beyond yourself. Now you can connect yourself to the power of the universe and seek transformation. People look at the owl and say, 'Look how well camouflaged she is.' However, they are wrong. She is not camouflaged at all: the owl doesn't live in the tree; the owl is the tree… the tree has gone beyond itself.'

Eventually, it all began to make sense to her: 'Flying is in the mind. It is something that I am capable of when I see my identity as a universal soul.' Then she closed her eyes, put her legs astride her broomstick and imagined such a thought. After that, she went outside to sweep some leaves. Whilst she was doing this, something else that could make one fly caught her eye. It was half-hidden under a rock: something shiny, something green, red and white. Apolline bent over and picked it up. It felt like the thread from a spider's web. It was an airline ticket stub: 'Alitalia. Rome to Delhi. Ms Olivia Lascaux.' She re-read it, placed it into her apron pocket and hurried back to speak to Sollie.

> Your purpose is not something that you decide. It's what you find under a rock when you sweep the leaves.

PICTURES AND SYMBOLS

Religious traditions – Mantras – Annual events – Entrapment

> "A tree is known by its fruits… no good tree bears bad fruit, nor does a bad tree bear good fruit."
>
> Luke

The situation in Bhopal might have been grave, but that did not put a stop to Sollie's activity programme. They had just enjoyed a 'dancing frogs' event, packed with lessons on life for the children.

Afterwards, Komodo and the ladies began to pack the silk and taffeta frog costumes away in boxes. Ling was admiring the outfits; there were red, yellow, purple, pink and crimson bodies, embellished with stripes, spots, dashes and flashes. She assumed that they would repeat the event next year.

Then Sollie breezed in: "Would it not be better if we gave the costumes to the local villagers?"

"What?"

"We don't want this to become an annual event, do we?"

"Ling put her head down in disappointment: "It was so much fun."

"It was more than fun. It was amazing. However, we don't want to fall into the tradition and ritual trap and become conditioned. Religion uses holy dates, holy places and holy rituals to put you to sleep and trap you. For this reason, I try and avoid repeating my events. Save your repetition for mantras and imagining your success."

Ling frowned and then teased, "You are very suspicious. Are you not just spoiling some innocent fun?"

Sollie glared at her with demonic eyes: "Maybe. Most rituals and traditions are probably harmless… in comparison to the very dangerous traps."

"What are they?"

"Symbols. Symbols on a chain that people wear around their neck or wrists. Symbols that condition people and remove their freewill. Symbols which make some people feel that they are close to God or close to the devil."

Ling picked up the crimson silk costume that Yutika had worn. She wafted it in Sollie's direction, so that it nearly hit him. As she did, a small photograph fluttered to the ground. It settled face down on the floor. Komodo pounced upon it. Then surprisingly, Yutika pounced on Komodo. Her desperate demand seemed very out of character: "Give me that back."

However, Komodo was not accommodating. He showed everyone the photo of a little girl, with coal black eyes, wearing a little pink and cream dress. Coincidentally, the little girl was holding a symbol very tightly in her hand. It was a gold spinning disk with lots of serrated edges attached to a chain.

Ling's mouth opened in astonishment. She looked at Sollie: "Wow, how did you know that was going to happen?" He didn't answer.

Now all eyes were focused on Komodo and Yutika. He challenged her, devoid of any sensitivity: "Is the little girl in the photo one of your daughters?"

Yutika was now visibly distressed. She held out an outstretched, shaking arm towards Komodo and replied with trembling lips, "No. It is not one of my daughters."

"I didn't think so, because she has evil eyes. I think that the devil might be inside her."

However, the other adults knew who it was, because they had seen Yutika's name stamped on the back of the photograph. They said nothing. Eventually, Yutika snatched the photograph back and placed it in her dress pocket.

PAINTING A SOLUTION

Spiritual and compelling art - Miracles - Logic - Experience Beliefs - Creativity - Change - Transformation - Out of your mind

When you accept that all things are possible, the answers that you need may come to you in a dream.

Sollie invited Ling to accompany him on a late-night, jasmine-scented walk around the garden. Ling presumed that he would discuss something important with her. That warranted some extra preparation; the conditioner would be left on her hair a little longer before they met.

He spoke in a deep, hushed voice, drawn from the very bottom of his inner caves: "I have an important project for you. One that you will never execute if you attempt to use logic, limited experiences or limiting beliefs."

"Are you telling me that the opportunity to paint some 'spiritual art' has finally arrived?"

"Yes. We need to find a solution to the drought and famine and find a way to end the widows' suffering. We also need some people to change their thinking. I would like you to paint this work with the help of Komodo."

"A persuasive, transformative work of art?"

"Yes, exactly. Sometimes, we need to feel differently about things, if we want to change our actions. One way to do this is to present things to ourselves in a medium that we do not normally use. **If you usually think a challenge through, write it down instead. If you normally write it down, paint a picture of it. If you generally paint a picture of it, present your challenge to music.** I am sure that we talked about this before. Now, can you remember what I said about high art?"

"You said that to produce a masterpiece, the artist only chooses the paintbrushes and the colours. Something higher determines the details in the painting. You also said that on some ancient Chinese scrolls, the viewer would only be rewarded if they took the time to view the art from a variety of different perspectives."

"Correct. Oh... and of course it needs to be grand, ambitious and full of intrigue."

"How exactly?"

"Intriguing enough to hypnotise. Ambitious enough to be painted over eight frames. Grand enough for a Prime Minister [PM] to wear, should they see fit."

"Should the painting also provoke the PM into taking new action?"

"I think that this piece of art must do more than provoke; it will need to swarm on much of what he holds dear. It will need to chisel out his soul and bring it to the surface. Each of its eight frames must feel like a pair of pliers slowly pulling out his fingernails, until his beliefs are uprooted like a storm-ravaged tree lying on its side."

"That is asking a lot! How will I do that?"

"The Prime Minister is a Hindu. Hindus believe the Gods are alive in their statues. You must make him believe that the Gods are talking to him through your painting."

"How will Komodo and I produce the artwork?"

"We will inform Komodo of our goals. Then we will ask him to act as a vessel and paint some outline sketches. Afterwards, I want you to flush out the detail of Komodo's work and transfer it onto a bigger canvas."

"When do I start?"

"You can start as soon as you have acquired a suitable canvas and Komodo's outline work is complete."

Then he squeezed her nose: "Don't forget to leave a gap in the painting."

"Why?"

OUR CREATOR'S CANVAS

Incompletion - Art - Goals - Success - Peace of mind

Talisman - Challenges - Injustice

Don't think completion, it is too near the devil that exists in perfection.

"It's obligatory for all artists to leave their work unfinished. Remember that worthwhile work is not yours. It's there to be passed on, so that others can add to it."

Ling did not reply. Her frown said that she was a little puzzled.

"Allow me to explain this in a slightly different way. Life can be full of challenges and suffering. It can appear that the world is unjust. We can conclude from this that the ultimate creator has trusted us with the ultimate responsibility…**The creator has left a gap on their own canvas, for us to make the world a better place to live in.**"

"Really?"

"Why else would you have choices, gifts and purpose? The creator's canvas is there for you to add to their story. Surely this is not an opportunity that we can turn down?"

DOUBT AND CONFIDENCE

Art - Fear - Skills - Faith outside ourselves - Best you can be
Ego - Space – Higher self - Self-love - Self-worth

Ling sat alone at her desk and stared at a shoebox full of paint pots. A minute later worries began to march… Then her confidence seemed to drain away. She rushed back to see Sollie: "I think that this is beyond me."

"I agree. It is beyond YOU! That is why you must become a vessel for something higher to flow through you."

Ling scrunched her nose: "I am still not sure that I can paint what you want me to, even if I do become a vessel. I lack confidence, it has held me back all my life."

Sollie tapped her nose: "What exactly do you think that confidence is?"

"The good feelings that I experience at work when I am doing what I am best at."

Sollie tutted: "I don't think that work skills have anything to do with confidence. Confidence is not something that comes and goes. True confidence is a quality that once acquired will always be at your side. It works like a rainbow: overarching all that you do, wherever you go. If your confidence was based on your skills, every time you were asked to learn a new skill or move to a new job your confidence would desert you."

"Then I will just try and do my best."

"No, you must not 'try and do your best.' If you do, you will place your emphasis on your experience, knowledge and effort. Then your ego will surface. This may result in you seeking the approval of others. This will make you anxious. If you are anxious, you won't be confident."

She laughed, "Then what must we do?"

"We must be 'the best that we can be'. However, To be the best that we can be, we must *not* try and do our best**!** We must *not* try our hardest! We must put aside our experience, logic and knowledge. We must *not* rely on effort… we must consciously leave space for something greater to flow through us than our individual capabilities. This is what we call surrender. We work in partnership with our higher-self. In this union all things are possible. **It is for this reason that we must develop faith outside ourselves**."

"So I must not work as an individual?"

"Correct. Work in partnership with God instead. This way, your self-worth will increase and your work will blossom."

"Why was my thinking so wrong before?"

"You were taught badly. I constantly hear people say, 'I am confident when I am doing what I am good at.' However, as I said, that is not confidence. Confidence is not about taking a deep breath. It is not about rehearsing your lines or practising skills."

CONFIDENCE

Confidence has nothing to do with your skills. It is not temporary or limited either; real confidence bubbles and froths up so much, that it cannot all fit into the jar. It emerges from your relationship with your higher self. It is not a performance to win a trophy or applause. It is not about wiping the sweat from your brow. No, it is not like this. Nor does it make a loud noise or announce itself with a gong. It is no more than a pitter-patter and a splish and splash. It is a thing of beauty like the robin's breast. It does not run; it hops around.

PERSUASION

Art - Yoga - Meditation - Attendance - Commitment

Purpose - Inspiration - Intervention - Change

Frames are like rules…. they limit you. Remove them and all things are possible.

Sollie spoke to Komodo and outlined his role in helping Ling with some high art. Meanwhile Ling began to think about the materials that she might need.

Her first question was an obvious one for an artist but not the rest of us… Should she paint it portrait or landscape? This is of vital importance, because if a painting tells a life story, whether you paint it vertically or horizontally determines what you put in the painting and what you leave out.

The decision to frame or not frame your painting or your life is of equal importance; it means that you either shut things out or you let things in.

She reminded herself that the painting must be persuasive. That, she reasoned, might be easier to achieve if the art was painted on an interesting canvas or base. Suddenly, her lips curled and exactly what she needed entered her mind like a magic carpet flying through an open window. She also knew where to find it - a shop selling old photographs and paintings on a dusty, winding road. Ling persuaded Yutika to accompany her.

They arrived in the afternoon. It was a curious-looking shop with faded-pink wooden shutters either side of a horseshoe-shaped carved doorway. On the wall outside there were paintings of film stars, religious buildings and gaudy idols. They were met at the entrance by the owner, a very tall, straight-backed old lady. She ushered them in with the sort of welcome that you might hope for at the gates of heaven.

At the far end of the shop, there was a yellow mattress. Sitting on it, whilst practising his yoga, was an old man with a creamy-white beard and long hair. His appearance was in keeping with the mystery that swirled around him: a short, vivid-red skirt revealed bare legs and arms that appeared too long for his body. When he had finished scrutinising Ling and Yutika, one of his long arms went up in the air. It caught the old lady's attention and she led Ling and Yutika through a honeycombed doorway. On the other side, they found themselves standing on a roofless stone courtyard, surrounded by ancient, crumbling pillars. Paintings in old wooden frames, tapestries and scrolls decorated the walls.

It seemed that they were the ornaments of a courtyard tea room, where no one was taking tea. Instantly, one of the wall hangings caught Ling's eye. It was of a Chinese rural landscape and ancient battle. The artwork did not have obvious charm. However, it had been painted on an ancient silk scroll. A scroll with intricate borders and some unusual-coloured ribbons that protruded from its corners and edges. This, she told herself, was a painting with a story to tell.

Ling took another look at the shopkeeper. The lady was serenely old; softness had settled on her, despite the ravages of the sun. Like the old man sitting on the bed, her hair was creamy white. Like the wooden shutters at the front of the shop, she was dressed in soft pink. Adorning her were beaded necklaces, more than an elderly lady would normally wear. The red sindhoor on her forehead belied her true marriage status but gave her an air of mysticism. The fact that she rarely seemed to open her eyes whilst she tiptoed around only added to her allure.

Yutika asked the lady if the mural was for sale. The old lady's eyes flickered; she appeared to be surprised at the request: "I am sorry, it is not for sale. However, you could stay for tea and admire it whilst you are here."

They sat down at a shady courtyard table with two chairs. Twenty minutes later the tea arrived; it was so sublime that it tickled their ears. It also prompted Ling to stand up and add a third chair to their table: "Will you join us?"

"Thank you. My name is Sahana."

"Is that your husband sitting on the bed at the back of the shop?"

"No. It's my brother Bodhi. My husband passed away many years ago. Now I am one of Krishna's soldiers; a widow with a very important job to do."

However, before they could ask what that job might be, Sahana suddenly became tearful: "I am sorry. It is my grandson's birthday today; he would be eight if he was still here."

"Do you have a photo of him?"

The lady immediately dipped into her bag and brought out a picture. Ling had a thought… She disappeared for a minute and then returned with a sketchpad and some crayons.

"Using your photograph, I could sketch a picture of your grandson. Perhaps you could hang that up on the wall as well."

Sahana touched Ling's hand. "If you would, I know exactly where it should be displayed."

Two minutes later the painted scroll that they had been admiring was rolled up and handed over. Yutika thought that Ling had been clever. Then she quickly changed her mind... As they stood up to leave, Sahana whispered something most unexpected: "I want you to know that the scroll's unusual folds and ribbons harbour an important message. My brother Bodhi and I have been waiting many years to pass this on."

Yutika's eyes sparkled: "Many years?"

"Yes, many years. Bodhi is 105 years old. We have had to do a lot of yoga and meditation to make sure that we were still alive when you arrived."

"How many lessons of yoga and meditation per week?"

"I think that you misunderstand me. I don't mean to stay alive; I mean to be alive. To be alive and awake, you must do more than attend a few classes a week. You must do your other work whilst you are practising your yoga and meditation.

FRAGRANCES OF FARAWAY LANDS

When they arrived back at the Mustard Garden, Ling took the silk canvas and rolled it out on the floor. To her surprise, it was much bigger than she had imagined. That was because it was folded into eight frames and only two of the frames had been displayed on the courtyard wall. Although one could view the entire canvas when it was spread out, each of the eight frames told a different story. The canvas' background was light green. In each corner, there was some Chinese writing in pale-blue ink. There was a barely distinguishable silk border around each of the eight frames… Tucked into the border, there were bright green, red and orange ribbons tied in bows. There were also some flaps and hooks for securing some of the folds that were not apparent when it was hanging up in the courtyard.

She recalled what Sollie had told her about ancient Chinese art: 'Vertical silk scrolls with separate frames… frames that reveal the storyline very slowly… in order to keep the admirers in suspense.' She stared at the vast piece of art spread out on the floor. 'This canvas does exactly that,' she thought. She walked around the edges once again and studied the detail of the brushstrokes with her eyes and nostrils. The fragrance was of a faraway land. The backdrop was a wide wilderness and a starlit sky. Despairing warriors were retreating towards the mountains on galloping horses.

However, Ling decided that what mattered was the canvas and the frippery; not the painting… She recalled what Sollie had told her: **'You don't need to start again on a blank canvas from scratch, you just need to focus on creating a happy ending.'** With that in mind, she quickly decided the methodology. Komodo would sketch his vision on some paper using his pencils, crayons and paints. Afterwards, she would copy and paint his work over the original artwork on the silk scroll.

KOMODO'S ART

Devotion - Challenges - God - Hidden resources
Risks - Vessels - Possibilities - Ego

Komodo consulted Bongo to find out what the birds had been singing. Then he joined Ling and Sollie in the art studio. He was aware that the purpose of the art was to help find a solution for the famine, drought and the widows' suffering. It was a tall task… 'This isn't just a challenging time for me, this is also a challenging time for God!' he said to himself. At this point he recalled someone saying, **'God cannot do his work without you and you cannot do your work without him.'** That thought reassured him … now he didn't feel alone.

Komodo looked up at Sollie: "Can you tell me again what you want me to do?"

"Make sure that you paint with lots of splodgery."

"How do I paint with splodgery?"

"Look inwards. Paint without desire for approval. Let your brushes and crayons touch the paper before you do any thinking. Take risks; walk across rope ladders. Make your colours fly and splash across the page. Let the viewer taste the salty water of your seas. Paint corn fields like calling bells that ring out and persuade people to change the ending of their stories. Paint with love and devotion and you will see the evidence of God's light in your outstretched hand."

From the cupboards Komodo collected calligraphy brushes, coloured crayons and watercolours. He wiped the soft hairs of the brushes and gently blew on his painting paper. Then he started with an outline of the earth in rich and fluid ink tones. He did all his other work inside this circle. At the bottom, his brushes created a foreboding, stormy sea. Above the hills, lines of cloud chariots sucked their energy from a growling volcano. Both the sky and the seas were covered in birds of all shapes and sizes. The cranes guarded the caves on the dry lakes of Bhopal and the Buddhist stupa at Sanchi. Others dropped red dots from the sky. At the very edges of his paper, he daubed flocks of huge white-winged birds flying in opposite directions.

Then he painted a colourful gathering of elderly ladies. They were chanting joyfully, striking tambourines and bowing before what appeared to be India's opposition leader. Only one person in the scene appeared unhappy: a man with a white beard. The faint line of a dangling rope coiled above his head. Now he was absorbed into his own painting; working so close to the surface that his nose was flecked in rainbow colours. Outside the city, he painted hedgerows so beautiful that they had no choice but to flower. Finally, he added the smaller details, including the sadhu's charms's.

"Ling, I have finished."

"Are you happy with it Komodo?"

"If I wasn't happy with it, I would chop off my ears, like any other great artist." He pinged one of them with his fingers. "However, as you can see, they are both still in place."

OVERLOOKED COLOURS

Art - Change - Empathy - New perspectives

Shared joy - Vessels - Approval – Ego

KOMODO'S COLOURS

The strong, impregnable colours have been fortified through meditation. The fair ones represent the future. The shy ones will not mix. The saturated and bloated ones can no longer learn. The occupied ones can't reflect. The troubled and overlooked ones need some help.

The time arrived for Ling to convert Komodo's smaller painting onto the silk scroll. She reminded herself of Sollie's brief: 'The painting must grab the PM by the ankles and pull him in. He needs to gargle on the paint.' Then, for the next four days, all she did was paint. Only at the very end did she lift the corner flaps up and paint on the charms from the sadhu's bracelet.

Then it was time to scrutinize the art. She climbed onto the table and screwed some cup hooks into the ceiling. A minute later the canvas was a sail and a kite. After that, she took a cushion for her head and looked up at it from the floor. From here things looked very different. Finally, the canvas was wrapped around her body. When she did this, some paper-thin silk buttons on the reverse side became apparent. Undoing these revealed some slits for a head and two arms so that the scroll could be worn as a coat.

Now Ling felt light. More importantly, she discovered what happens when you allow yourself to be a vessel instead of seeking approval and recognition through the ego: **Anxiety floats away but you still get to share the joy.** Apolline had told her that, in French, there was a special verb for 'deeper joy'. She could not remember what it was; however, she did now understand why it existed.

MIND, BODY AND SPIRIT

Who am I? - Joy and excitement - Sacrifice - Surrender - God - Diet

Life should be boiling, not simmering.

Sollie and Apolline were returning home after a visit to the magnificent 12th century Shiva temple at Bhojpur. "Sollie, you told me that you would tell me more about the mind, body and spirit?"

Five minutes later, he put the brakes on abruptly and pulled the truck up in front of a cake shop: "Follow me."

The interior was what you might imagine heaven to be made of, if you were a lover of sweet baking. Stuffed on the shelves, from floor to ceiling, were multi-coloured pastries, sponges, gateaux and cakes. There were browns, pinks and purples, reds, oranges and lemons. At the counter and at the tables, the air was full of liquorice, marzipan, chocolate and strawberries.

The pale-green tables were quite grubby but the bright-red benches looked freshly painted. It was busy. Busy with extremely large people that liked sweet baking. The jolly-looking lady behind the counter was an extremely generous size too. She smiled and walked them to a table. Apolline wanted to see a menu. However, before she could ask, the lady walked away. Two minutes later she returned with two bananas, two oranges and a very large coconut. Now all the other people in the cake shop were staring. Apolline assumed that they were wondering why anyone would buy these plain items when the wonders of the world were all about them.

Sollie smiled at the man sitting at the adjacent table and listened to the cake-room gossip. Then the man turned to face Apolline and whispered to her in English, "Have you guessed what these customers are all talking about?"

"I have no idea."

His eyes widened and he replied in a knowing voice, "They are all talking about food. They are chatting about what they are going to cook for their next dinner party, which cakes are the sweetest and which are the healthiest. They

BHOJPUR TEMPLE

are discussing their diets and talking about calories." Then he doffed his hat, stood up and left.

Apolline turned towards Sollie: "Most of the customers are huge, why are they all talking about diets in a cake shop?"

Sollie laughed but didn't answer. Then he had a thought… There was someone else who would benefit from a visit to this cake shop, even if they didn't have a weight problem.

Apolline tapped his shoulder to bring him out of his daydream; "So, are you going to tell me who I am and help me understand the workings of the mind, body and spirit?"

"You must quieten the soul to release the spirit that brings you joy."

"What about discovering who I am?"

"I can't help you with that. That is your quest. However, I can help you understand who you are not.

"You are certainly not your body. Think of your body as your senses and a temporary home; somewhere you will move on from. Know that you can't be your mind, because you can observe and witness your thoughts and you can't be something that you can watch."

Apolline looked confused, so he picked up the big green coconut: "Think of the coconut's green outer casing as the body and mind. Remove this casing and you will find the brown, rough and fibrous casing of the inner coconut: think of that as your 'soul'. It is the soul that prevents you accessing the sweet milk of the 'spirit', which is in the centre. However, you don't need to remove the soul; you just need to convert it from a troublesome one to a peaceful one."

"How do I manage to make my soul peaceful?"

"The obvious way to make the soul peaceful would be to search for tranquillity. However, this might exchange troubles for dullness, and what is life without joy? Therefore, **We don't try and quieten the mind, we simply drop it. The dragon is not slayed with a sword but an act of surrender**."

"What happens after that?"

"**As your soul becomes peaceful, so your spirit begins to jump.** Now you experience joy. The order of your desires switches around too; now you desire to dine on spiritual food before you have a desire to feed the body. **Now you stop asking yourself how you can satisfy your own needs. Instead, you ask how you can help satisfy the needs of others.**"

Then he changed the subject.

FAVOURITISM

Overlooked - Mind - Body - Spirit - Sharing - Poverty

"Apolline, can you tell me why you think that your parents should have treated all their children equally?"

She immediately crossed her legs and arms: "Is that not obvious? Did I not tell you that I was frequently overlooked and treated unfavourably? My parents looked after my sisters differently… They had concerns about me… they had hopes for them. They fed and clothed me, but they loved my sisters. My father held my sisters' hand, my mother combed their hair… but never mine. I can't put it all into words. I can only tell you that my childhood left me feeling empty, unloved and distraught."

He began to juggle the oranges and the bananas: "When the Titans were defeated, Atlas was given the job of holding the heavens on his shoulders. It was a difficult task, not unlike juggling fruit or bringing up several children in a family. This is because each one of us is different. Each of us has different needs. Surely, good parents cannot possibly treat all their children the same if each child has different needs? Now tell me, is it possible that some people find juggling fruit and coconuts easy and some people find it difficult? Is it possible that you were not overlooked or treated unfavourably but just treated differently?"

"I will need to think about that."

However, Sollie wanted her to think about that another time, so once again, he changed the subject. This time he stared right into her eyes: "Which do you think that we should feed first, the body or the soul?"

"I don't know and I do not want to guess."

"Then we should leave."

He picked up the fruit and the coconuts and they walked out of the cake shop. Just as they were approaching the truck, he changed direction. He walked up to an old lady who was sat behind a large hole in the wall. She was trying to sell fruit juice. The juice was stored in a large, pink pot and served in stainless steel tumblers. Sollie suspected that no one was buying any. He knelt down, smiled and pulled out a banana from his bag. The old lady accepted with a toothless smile. Then she waved at Apolline and beckoned her over.

Apolline stared at Sollie and paused for guidance. He encouraged her to walk over.

"Sit down here, my dear. My name is Tanmayi."

Tanmayi put a jug into the painted pot and drew some of the juice. Slowly she poured it into one of the tumblers and passed it to Apolline. However, the performance was not over. After bending down to pick something up, Tanmayi swivelled around and handed Apolline a paper-wrapped parcel. Inside was a small, iced cake. Tanmayi took a bone-handled knife, cut the cake down the middle and handed Apolline the largest piece. Apolline accepted. When the cake was eaten, Apolline stood up. Her first reaction was to touch her pocket. Her second reaction was to give the lady a hug… Clearly, despite having nothing, Tanmayi didn't want anything from her.

They climbed back into the truck, and Sollie threw Apolline an orange.

"Sollie, why did Tanmayi do that?"

"**She knew the importance of feeding her soul before her body.** She knew that if you share your last piece of cake with a stranger, you can never imagine yourself as being poor. Even if you have no teeth, your smile will always be beautiful."

Tanmayi – a Sanskrit name meaning wholly absorbed in God

LOSING AND FINDING YOURSELF

Giving up habits – Control – Imagined success – Meditation

Do you want to lose yourself, or do you want to find yourself? Do you want to give up, or do you want to do more with your life than just give up?

Tom approached Sollie at the edge of the Mustard Garden forest: "I have come to tell you that I am ready to stop drinking whisky. Now I am totally committed. Now I want to reclaim my life. What must I do next?"

"Imagine and feel your success… People say to me all the time, 'I can't imagine myself without a pill, a cigarette or a drink in my hand. I would not be able to enjoy myself, cope with my problems or let go and dance.' Many of them are right. They cannot do these things until they first believe that it is possible. **Therefore, they must practise their success in their mind and imagine how good it will feel before they attempt the reality.**"

FALLING OUT OF LOVE

Giving up habits – Diets – Changing feelings

Your challenge will not be overcome with just effort and persistence; you need to change how you feel and think about it.

The next day Sollie enticed Tom to the cake shop. The pleasant shopkeeper arrived at their table. However, this time, instead of bringing fruit and coconuts, she curtsied and gave them small cups of delicate green tea.

"Tom, listen to all the chattering people around you, and then try and guess what they are talking about."

"I have no idea what the subject is, but they seem to be in love with whatever they are talking about."

"You are right. They are talking about what they love: food. Now tell me something Tom, is whisky something that you love, or is whisky something that you dislike but which you can't help drinking?"

Tom thought about that for a minute: "It's not just a coping mechanism… I adore whisky. I love the taste. I like the chink of the glasses that I drink it from."

"What don't you like about whisky?"

"I don't like my behaviour when I am drinking."

"Now tell me, apart from talking about their love of food, what else do most of the people in this shop have in common?"

Tom surveyed the room. "It appears that many of them are overweight."

"Why do you think that they are overweight, even though many of them are discussing diets?"

"Is it because they are too much in love with what they want to give up?"

"It could be. What do you think that they need to do in order to change their habit?"

"I would imagine that they would need to fall out of love with food and think and feel about it differently."

THREE ST-MARTINS

Orphans - Belonging - Decisions - Positive interpretations
Adversity - Difficult pasts

The children had seen the famine and the drought on television. Now Sollie was taking them to the countryside to see and feel the tragedy for themselves. On the way, Phi Phi sat next to him. She wasn't very talkative.

"You are very quiet today Phi Phi, is everything okay?"

"The children at the village school have been laughing at us because we are named after islands. They said that we don't belong."

"You should ignore what they say, your name is exotic."

"It is not easy to ignore."

"Are you aware that my name is also an island?"

He received a blank look.

"It is true. Sollie is short for Solomon and the Solomon Islands."

"If you are also named after an island, does that mean we are all related?"

"Of course we are. We are all related and connected to each other, whether we share a name or not."

"I can't wait to tell everyone. What is your full name?"

"Solomon St-Martin."

"That is the same family name as Gabriel."

"I know, but it is just a coincidence."

"When I went with Apolline to meet Olivia at the train station, I saw Olivia's address label on her suitcase. She comes from a place in France near Lascaux called Lamonzie-St-Martin. Is that just a coincidence as well?"

Sollie didn't answer. He changed the subject: "Tell me Phi Phi, are you happy with the lessons at the village school."

"Yes, but I am not happy being an orphan. My circumstances will limit me for the rest of my life."

"Or your circumstances could make you and many others very happy. **It all depends on how you interpret your experiences and how you respond to adversity. It is this that ultimately determines your happiness.**"

"What does that mean?"

"Great adversity can give people the fortitude that they need to face certain challenges. Challenges that perhaps they could not have overcome if they had lived a charmed life."

"I am not convinced. It seems to me that orphans are unlikely to do anything meaningful with their lives."

"What about Moses? Was he not placed in a basket and pushed down the river?"

"That was a one off."

"What about Muhammad?"

"What about him?"

"He was orphaned not once, but twice."

"Was he?" she asked in a startled voice.

"By the time he was six, he had lost both his parents. Then he was placed in the care of his grandfather, who also died a few years later. Finally, he was looked after by his uncle. We don't know why these things happen, and it is not wise to ask. However, it is possible that those who suffer become stronger because of their endurances. In some cases, so strong that others feel compelled to follow them."

MUDDY WATER

Empathy - Emotional feelings - Changing thinking - Shared pain and joy Desensitised - Reaching out - Redemption - Opening hearts

The children arrived at their destination in the countryside. By working alongside some of the destitute local women, Sollie hoped the children would make an 'emotional connection'.

Things were not pleasant. On the farmlands there were no smiling faces; only sorrow, bent shoulders and furrowed brows. In the fields, there were no swinging udders or happy cowbells; only dead cattle and abandoned crops. They watched mothers and grandmothers searching for water. The ladies dug holes in the ground with their bare hands that left them sore, cut and bleeding. If any watery mud appeared, they spooned it into their water carriers.

The children helped the women as best they could. They helped strain the muddy water and carry the heavy containers back to the village. They could not, however, help them with the real problem; they could not make it rain.

Despite this, Sollie viewed the trip as a success. The children had crawled in the dust on their hands and knees and had felt the weight of the villagers' heavy loads on their backs. They had stared into the recesses of sunken, hollow eyes, held bony hands and touched frail skin. The children no longer had to imagine how these old ladies felt.

There was something else that brightened Sollie's eyes. The children were visibly upset by what they had experienced. He wasn't pleased because they were upset; he was pleased because they could be upset. This told him that they had not been completely desensitised by their early childhood experiences… **There was hope for them… for if you take the time to fully understand another person's pain, one day it may help you overcome your own**.

One child in particular, Stromboli, who had once lacked empathy, seemed to feel the villagers' pain more than most. On the drive home he had to be comforted by Tom's long arm, as tears streamed down his cheeks.

"I will never forget what I have experienced and learnt today."

"What did you learn?"

"**Don't be scared to visit poverty and suffering, for it is here that you can find your heart.** Find some sisters and brothers that you didn't know you had. Share their sorrow. For then you will surely share their joy."

HATCHING, MATCHING AND DISPATCHING

Priorities - Umbilical - Self-love - Touching - Learned behaviour
Bereavement - Afterlife - Being present - The circle of love

Hands should be an extension of the heart, like branches are to the tree.

Yutika brought Sollie some tea: "You asked me to remind you about something."

"I did, thank you, please sit down. The time has arrived for us to connect some of our cords and become umbilical. I would like you to gather 14 widows from the surrounding area. They will come and live with us."

"Are you sure that this is the right time, what with all the other things going on?"

"If we put off the very important things, because there are other important things going on, we will never make progress, will we?"

"What will the widows do?"

"Some of them will already be putting their gifts to good use and will only need food and shelter. We may need to help others reconnect to society and re-find themselves. However, ultimately they must dance. There is no place for the distribution of soup in my dreams."

"How will we help them do that?"

"In the first instance, we will concentrate on giving them lots of simple, selfless tasks, like cooking and cleaning for other people. This unblocks the obstacles covering the true will of the heart. It is also one of the first steps towards loving ourselves again. We will also encourage them to participate in some group therapy, to help them come to terms with their anguish and rejection. Later, we will help them acquire the desire to imagine other people being happy, instead of just themselves."

"What comes after that?"

"You, Ling and Apolline will help train them to start a new career."

"What exactly will this involve?"

"**Hatching, matching and dispatching**...It's part of my mission."

"What does that mean?"

"The first 14 homeless widows to arrive at the Mustard Garden will become **matchers**. They will be like grandmothers to the orphaned children here. This will turn the wheels of love in both directions. Then the real work starts! We are going to set up a much bigger programme where homeless widows are taken off the streets of Varanasi and Vrindavan and given training in midwifery, orphan and hospice care.

"As **hatchers**, the widows will be trained to work in the local villages as midwives. In this job, they will also be on the lookout for any unwanted babies. Then, during pregnancy and after birth they will help cradle, hug and touch them. **Dispatchers** complete the circle of love. They will give a special programme of palliative and hospice care to the dying, in line with Emperor Huizong's instructions for eternal life."

"Why those particular jobs?"

"You once said that you could not imagine being in a loving embrace. I think that you said that your parents never touched or held you. We want to limit the spread of this disease. And, when you believe in eternal life, you are more likely to plant seeds that continue to blossom after your body has gone."

"Is that it?"

"No, this is just the start. Emperor Huizong's ultimate goal is for the poor to become rich. This will require us to recruit a huge army of widows and transform them into spiritual teachers. However, I will probably have departed by the time this task is completed."

You will hear well-meaning people tell you that you must live in the present and not in the past or the future. However, they are not entirely right. You must live in a way that makes you present, after you have gone.

FABLES AND MYTHS

Commitment - Beyond imagination

The goal is to go beyond ourselves; to progress from being the storyteller to being the story.

Apolline knocked on Sollie's door: "Sollie, you asked to see me."

He motioned for her to sit down: "Apolline, I would like you to cut down your teaching hours and go part-time."

Apolline looked down at her feet despondently: "Why? I left France because my teaching hours were reduced."

"I think that the time has arrived for you to start doing the things that you talked of in your application letter."

"What exactly?"

"I want you to write the very best stories that you can. A meaty stew of stories with vegetarian options. Tales that the children can pass on to their own children. Fables that will plant seeds of hope. Myths and legends that will help people re-find their pure, loving hearts. Parables that will make people take their shoes and socks off and set out on a pilgrimage to Bhopal."

"Where will I find these stories?"

"Speak to your higher self before you place your head on your pillow… Then they will drift in through the open window and fall about you as you sleep."

Then she fell silent for a few moments.

"Why have you gone quiet?"

"I was thinking about what the book cover should look like."

"I wouldn't worry about that. What the book cover looks like will not matter. People will be drawn to the book regardless. It will have its own perfume. It will be like riding through the woods and smelling wafts of lilac. This book will illuminate bookcases even when there is no light. This is what happens when you allow something higher to flow through your pen."

Now the smile had returned to her face: "I thought that you had forgotten my dreams. Did you always have this planned for me?"

"Of course."

"I cannot wait for the day to arrive when I can read my stories out."

Sollie did not reply, and a silence fell about the room.

Apolline looked incredulous: "What? Don't you want me to read out my stories?"

"Not exactly... We are going to invite some widows to live here. I want you to teach the widows all the stories that you write so that they can pass the tales down to the children."

She wrung her hands in frustration. He stretched out his arm towards her: "Don't be disappointed, I told you once before that, **You must prepare to go beyond the role of storyteller and become the story; to go beyond yourself and to live a life that others feel compelled to write about.** The time for that is fast approaching."

Apolline paled slightly and replied nervously, "You make it sound as if something terrible is going to happen to me."

DANCING AND MUSIC

Gifts - Pain - Discipline and reward

"I also want you to plan a dance and music programme. First you will teach the widows that come to live here how to dance. Then one day, you must find a way to teach all the destitute people of the world how to sway and raise their heads towards the sky."

"How?"

"With your gifts! However, your responsibilities will go beyond playing a violin in a world class orchestra... you will be the orchestra's conductor."

Apolline went quiet for a few minutes and started to imagine her tasks; the gathering of stories, the training of the widows, conducting a great symphony and choosing appropriate dances: "What type of dances did you have in mind?"

"I was thinking of something like the cha-cha-cha and the Beryozka; one to breathe life, the other to settle serenity."

"What is the Beryozka?"

"It is 'The Dance of the Birch Trees', a dance of grace and propriety that I witnessed during a recent visit to Russia. It is also a transformative dance of meditation that will make the troupe float and levitate before turning them into a ring of trees. I suggest that you go and watch a film clip of it."

As she imagined the smiling faces and dancing feet, she saw her heart. Finally her burning bush was on fire.

There are no sacrifices worth dying for, only sacrifices worth living for.

RISHI BACK IN AUSTRALIA

Rishi was now back in Kakadu, Australia. He sent photographs and explanations to show everyone what was unfolding there.

Hubert provided a passionate commentary: "The first photograph is of several hundred sarus cranes milling around the Kakadu National Park and cave entrances. The second one is taken in the city of Darwin a few miles away. Here birds of every species have taken over the town; the traffic can't move and every rooftop is full of birds.

"Now look at this picture, taken the following day on the coast at Darwin by the Timor sea. Given a choice, most migrating birds will avoid flying over the sea. Here, thousands of birds are sitting on the water and have made themselves into a bridge between Darwin and Melville Island. The rest of the birds are flying over them as if the floating birds are land. The next day's photographs show more bird bridges being formed in a north-easterly direction from Bali, Malaysia and Thailand.

"In Europe we are informed that millions of birds had descended on southern Spain and Gibraltar. They are heading across the water to North Africa. Others can be seen flying to Eritrea and across the Red Sea into Yemen.

"It is evident that two huge masses of birds are on the move. One is heading east and the other is heading west. Now it is no longer difficult to work out where they are heading. They are moving towards India; it seems that their destination is Bhopal."

IRRUPTIONS, SUPERFLIGHTS AND MEDITATING BIRDS

Sollie lifted himself up onto the desk: "Hubert, can you tell us how migrating birds can fly thousands of miles with so little sleep and rest?"

"They travel in a meditative-like state. They rarely flap their wings. Their hearts barely beat. They are zen-like; they move, but they are undisturbed by their activity."

"How often do they migrate?"

"Normally birds will migrate twice a year: once forward and once back. However, there are also 'irruptions'. An irruption is a dramatic, irregular migration, when large numbers of birds are spotted in places that they do not normally visit. However, when several different species irrupt to the same region in one year, we call it a SUPERFLIGHT!"

Sollie raised his eyebrows: "Why did you take so long to tell us that?"

"I didn't rush to give it that name because I am not sure that it is a superflight that we are experiencing. It appears to be more than that."

Everyone lurched forward.

"The birds appear to be on something like a pilgrimage. It might be that the pilgrims are arriving to witness an extraordinary event. Alternatively, it might be that they are coming together to do something unexpected and astonishing."

Sollie straightened himself up: "I think that Bongo might have been right when he said that the birds are planning a big dance. Now tell us Hubert, is it possible to have a superflight linked to the movements of the stars, maybe a huge one that only happens sporadically, maybe every few thousand years?"

"I am not aware of any superflights that take place that infrequently. If there had been, I am sure that they would have been recorded."

"Perhaps it has been. Perhaps that is what the cave paintings going back all those thousands of years are trying to tell us."

TRAVELLING

Synthesis - Problems - Small steps - Challenges
Sharing - Meeting people - Spiritual preparation

The traveller needs to exercise thanksgiving like the farmer. Whilst they travel and harvest all this world's beauty, they should ask themselves how they can give something back.

Later Tom and Sollie chatted about human pilgrimages and travel.

"Sollie, what advice would you give to those travelling around the world with rucksacks on their back?"

"Before you set off, **Identify the pain and fears that you would like to unload and the challenges that you need to air.** If your bag or rucksack is already full, throw out your mosquito spray and excess clothes. Fill it instead with good questions that will help you overcome your challenges."

"Like what?"

"Like your fear of rejection, need for approval, desire for belonging, fear of loss and any other anxieties."

"How exactly?"

"Wherever you go, ask for help. Do this as soon as you set out, so that you build up momentum. Let the foothills of your journey be your testing ground."

"Are you suggesting that I should ask strangers to help me with my big challenges and offer something similar in return?"

"No. Not at all."

"Then what?"

"**Start by asking for help with the smallest things... Ask where to put your bag, for help with pulling your boots off and doing up your fiddly buttons.**

"The healing of emotional challenges doesn't start in the operating theatre. It starts outside your tent, on your bunk and at the coffee station. Then you can move to the next stage; now you can lend your ears instead of socks, now you can ask to borrow opinions and advice instead of bars of soap."

"What comes next?"

"Some people share their soup and sandwiches, but I think it's more beneficial to share your hopes and your vulnerabilities."

"When do I ask for help with solving my big problems?"

"You don't. Look to meditate on these and synthesise them through a support group."

"What attractions should a pilgrim visit?"

"It's not important; **It would be better to be one of the attractions yourself.** Imagine yourself as a tree; stand still more often, offer shade, be a bird table. However, remember that self-love must precede looking out for others. If you must help, keep it small: offer to lift up bags, lend socks and give out kind looks."

"What other preparation should I do before I set out on my pilgrimage?"

"You must plan some of your communication. Don't leave it all to chance. Remember the winning formula; **Imagine and practise your success in your mind before you practise in reality.**"

"What communication? Do you mean the things that I am going to say to the people that I meet in hostels and at train stations?"

"More than that. Anticipate injustice and disappointment. Don't let these be a surprise; prepare in advance for them."

"What does that mean?"

"Be aware that in all your daily meetings there is the potential of someone winning and someone losing. There is an opportunity for joy or for sadness. **You are ready to depart on your pilgrimage when you can picture in your mind's eye all your meetings and transactions ending with hugs and heartfelt goodbyes.** This is one of the measurements that tells you that you are spiritually ready to set out on your journey."

HOPES FOR THE FUTURE

Giving up habits - Luck - Action - Dreams - Shock treatment - Fate

> Faith is not the same as hope. Don't dream in hope. Know that dreams come true because of your faith, your thoughts and your actions.

Afterwards, Sollie and Tom walked through the forest.

"Tom, I want you to look carefully at that tree and tell me what you see."

"I see a camouflaged stick insect and a long line of ants carrying leaves. At the top a gecko is taking its lunch."

"Good, now we can continue."

However, just as they turned around, Tom jumped two foot in the air: "HELP!" He grabbed Sollie's arm, as if his life depended on it.

"What's wrong?"

No words came out of Tom's mouth … so he pointed at the tree. A huge, fat green snake lay coiled around the branches… it glared menacingly at Tom and flicked out its tongue… Tom's heart jumped out of his chest. He let go of Sollie's arm and ran.

When they reached the Mustard Garden, Sollie sat Tom down: "Before we talk more about the wildlife in the trees, tell me a happy ending that you would like, if you could choose one."

"I would like to be with Apolline. If it was God's will, I would feel very lucky if I was."

Then Sollie burst into a little tirade of shock treatment that both surprised and shook Tom… "It's not about luck, fate or God's will, Tom; it's about taking responsibility and carrying your own cross. It's about your decisions and your actions."

GECKOS ON THE CEILING

Giving up habits - Boundaries - Addictions

> If you are troubled, don't give up... This might just be your chrysalis stage before you begin to flutter.

"Now let us talk about what we saw in the forest. I want you to understand that the camouflaged stick insect is like your diseased liver. It might not be easy to see, but it doesn't mean it is not there.

"You also saw a little gecko climbing to the top of the tree. Geckos have special sticky pads on their feet. This adhesive gives them something to hold on to and stops them falling off. Geckos' feet are like parameters or boundaries; if they are absent, there is no limit to how far you can fall. This is something that I learnt from my short stay in prison. "Many of the prisoners were addicted to drugs, cigarettes, alcohol and gambling. It seemed that the only prisoners that could be helped were those that had set out some boundaries. They had a limit to how much they would gamble; they would never smoke or drink before certain times of the day or never go beyond a certain amount. However, those without any boundaries were difficult to save.

"You must make friends with the little guys that you saw in the trees, because there are some bigger guys lurking around who are out to harm you. Huge guys like the snake that made you jump in the air. Anaconda-like addictions coiled around the branches, waiting for you to pass by. When they wrap themselves around you, they will not let go."

Tom laughed nervously: "That is how my addiction feels. The anaconda has me in a vice-like grip and is crushing the life out of me. I feel as if I have no control."

"Then we need to find a way to loosen the anaconda's grip and shake it off right away."

> When you are all at sea, don't wait until you are scraping the rocks and there are holes in the bottom of your boat before you act.

ORGANIC FARMING

Giving up habits - Synthesis - Transformation - Steeping - Staring Silence - Meditation - Coping mechanisms - Self-love

"Tell me Tom, do you want to change or transform your behaviour? For if you only change, I cannot guarantee that at some point, the tide will not come back in and wash away all your good work. However, if you want a permanent solution, I ask you to think of transformation by synthesis. **Look to convert bad things into good things, instead of pursuing avoidance.** For this is nature's way. This way there is no way of turning back. This way you choose to farm your habits and your mind organically. Here nothing is forced; everything is laid out for the sun to warm and for the wind to pass through, in the same way that we sun dry tomatoes."

"How do you do that?"

"In the early stages of making whisky, the barley is steeped in water in preparation for its transformation. You need to do some steeping too."

"In what?"

"Steep yourself in silence, meditation and staring."

"What can staring do for me?"

"It will take you to the present and away from your thoughts. **If you stare at something for long enough, it alters your consciousness.** Stare and you will witness and confront your habits. Stare deeply and for longer and the consequences of your behaviour will march into view, like the long line of ants that we saw climbing down the tree.

"Is that it?"

"That is a lot. However, if you need additional motivation, **I recommend a transference from the mind to the heart**. To understand this, I suggest that you go and watch Stromboli. He has been playing in the position of goalkeeper for the football team. Now no one can score a goal against him. Perhaps you should find out what has transformed him into a sporting phenomenon."

THE GOALKEEPER

Giving up habits – Emotional connection – Changing feelings
Reaching out – Transformation from mind to heart – Goals

> Don't say, 'I can be whatever I want to be'; say, 'I need to transform myself into something that God needs me to be.'

Tom made his way to the dusty field where the children were playing football. It was as Sollie had said. No one could score a goal against Stromboli. When the game was over, Tom sat down with him in the dust: "Stromboli, you were amazing. What is your secret?"

"I have just changed how I feel about something."

"How did you do that?"

"Sollie called it synthesising my problems. It started with helping the old ladies who had no water; I shared their pain. It made me realise how lucky I am. After my visit I made a promise to myself. I vowed that I would do all that I could to ensure that not one drop of water is spilt or wasted during the drought. Then I imagined that my goal line was a bucket of water. Every time I look at my goal line, I see the sore hands and hunched shoulders that I witnessed in the fields. Now when I am in goal my concentration never falters. No one is going to score a goal or kick my imaginary bucket of water over. **Now I am shifting my focus away from my own challenges so that I can be something that other people need.**"

> If you transform yourself into something that can help others, you inadvertently help and transform yourself too.

TREASURE

Death – Peace – Success – Persistence

> If you can live close to death whilst still taking care of your life, your worries will retreat. If you can live with non-attachment, your anxiety will melt. When you have found your own peace, you can be peaceful with others and you will not seek to control anyone. When you have triumphed over the fear of your own death, you will not seek to triumph over the death of others.

The children were intrigued by Komodo and Ling's joint art project. They concluded that it was something to do with treasure hidden in the caves at the bottom of the dried-up lake. Then, an opportunity to find the treasure presented itself... They were all going on a trip to Bhopal's multi-art centre. It was a short walk from the lakes. A school bus had been arranged to take them there. The night before the trip, they smuggled torches, ropes and digging equipment into their backpacks.

As soon as the school bus set them down and was out of view, the children made their way towards the caves. There were thousands of birds walking on the lakebed. However, the birds ignored the children, and they encountered none of the attacks experienced by the adults. Eventually, they reached their destination and climbed on top of the cave. They quickly gave up on the idea of trying to remove the boulder. They searched instead for a soft spot and dug their own entrance.

Bongo volunteered to go down first: "I will be able to find my way in the dark caves."

Ascension accompanied him. They had been walking for an hour when Ascension suddenly stopped: "There are some paintings on the cave ceiling."

"What paintings?"

"The sky is full of chariots racing across the heavens. A volcano is erupting in the distance. Warriors are riding horses and throwing spears at some soaring birds. Other large-winged birds are flying around the edge of a planet."

"Anything else?"

Ascension looked at another wall around the corner: "There is also a temple with a domed roof next to some umbrellas. A figure is standing on the roof. It is a human body standing up in a trellised cage, and it has a big bird's head. On the left and right of the main image there are thousands of cranes sitting on the ground..." However, before he could continue with the description of the drawings, they were interrupted by a noise.

Bongo sniffed: "Shine the torch on the ground. Tell me what is there."

Ascension did as he was told. Then he screamed… "SNAKES!"

Bongo felt the pain before he heard the warning. Ascension's torch illuminated large fangs and dark, triangular marks on beige bodies. There must have been two dozen. Bongo fell to the ground. Ascension dragged him away from the danger by his feet.

"Where does it hurt?"

Bongo pointed to both his legs. Ascension ripped off his shirt and wrapped it tightly around the bite areas: "How do you feel?"

"A bit dizzy."

"Then we need to leave."

Bongo managed to stand up and walk. However, after 15 minutes he had to stop: "You go ahead and find help."

As soon as Ascension ran off, Bongo crouched down. He rested his back against the cold cave wall. For a few moments his pain disappeared; his worries retreated too. He concluded that he must be close to death because suddenly everything felt so good.

Ascension had seen photographs of snakes similar to the ones that he had just witnessed. He hoped with all his heart that he had been mistaken and that the bites had not been made by a Russell's viper, one of India's most deadly snakes. As he ran, he recalled what he knew: 'The ancients referred to the snake as the personification of the devil, a reptile so evil that it is not content with killing you. Its wounds cause internal haemorrhaging, attack the pituitary gland and reverse puberty.' In truth, it was not normally a bite worth surviving.

Back at the cave entrance, the other children pulled Ascension through the opening. "Bongo has been attacked by some Russell's viper snakes. We need anti-venom straight away."

Then Ascension slid back down the hole with Stromboli, Curacao and Andaman to retrieve Bongo. Phi Phi rang Sollie and told him what had happened. Sollie's reply was urgent but calm: "Carry him to the road and flag down a taxi that will take you to the hospital. We will meet you there."

After that, there was a flurry of activity. Sollie rang Ajeet and asked him if he would arrange for Bongo to receive some immediate treatment on arrival at the hospital. Yutika called Tom, who was already in town, only a short distance from where Bongo was heading. Then, they jumped in the truck and headed for the hospital. On the way, Sollie recalled Fei Hung's warning about evil forces harming those dear to him. However, he kept his counsel.

MEASURES AND SEMIQUAVERS

Measures - Vibrations - Acceptance - Gratitude - Eternal life

Tom was waiting at the hospital gates when the taxi arrived. He picked up Bongo in his arms and hurriedly carried him inside. Bongo was taken straight to a bed and Tom sat down by his side. The doctor administered the anti-venom, put him on a drip and left the room. Tom held Bongo's hand. A nurse came in, checked his pulse and left again. As she left the room, Bongo spoke in a whisper: "I thought that a viper's bite was meant to reverse things; however, I still can't see!"

"You are going to recover; they have administered the anti-venom."

"Perhaps. However, it is not important anymore. I have completed my first measure."

"What do you mean?"

"I was trusted, as we all are, with a gift. I learnt the language of the birds, and I passed on the message to Komodo so that he could include it in his painting for Ling. That was all I had to do: master my art, hand myself over and carry out my calling. My first measure here on earth was short, like that of a butterfly. However, now it has reached its end. Now I am looking forward to someone picking up my thread and working with me when I become a young ancestor…Sollie will explain what that is."

"Bongo, you are much more than a measure. You have touched people's lives and you have inspired them."

Bongo smiled faintly: "I know. I am a semiquaver not just any old quaver. Soon I will tremble, shake and vibrate."

FORGIVING

> Forgiveness is like the settling of the snow; after forgiveness, all the footprints that went before it disappear.

"Bongo, can I ask you another question?"

"One last one, so I hope that this one is your best."

"You were abandoned, and you are blind. How can you be so forgiving and happy?"

"When it comes to forgiving, I had no choice. If I had not forgiven myself and those around me, I wouldn't have had any life at all. For I spent a lot of my early years hiding from terrors that even a blind person can see. However, I overcame these nightmares a long time ago. The more difficult challenge was coming to terms with my mother's decision to abandon me."

"How did you do that?"

"I learnt that we must not allow other people's mistakes to ruin our lives."

Half an hour later the rest of the adults arrived at the hospital. They all rushed to his bedside. Ling headed straight for Bongo. His eyes were shut, but he was smiling. Ling sighed with relief. Then she bent over and put the backs of her tiny hands on his cheeks before reaching out to touch his hands. They were all cold. Rivers of tears replaced her sighs… Bongo had gone.

They took him back to the Mustard Garden and laid his body down on a bench in one of the stores. Then, in a silence only illuminated by the sparks of their spades, the three men dug a grave, a thousand kisses deep.

COMPOSING SYMPHONIES

Music - Compost - Death - Diet - Surrender
Acceptance - Kind thoughts - Nature - Gardening

Do not let death get in the way of your purpose.

An hour or so later, Sollie went to investigate a sawing noise: "Tom, we won't be needing that coffin. It's not what Bongo wanted."

Tom looked puzzled: "Why not?"

"You told me that Bongo said, 'I am a semiquaver'."

"That's right. He also told me that he was looking forward to becoming a young ancestor."

"When the time is right, I will tell you all about young ancestors. However, tonight, let us talk about semiquavers... Bongo loved and protected nature, so much so that he worked on making himself into a special type of compost whilst he was alive... This was to ensure that his death would not get in the way of his work."

"Really?"

"Yes. We discussed it many times. We share the same views. A solid wood coffin can take quite a long time to breakdown and impedes a dead person's entry into the soil. Bongo didn't want any delays. He was keen for his remains to break down and fertilise the soil as soon as his body was dead."

"Are you being serious?"

"Deathly. He was also keen to use his own body to teach people that there are two stages of surrender. The first surrender is during our working life, so that we work alongside God. The second surrender, before death, is to demonstrate our acceptance that we are a universal soul and belong to the whole. **However, if we are buried in a coffin, it suggests that, even after death, we imagine ourselves to be separate and possibly superior to the whole.** This is a 'grave' misjudgement and will delay our loved ones from seeing us in the forests and in the gardens. Can you recall his exact words?"

"He said, 'I am a semiquaver not just any old quaver... soon I will tremble, shake and vibrate.' What did he mean?"

"He was saying that everything in life and death vibrates in its own unique way. More importantly, how everything vibrates determines the happiness of the whole. It seems that Bongo wasn't just in a hurry to be broken down into compost. He wanted to make sure that his compost heap would make the type of vibrations and music that would contribute to a better world. Do you know why Bongo was always putting his ears to the ground?"

"I have no idea."

"He was learning how the soil vibrates. He was preparing for the day that his body would join the 'whole' under the ground. He knew that if he could influence the constituents of his own compost heap, he could influence how it vibrated and what type of music it would make when he died. This, he knew, would determine the colour and the fragrance of the trees and flowers that sprung from his remains."

"Tell me you are joking."

"I assure you that I am not. I think that he chose his final words with great care. He knew that compost is made up of vibrating quavers, semiquavers and crotchets like any other music. Bongo wanted to compose his own symphony in the soil before he became a semibreve or a whole note again."

"How did he intend to do that?"

"He became a vegetarian and filled his constitution with kind thoughts and deeds."

Tom was silent. He still wasn't sure whether Sollie was playing with him. Sollie could see that he wasn't convinced: "If you doubt me, ask yourself where the expression 'a heap of pleasure' comes from. If you still doubt me, ask yourself where the expression 'to compose a symphony' originates from."

> Spend more time in and around the soil, so that when the day arrives for you to enter it, you will find it full of friends.

LEGACIES

Sacrifices – The past – Death – Fate

> "To live in the hearts of those you love is not to die." The inscription on my father's remembrance page.

Then they headed back to the house, bonded in grief, like the trees stripped of all their leaves. They didn't feel like sleeping and decided to reminisce with some tea.

"You know, Tom, all my worthwhile achievements were borne out of my parent's love and sacrifices. A legacy that I was not aware of when it was being spun. That is because great legacies, like Emperor Huizong's, are not always obvious at the time; sometimes they only come to life in death."

"I understand that."

"Do you think that you could say a few words at the funeral that would help everyone understand how Bongo's life will do something similar?"

* * *

Bongo's send-off would be in two parts: a simple burial with the adults in the morning and a celebration of Bongo's life with the children, later in the day. Tom said his discourse in the manner of a songbird, exactly how Bongo would have delivered it.

"In the Scottish Hebrides the salmon needs high water to climb from the sea and up into the river so that they can spawn. If there is no rain, while waiting for the water to rise, many of the salmon are eaten by the grey seals. Here the timing in their fortunes is not of their own making. One could say it is their fate. However, as the salmon perish, the seals feast; and in death the scales are balanced. Pacific salmon carry nitrogen in their bodies from the sea. When they die, their bodies fertilise the forests with nutrients that the forest would not otherwise have received. This ensures trees like the red cedar grow to such amazing heights. I think that Bongo is about to do something similar here, for he was not a boy who would let death get in the way of his work."

SUPERSTITION AND BELIEF

Art - Transformation - Miracles - Persuasion

The next day Ajeet came to the garden to see Sollie. Over tea, he told him that in the city and the villages, the poorest and the elderly were now dying from lack of water and starvation.

"We need water, we need food and we need the birds to leave."

"Why do we need the birds to leave?"

"The people believe that the birds are the cause of all the problems."

"Please wait here for a moment. I have something that I want to show you."

Sollie returned to the table with the photographs of the birds crossing the seas of the world. Then he took Ajeet to the art studio where Ling had been working on the silk scroll. It was spread out on the floor.

Ajeet stooped to study it: "What does it mean?"

"It means that what is happening has been foreseen. Now we need the PM to see it. Then he will understand that he has a role to play in the mural's prophecy. I have heard that he is coming to Bhopal on Thursday to address the state."

"He is coming, but don't expect any miracles. You must understand that there are other pressing needs in this country. Unfortunately, drought and famine are not rare occurrences in India. He will express his sympathy and promise some assistance, but he will not solve a crisis of this magnitude."

"If you can secure me an audience with the PM, let me worry about how I teach him to perform miracles."

"I am not sure that I will be able to convince him to see you."

"Sorry, Ajeet, I didn't make myself clear; it is the other way around. You need to tell the PM that he needs to persuade me to see him."

OPINIONS AND BELIEFS

Identity - Influencing - Art - Fear v possibility
Incompletion - Opportunity - Intervention

Sollie spent the next day studying the Prime Minister. He wondered, 'How does this man want to be remembered? What are his weaknesses and his fears? How exactly is he convinced? Is this man truly altruistic or does he desire recognition? What loss would hurt him most?'

It was evident that the PM was a religious man. Sollie knew that this would help him. A man with no beliefs is a difficult man to influence. However, a man who is a believer of one thing can be persuaded to be the believer of another. After just four hours, Sollie had seen enough. Now he felt that he knew what would make the PM flower and what would make him wilt.

Sollie's next important task was to talk to Ajeet again: "When the PM has seen how serious the drought and famine is, you can bring him to the Mustard Garden to meet his saviour. Inform him that we have unearthed an ancient piece of art that seems to explain what is happening."

"But you told me that the painting is only a few days old."

"True. However, the silk scroll that it is painted on isn't."

"And after that?"

"We set out our demands for the liberation of the widows."

"Then?"

"Then, I suspect that the PM will ask if he can take the silk scroll away with him to show it to Sudarshan his sadhu. Sudarshan will be convinced because the art on the scroll depicts what is painted on the cave walls under the lake."

"How do you know that?"

"The art on the cave walls under the lakebed is tattooed on Sudarshan's back."

"What do you hope for after that?"

"We want the PM to see that the canvas is not complete, and therefore the script doesn't have an ending yet. We want him to believe that there is an opportunity for a personal intervention."

THE REAL FAMILY TREE

Ancestors - Miracles - 'Past-Present-Future' - Beyond mindfulness
Overlooked - Not valued - Measures - Immortality - Legacy

> They say that jade will give you immortality, a mystical aura and enable you to talk to the Gods. Continue your ancestors' work and you can experience all this and more.

Sollie was talking to his pollinators; swinging elephant trunks were not going to halt his teaching plan.

"When we were planning the development of the Mustard Garden, I told you that history and genealogy were activities that would make our home fragrant and saintly. I also promised you miracles. Today I am going to tell you how... Previously, we discussed how we should live mindfully and in the present. Today we are going to discuss how we live 'beyond mindfulness'.

Simply put, this means 'linking the past, the present and the future together'. Beyond mindfulness takes us to resurrection and immortality.

"However, before you do this, you must review the makeup of your family tree. You are a universal soul. Therefore, everything in the universe that is dead is your ancestor; this includes your great grandmother and everyone else's. The aim is to weave your ancestors' work into yours. Picking up your ancestors' threads goes beyond venerating them, an occasional visit to their burial ground or displaying their keepsakes and photograph albums in your home. True genealogy is about discovering and bringing back to life sacrifices, hopes, unfinished and overlooked work from the past. The objective is to open up a relationship where 'the dead and the living' share each other's poetry, hopes and dinner. The aim is also to discover something that you can pour yourself into.

"The first task is to choose which ancestor(s) you are going to incorporate into your life. The options are endless. Pick up the thread of the famous, the overlooked, the marginalised or the misunderstood. Alternatively, you might want to choose a young person cut off in their prime. This is why Bongo said that he was looking forward to becoming a young ancestor."

"This thinking should also give rise to the question, **What must I do myself, so that others want to continue to turn the pages of my life's work after I am gone?** If you find all of this difficult to comprehend, just remind yourself of what we are already doing. We have picked up Emperor Huizong's thread. Soon we will make the birds on his canvas come to life. This should serve as a reminder that when someone is overlooked or not valued in one lifetime, it does not mean that they will be overlooked in another."

Be the waterer of the trees that your ancestors have been waiting to see blossom.

LOVING SACRIFICES

Talking to the dead - Gratitude - Fear of death
Resurrection - Eternal life - Albatross

> When you see something soaring to a great height, know that sometimes it has been built out of the sacrifices and love of others.

Life after death isn't the lightest of soufflés! Most of them left for a tea break after that… except Apolline.

"What did you mean when you referred to sharing your poetry and your thinking with your belated loved ones and ancestors?"

"I meant talk to your dead loved ones and ancestors directly."

"Surely it is too late for that?"

"It is never too late to thank, forgive or show gratitude; these words are not bound by time."

"How?"

"At a spiritualist church or séance, they say that a 'spiritual medium' can relay messages to you from the dead. It is not my intention to try and do that… I want you to speak to your ancestors and dead loved ones yourself. When you experienced the 'heart meditation', you were able to love, dance and hold your belated loved ones close to you again. You told me that you held your frail, old grandmother in your arms."

"Don't worry. I won't forget that."

"The 'resurrection' that I am about to tell you about is called 'loving sacrifices'. It is for the departed who made sacrifices for you when you were a child. Sacrifices and acts of love that you may have been too young to appreciate. Do you remember when I said that you should not seek other people's approval?"

"I won't forget that in a hurry either."

"What I should have said is, **Don't seek approval from the living; seek it from the dead,** particularly those that helped you as a child."

By now Apolline's bottom was barely on the seat: "What do I need to do?"

"Write a story of your early life… This is something that everyone should do. You can put your story to music, write it, paint it, sew it or knit it. Very quickly, certain sentences will jump off the pages and balls of wool will unravel. The love and sacrifices that were made for you will jump out at you. After that, you may be left with a burning desire to say thank you."

"How do I say thank you?"

"Imagine those who loved you and who made sacrifices for you are standing in front or above you. Reach out to them. Speak to them and express your heartfelt gratitude.

"Then have faith."

"Faith in what?"

"Faith that if you can look up and speak to the dead. The deceased must be able to look down and see you thanking them. The symbol of this faith is the albatross … That what can go one way, must be able to go the other. As I am fond of saying,

There are no sacrifices, only falling leaves.

LEARNT BEHAVIOUR

The gift of life – Forgiveness – Expressing feelings

Apolline was back at Sollie's table the following day: "I have not stopped thinking about my childhood, eternal life and communicating with the dead!"

"Good. Perhaps you realise now that making sacrifices and exercising tough love is not always easy. Therefore, sometimes those nurturing us make mistakes. Maybe your father was just trying to do his best?"

"What could have gone wrong?"

"**Sometimes important things like 'demonstrating how to love' are not passed down. Perhaps your father wasn't taught 'how to demonstrate his love' by his own parents.** However, this does not mean that he didn't love you. He may have just kept his love inside and was unable to express it externally. If you do feel hurt and upset, remember this… **Your parents may have left you feeling unloved, but they did give you the wonderful gift of life.** They also helped you become a lovely person."

She wasn't sure what to say. He smiled and broke the silence for her: "Remember, you only ever have to forgive yourself. If you cannot forgive your father, just say, **Thank you for looking after me as a child, or thank you for the wonderful gift of life**."

PARENTAL PRESSURE

Careers - Expectation - Success - Vessels

Apolline wiped a tear: "On reflection, I think that my father did love me, he just expected too much."

"As I said, mistakes are made."

"What do I need to do in order to avoid making the same mistakes?"

"Most parents want the best for their children. Many parents tell their children that they will be successful. However, some children may find the weight of this expectation suffocating. Sometimes children suffer from the opposite. If you speak to Ling, she will tell you that her mother did not want her to be a success. It seems that expectation is a disease that many parents suffer from. However, it is their illness. **The road to happiness starts with the courage to stand up to parents with misguided expectations.**" Then there was a long pause: "Of course, I could be wrong."

"How might you be wrong?"

"There is always the possibility that your father was trying to help you become an amazing violinist for a reason."

PIED PIPERS

Mystery - Logic - Effort - Faith v belief - Prayers - Leadership

The Prime Minister would speak to the people of Bhopal at the Lal parade ground. The day before his planned speech, Ajeet took him on a tour of the city and surrounding countryside. After his tour, he came to a swift conclusion. The three trusty weapons of logic, effort and faith that he had used so successfully all his life were not the answer. The answer appeared to be a mystery.

"Ajeet, what would you do if you were in my position?"

"I think that we have to find someone whose weapon isn't logic; a mystic to fight mystery, someone like a Pied Piper."

"What is a Pied Piper?"

"It is a legend from the Middle Ages. It tells the tale of a small town in Germany that was plagued by rats. The authorities hired a Pied Piper wearing multi-coloured clothing to clear the vermin. When he did so, the town failed to pay him and so he used his magic flute to take all the town's children away."

"I think that you are going to tell me that you know where one exists."

"I may."

"Does he have a magic flute?"

"No, but he does blow a conch and wear a strange multi-coloured coat."

The PM did not blink: "Arrange a meeting."

PRESIDENTS

Risk - Luck - War - Inspiration - Leadership - Misunderstandings
Disputes - Judgment - Reflection - Of no mind

True Facts

If you look at Russian history, you will see that normally presidents and tsars are sent to Siberia. They do not normally go there willingly. However, in September 2012 a Russian president visited an endangered crane sanctuary in Yamal, Siberia and did something quite extraordinary. He played a principal role in a project called, 'The Flight of Hope.'

Hunting had reduced the numbers of adult cranes able to pass on information of migratory routes. The Siberian sanctuary exists to train the birds to navigate the sky before they attempt their winter migration to India and China. The president went up into the sky in a motorized hang-glider. He led the way so that a flock of Siberian white cranes could follow him in their final practice before they were released. The cranes now remain under the supervision of the Russian presidential administration.

When the PM arrived at the Mustard Garden, Sollie suggested that they take tea on the lawn. After a few minutes, Yutika arrived with some mystical tea that followed Emperor Huizong's instruction.

Sollie handed the PM a photograph of a Russian president flying in the sky: "If it eases your mind, don't think that you will be the only presidential leader to be involved in this mystery."

"What do you mean?"

True Facts

"In 2012 a Russian president went up into the sky and piloted a motorised hang-glider to help the Siberian cranes on their migratory paths. If you go back to 1963, you will find a French president heavily involved in the closure of the Lascaux caves, which the French government still guard over today. If you must go back even further, look at Emperor Huizong, emperor of the Song dynasty who reigned from 1100 to 1126. It was this emperor that painted the Auspicious CranesC. A copy of his original is hanging on one of the walls in this house. These are not stories, these are facts."

"What might my role be?"

"Sometimes it is not enough for a leader to secure the votes of their supporters; they also need the support of their opposers. This can only be achieved when a leader puts their hopes, politics, experience, knowledge and even any attempt at reflection to the side... **This is unlearning and being in a state of no mind.** It is this that delivers the response that brings all misunderstandings and disputes to a close."

A KINGMAKER

Difficult pasts - Equality - Courage - Rapport

Knowledge - Beliefs - Experience - Transformation

Sollie poured more tea: "For this reason, you must be neither politician, Prime Minister nor servant. You must be a kingmaker."

"Surely I couldn't do more than place myself at the service of India's people?"

"I am not talking about the people of India. I am referring to the people of Bhopal. They have an 11th century king that they can relate to: Raja Bhoj. It would not be difficult for them to support an event that built on Raja Bhoj's legend."

"You mean I use their history to create a brighter future?"

"Yes. You use the same formula that a therapist uses with a person who has experienced a troubled past. **You don't focus on understanding the problem; you focus on helping the people see how their past can be a catalyst for a**

brighter future. A future that they could not enjoy if they had not experienced their past. This will establish rapport. Momentum and spades will follow."

"Is there anything else that a kingmaker must do?"

"Set the widows free. It is this that will make you truly majestic."

The PM peered into the bottom of his tea cup. He wasn't worried about being poisoned. He did, however, consider that the tea might contain some mysterious, persuasive qualities.

Sollie seemed to read his mind: "Now please come with me, I have something mysterious to show you; something that perhaps only a kingmaker will understand."

TRANSFORMATIVE ART

God within – Incompletion

For mystery and superstition are not out of the same jar.

Sollie led the PM away from the lawn and into the studio. Here he lifted Ling's painted silk scroll onto a long table and carefully rolled it out.

The PM appeared to be impressed; his eyebrows straightened. Then the clicking of a latch startled him and broke his study. It was Ling and Komodo.

The PM smiled warmly: "Please come in. Tell me what you know about this work of art."

Ling did the talking: "It is an ancient canvas whose art originates from the highest source."

"What is the art's significance?"

"It is a painted scroll that can be worn as an emperor's ceremonial coat. It also has a story to tell. It will reveal different secrets when it is experienced from a variety of perspectives."

Suddenly, the PM stepped back from the table; one might have thought that he had been bitten. It seemed that the prominent saffron, indigo and red colours in the painting matched those of his own tunic and scarf. Mercifully, and contrary to his wishes, the painting pulled him back. Now his face was merely a centimetre away from the brushstrokes and the warmer pinks and violets. However, there was no time to protest; he was immediately tossed onto the frothy waves of the sea. At first he was washed ashore to witness the joyful widows. Then, before he had time to spit out the salty water, he was dropped in front of the domed stupas at Sanchi. The first objective had been achieved; he had been poured into the painting. Now they had to hope that the light in Ling's brushes would help him see his God within.

Then, Komodo disturbed the hypnosis and turned towards the door: "I would like to leave now."

The PM blocked his path: "Before you leave, young man, I have a question for you. In the bottom right-hand corner of the scroll, I can see the faint outline of a little frog with a rucksack on its back. The frog seems to have been rubbed out, leaving a gap. Can you explain what this means?"

"The gap is there so that another person can add to the story or change the ending... That other person could be you, Sir!"

"What does the faint outline of the frog and its rucksack represent?"

Komodo clambered onto the table before whispering into the PM's ear, "... and that is a very important message."

Ling took over again. She showed the PM the coloured ribbons tucked into the borders of the scroll. Then she unfastened the silk buttons to reveal the openings for a person's head and arms: "Now, if you will permit me, I will help you wear the scroll as a ceremonial coat. Then you will see how it may have adorned a great Chinese emperor hundreds of years ago."

The PM nodded his agreement, and she proceeded to dress him in the scroll. This impressed him. However, delight turned to astonishment when he lifted up one of the flaps to reveal Sudarshan's wrist charms. "Tell me Sollie, what do you make of all of this?"

"I think that the birds are on a pilgrimage to honour their leader, a leader who represents the birds and the spiritually enlightened. A leader depicted on the cave walls as 'The Birdman of Lascaux'."

"Do you think that the widows will be freed from their suffering during this gathering of the birds?"

"I don't know. I assume that you will do all that you can. However, there will be others who will try and ensure that the widows' suffering continues. For let us not forget that it is in the name of religion that the widows are imprisoned. However, you must know that Emperor Huizong did not set out to help the widows specifically. His aim is just to make the poor rich. My mission is to help him achieve this. When I stumbled across the widows' plight, I realised that they could be the first battalion in the spiritual army needed to achieve his goal."

"How rich will the poor become?"

"Wealthier than anyone could imagine. You must understand that when Emperor Huizong referred to the poor, he meant the spiritually poor, regardless of how much money they have."

"You should also be aware that the gathering of the birds that you are witnessing is not the main event; it is merely a test flight for a bigger pilgrimage. A practice run for the birds and an act of inspiration to show someone else the way. When a larger army of spiritual teachers has been recruited, there will be a superflight and an act of sacrifice like no other. It will be an event that demonstrates that our well-being and our happiness are dependent on the birds and the trees. Prehistoric star charts in the caves of Lascaux tell us this will take place in half a century."

"I would like to take the scroll away with me. Be assured that I will look at all your requests."

And God has left his messages in the caves and in the trees.

CIRCLES OF LOVE

With that the PM departed, and Ling and Sollie were left alone in the room together.

"Perhaps you should try the painted scroll on, Sollie."

"Why?"

"I would like to see what you look like when you arc wearing it."

Ling stood on a little stool and helped him put his arms through the holes. Then she smoothed the cloth over his chest.

"You taught Bruno some amazing things about love. Why didn't you share those teachings with me?"

"I was sure that he would pass them on to you."

"Perhaps I need a practical lesson." With that she pressed two of her tiny fingers on the inside of his leg and made some circles.

"But I thought that you were happy with Bruno?"

She blew out some hot air: "I have been on the same diet for too long; I need some chilli in my soup." She pulled herself up and sat astride his left leg: "No one needs to know."

Ten minutes later they lay on their backs flushed and breathless.

"Well, you did promise some of that in your advert Sollie. It seems that you finally delivered." He laughed. She squeezed his nose: "But never tell Bruno. He did say to me that if another man tried to kiss me, he would chop them up. Although I am sure that he was only joking."

"Thank you for telling me that. However, I don't think that he was."

SMOKE AND FLAMES

Adversity - Decisions

They heard the birds squawking before they saw the fire. The orange flames were coming from the direction of the children's sleeping accommodation. Sollie looked out of the window: "Oh my God." He immediately grabbed his conch and led the charge through the smoke. They shooed the children out as quickly as they could. Mercifully, it seemed that no one was hurt.

Then they realised that Bruno was missing… Ling's heart sank. Sollie closed his eyes: 'I did this! Bruno must have found out. Now he has tried to set the children on fire in his rage.' He motioned for the girls to stay with the children and grabbed Tom's arm: "We need to go and search for Bruno." It only took a minute to find him. He was lying in the burnt-out long grass behind the children's block… lifeless and charred from head to foot. Bruno hadn't attempted to set fire to the children; he had set fire to himself.

For the next seven nights, Sollie could not sleep and was deeply troubled. He concluded that he was culpable. Would he sink into a black hole or would he redouble his efforts and try and complete the mission? **Sollie's future, and those that relied on him, would not be determined by what had happened but by his response to adversity.**

ANCIENT SECRETS

Sudarshan entered the PM's chamber and studied the scroll spread out on the floor. "The canvas picture tells of a great story. Of an event that has happened before, many thousands of years ago. An event to be repeated. One which will sweep in great change."

"Are we safe, or will we perish?"

"Our fate is not clear because a gap has been left in the painting. What happens next depends on the courage of those that can influence the outcome."

"Sudarshan, whilst you are here, I would like to take the opportunity to thank you for your guidance and your sacrifices."

Sudarshan laughed laconically: "Is that what you believe? That one sadhu after another spends his life in isolation and silence outside a cave, in return for a few charas? Let me ask you a question. What do you think the caves in Bhopal, Australia and France have in common?"

The PM grimaced. He detected impudence. "I believe that they are all UNESCO World Heritage Sites."

"And do you think UNESCO is an organisation that preserves historical sites or a brotherhood that protects ancient secrets? If you guess correctly, you might understand why my ancestors and I have devoted our lives to protecting these ancient caves."

The PM was speechless and backed himself against the wall. Sudarshan moved towards him: "It is time that you understood something else. I didn't work for you; you worked for me. You gave me protection whilst I carried out my work. However, I no longer need you." At which point Sudarshan left the room.

KARMA AND AUSPICIOUS LANDINGS

Death

Ling and Sollie were discussing the PM's visit.

"Sollie, do you think that the PM will free the widows from their suffering if the famine and drought ends?"

"Yes. When your body dies your spirit will remain alive. It will simply jump out of one body and into a new one. You must ask yourself if your wrong-doings and good work will die with that body or jump on your spirit's back and accompany you in your next life. When Komodo whispered into the PM's ear, and told him about the rubbed-out frog; he suggested that only by putting his wrongs right would he be able to empty his burdens and enjoy a fresh start."

However, before they could continue with their conversation, the Mustard Garden became a flurry of activity. It started with Yutika. "Sollie, you have an email from China. It appears that the roofs of the Imperial Palace and the Liaoning Provincial Museum in China are covered in cranes."

Then Hubert arrived: "Rishi and Dominique have just contacted me. The cranes are dancing around the Kakadu and Lascaux caves."

Ajeet put his phone down: "I have just been informed that millions of migrating birds have landed on the dry lakebed. The people don't know whether to stay and watch or run for their lives."

The last person to run frantically into the room was Apolline. Not because she had received a message, but because she hadn't: "Has anyone seen Olivia?"

No one had, so Apolline took another look at Olivia's room. A few minutes later she returned with a note in her hand and tears in her eyes.

Sollie put her arm around her "What does it say?"

Apolline did not reply; she just handed him the note... 'Don't fear for me... Just follow me.'

A waterfall of tears cascaded down: "Olivia has departed and deceived me."

However, before she had the opportunity to soak in her misery, a surprise call came in from Rishi. "Apolline, I have just seen some cave paintings in Kakadu that suggest that you should go to Sanchi."

THE THREE STONE UMBRELLAS/CHATAVALI AT SANCHI TEMPLE

ACCEPTANCE

They decided that they would all go to Sanchi. It was approximately 45 kilometres away from Bhopal on a road cutting through the wheat fields.

Sollie sat in the back with Ajeet: "Do you think that you could arrange a television crew to be present? I think that the world may want to share the forthcoming event."

Ninety minutes later they turned off the main road and parked the truck opposite the Sanchi museum. When they arrived at the temples, the grounds and domes were covered in strutting cranes. They tried to move forward but to no avail; the cranes were too big and too numerous to argue with. Ling jumped up in order to be seen: "I think that this might be the prelude to the big bird dance that Bongo told Komodo about. I have a transcript here."

PREPARING TO DANCE

The trouble with most humans is that they don't study birds carefully enough. They see a bird, try and guess its breed and then they look away. Rarely do they wonder what the bird might be up to. People assume that humans are the only ones that practise in front of the mirror before they attend a dance. However, keen observers would know that the sparrows like to take a bath and that the magpie goes in search of a tiara before a big night out. Listen carefully and you will hear them practising the singing of a dance-floor anthem. Watch carefully and you will see them shuffle their feet, gyrate their beaks and shake their wings. I saw and heard all this. Therefore, I have no doubt that they are preparing for a big event and a celebratory dance.

As she finished her recital, three bright stars appeared over the temple. Then a large flock of cranes took off and filled the sky. After that their attention was drawn to the stone staircase that ran around the stupa's dome. It was being used as a processional route by some snowy-white cranes. Tom suddenly held Apolline tightly… for the cranes appeared to be carrying Olivia. They stopped when they reached the three stone chatavali or umbrellas, Olivia appeared to grab one. At which point, something Olivia had said a long time ago came into Apolline's mind: 'I will make sure that I take an umbrella to my own funeral.'

A minute later, Olivia was no longer recognisable. Now the whites of her eyes were yellow and the blue in her eyes was black. Now she was a bird's head on a stick and her true identity was apparent. Olivia was indeed 'The Bird Woman of Lascaux, just as the drawing had been depicted on the caves of Lascaux 17,000 years ago. The birds, it seemed, were here to honour her. The birds raised her into the air. Then, in a blink, Olivia disappeared. This was the cue for the cranes to flutter to the floor and begin their dancing… Wow… how they danced! They threw themselves in the air. They arched their wings. They bobbed like buoys on the waves of the stormiest seas.

Then the sky filled with the sound of more flapping wings, although this time it wasn't in Bhopal. It was in the southern hemisphere and northern pacific. It wasn't the cranes taking flight either. This was their distant cousins; the albatrosses. They took to the sky before setting off in defiance of their normal flying patterns; those that should have flown north and clockwise went anti-clockwise. Those that should have flown south also flew the other way.

Sollie's phone rang. He moved away from the throng. The PM spoke to him: "What are you thinking, Mr Sollie?"

"I am imagining a wonderful future for Bhopal. I see a light show on the city's two great lakes. I can smell donuts and taste candyfloss. I hear trainloads of pilgrims and tourists pulling into Bhopal's train station. I have also seen the albatross fly in the opposite direction; this tells me that the fortunes of the widows will soon be turning too."

* * *

It was the frogs that convinced the PM that change was on its way. They surged onto the streets in anticipation of the rain that was about to cascade from the sky. His driver took him to the lakes and stopped the car on the bridge. The rain started to fall. He knew that it wouldn't stop until the cave entrance on the lakebed of Bhopal disappeared from view. As it did, the sky went black. The birds were on the move; they were going home.

THE MAKING OF A GENTLE GIANT

Surrender - Sacred things - Diet - Religion

> "For as long as men massacre animals, they will kill each other. Indeed, he who sows the seed of murder and pain cannot reap joy and love."
>
> Pythagoras

Back at the Mustard Garden's smaller lake, the water was also lapping once more against its bank. Sollie was standing at its edge when his thoughts were disturbed by the sound of some oars scraping the gravely bottom. A blurry figure sitting in a small wooden boat glided towards him.

"Parminder, what a wonderful surprise. Where are you heading?"

Parminder shook his big, duck-like feet and walked slowly towards him: "I have come to see you. I have a proposition… You once told me that you hoped that everything at the Mustard Garden could be sustainable and continue after you had gone. My proposal is simple. I would like to move into the Mustard Garden."

Sollie stared at him in bewilderment: "Why would you want to do that?"

"My wealth is obscuring my happiness. I want it to be put to a better use.

"I would like to hand all my money over to the Mustard Garden so that more children and widows can be helped. However, in exchange for your lease, I am handing my palace over to you personally. You can do what you want with it."

"Do you want to manage the Mustard Garden, Parminder?"

Parminder's laughter made some of the fishes jump out of the water: "Not personally. However, I am sure my management team would like to assist the pollinators. I was rather hoping that Apolline would become the manager."

"I think it might be better if you put Ling in charge. Apolline needs to prepare herself for some other very important work. Now tell me, Parminder, what do you want to do personally?"

"I would like to live at the Mustard Garden and work as a leaf sweeper."

"Are you sure that you don't want anything else in exchange for the palace?"

"Perhaps you could share with me the recipe for your woodland soup?"

"It would be a pleasure. The recipe reads the same in all languages and faiths."

"Some people might not wish to eat a kangaroo because they are kind of cute. However, that is not a good reason for keeping it off the barbeque. Korean folklore regards the tiger as a divine spirit; the Himalayan mountain people feel likewise about the snow leopard. Lower down the mountains, elephants are loved by the Hindus. However, many Chinese are happy to see them slaughtered for the ivory that they believe will bring them prestige and good luck. Tell me what good luck might come from someone else's pain and suffering?" Sollie cleared his throat before continuing.

"Christianity associates snakes with the devil. In India snakes are celebrated at festivals and adorn the Gods. Jewish faith, however, forbids the eating of those things that crawl on the floor. The Christians will eat any part of the cow. The Jews will only eat half of the cow because they are prohibited from eating the gelatine and the hind-quarter. However, the Hindus will not eat any beef for they deem the cow to be sacred. It seems that some Jews would rather sacrifice an Arab than eat shellfish, whilst some Muslims would eat a Christian, Jew or Hindu before they ate some pork. In parts of central Africa and Asia, people believe that when you eat the flesh of a great animal like a lion, gorilla or tiger, you also consume the animal's spirit and that this makes you powerful and indomitable.

"WHAT IS THIS MADNESS? Is it so difficult to comprehend that all animals are sacred? Can we not understand that no living thing is superior to another, that comparison leads to hierarchies and that hierarchies lead to misery? Is it not obvious that a human's indifference to certain animals is the catalyst for their indifference to the suffering of their fellowmen? Therefore, I conclude that my woodland soup's recipe is simple… All animals are sacred, none are to be hurt and none are to be eaten. After that you can eat whatever takes your fancy…providing it is good for you."

PARMINDER'S TRANSFORMATION

Needs – Anger – Meditation – Sacredness – Kind thoughts v actions

Every time you have a kind thought, a pigeon turns into a dove.

Then Sollie exchanged his growl for a gentler voice: "Now Parminder, perhaps you can tell me what transformed you?"

"By sweeping the leaves back into the forest, **I have learnt that if I give up what I don't need, I will acquire those things that I do.** I have also learnt that I should not try and control my anger; what I need to do is prevent it from arising. For this reason, I must practise meditation."

"Your thinking is enlightened."

"I know. However, I now need to exchange my good intentions and kind thoughts for good actions."

Sollie tutted: "Those comments are less enlightened."

"What do you mean?"

"Don't exchange good intentions and kind thoughts for good actions... COMPLEMENT good intentions and kind thoughts with good actions. Now you have three arrows in your quiver."

Then Parminder took a notepad out: "I have made some basic calculations. It seems that we can fund about 60,000 widows and about the same number of children."

"Parminder, please tell me, if you do become like King Sagara and have 60,000 children at your beckoning, what will you teach them?"

"I will put my energy into teaching them that all the world is sacred. I will encourage them to search for God and work in partnership with him. From this, everything else will flow."

THE HONEY BADGER'S STRIPES

Surrender – Inspiration

Many of your small successes are borne out of discipline. All your real successes are borne out of surrender. It is surrender that will make you loving.

Parminder also passed Sollie a letter for Apolline. She lit a candle and lay on her bed to read it.

THE HONEY BADGER

I was striped like the honey badger, springy like the hare, empty like the hollow, angry like the bear.
My sett was full of gold coins, my larder full of meats, my thoughts were full of wonders yet my heart was blocked with grief.
My head was in the beehive, my direction unknown and fraught,
I was choking on the snake bones of the life that I had bought.
Then I grabbed a sweeping brush and swept away my wrath.
No longer was I skulking along the honey badger's path.
I woke to find my stripes had gone; my snare had come unlocked.
No longer am I cunning or thinking like the fox.

Parminder

A PROCESSION OF ELEPHANTS

Inspiration

Soon afterwards there was a formal announcement that Parminder was to exchange a life of servants for a life of service. It seemed that all of India wanted to celebrate with him. There was to be the mother of all parades and parties, the likes of which Bhopal had never seen before. It was to start and finish at the Mustard Garden.

On the day of the parade there was a carnival of colour. It started with a procession of turbaned elephants strolling through the Mustard Garden's entrance gates, just as Sollie had predicted. They were decked out in green, cerise and yellow sashes. Marching bands filled the streets. Monkeys found a vantage point at the top of the tallest trees and tigers came to the edge of the forest to inquire of the noise.

Parminder was forced to be the focus of attention for one last time. They tried to sit him on one of the elephants but he refused; now he had exchanged his finery for a saffron robe. He walked along the path, and the huge crowds lining the route saluted him. Sollie's face was a picture of glee and colour too: 'Sollie, I think that your mission is going to be a great success… The finishing line appears to be in view,' he said to himself.

PARMINDER'S LOVING PLACE

Parminder chose a sweeping brush. From that day on, he pootled along no faster than a beetle.

He brushed the ground in front of him before he ever planted a foot.

This ensured that not even the tiniest insect was ever stepped upon.

Indeed, as Apolline had written, everything in his life had become precious;

Nothing was harmed and everything was helped on its way.

Parminder had found a way to live, a place where he belonged and a loving place to stay.

PARTINGS

Leadership - Renewal - Loss

They were joyful. They had been rewarded for pursuing what they needed to do instead of pursuing what they wanted to have.

Sollie tweaked Ling's nose: "When I leave, you will be in charge."

"You don't seem very happy for me."

"I do not doubt that you can do the job. I am concerned that you have aspired to a position that might make you lonely and melt your sweetness."

She kissed him on the lips: "Don't worry about me."

Then Sollie approached Tom, who hugged him as firmly as he could: "You can rely on me Sollie. I will be there for her, whatever happens."

Then Sollie sought out Yutika, who was sitting alone at the dining room table. He pulled up a chair and sat beside her. Her heart knew what he would say.

"Yutika, the time has come for me to leave. Parminder's resources are much greater than mine..." Yutika didn't respond. They sat together in an uncomfortable silence for a while, and then he walked to the door. He headed for the garden. The rain was falling like noisy tin tacks onto metal tables.

Komodo was dancing in the puddles. He approached Sollie with an earnest question: "Why do some trees lose their leaves?"

"Trees don't lose their leaves. They surrender them in autumn and new ones return to them in the spring."

"Why is that?"

"The falling leaves tell us that we must learn to let the things that we love go. That no matter how much pain and hurt we experience…there will be renewal and other good things to look forward to. The falling and renewal of the leaves is another way of telling us that, **Pain is unavoidable, but suffering is a choice.**" However, when it came to saying goodbye to the rest of the children, in addition to his hugs, he left a brief message. One that he had learnt from his own father.

SHEPHERDING

Most things would like to be set free, even if they enjoy the feeling of being watched over. You rarely see the shepherd herding up the sheep. They prefer to stand at the gate waiting for the flock to come home. This way the shepherd has time to repair some of the broken fences that circle the earth.

Therefore, from this day on, shepherding is what I will do. Whether you stay or whether you stray, I will always be looking out for you. Wherever I am, I will always be waiting for you and I will always be here for you. Whilst I am doing this, I will try and make a small contribution, so that the world is a better place for you and all who follow.

Sollie

RAIN-SOAKED, MUDDY ROADS

Judging - Coincidences - Calling - Risk

Sollie walked towards the nearest village. On the way, he came across a familiar face, still dressed in vivid orange and sitting on the bonnet of his car. It was Souvik, the taxi driver who had brought him to Bhopal when he had first arrived in India.

"Souvik, what are you doing here?"

"Don't you remember, you told me to wait?"

Sollie laughed. Souvik told him to climb into the taxi whilst he packed his luggage in the boot. Then they headed for the airport. The rain was falling like ropes, and the road soon began to resemble a muddy field. At the point that he could no longer see out of the window, Souvik stopped the car and joined Sollie in the back of the taxi.

He coughed: "Did you enjoy your stay in prison Sollie?"

"I did thank you. I enjoyed a brief sojourn there after some false allegations that my protests were seditious."

"Were they?"

"They might have been. However, they were not my protests; they were the children's."

"I suppose that going to prison wasn't such a bad thing."

"What do you mean?"

"If you hadn't gone to prison, Gringe wouldn't have been able to help you... Without his help you wouldn't have met Dabeet and Ajeet. If you hadn't met Ajeet, you would never have met the Prime Minister. It was important that we arranged your stay in prison."

Sollie stood up and hit his head on the car roof: "What?! Was it you that made up those allegations?"

"Calm down. Everything worked out well, didn't it?"

"I suppose that it was you that left the motorbike?"

"I suppose that it may have been."

Sollie burst out laughing, and they both hugged each other.

"Sollie, if you don't mind, can you tell me how you acquired your limp?"

"I climbed a very tall tree in order to help some starving chicks. Then I fell.

I spent the next 20 years in a wheelchair, until I had a life-changing operation."

"Oh. I'm sorry."

"Don't be. Everything turned out wonderfully. Instead of going to school, I convalesced in a woodchopper's cottage, deep in the forest. I wouldn't swap my education for the world."

"One last question. How did you trick Parminder into giving you his palace?"

"There was no deception. I merely helped him remove his anxiety. He wanted to express his gratitude. If I hadn't helped him, he wouldn't be so happy now."

"But you have acquired his burden!"

"No. In fact, I have already sold it. I only have the money. And as long as I am not attached to it, I can enjoy it. Besides, if you want a thousand wives, you need to find a way of paying for their upkeep."

"But you could have taught Parminder to not be attached to his wealth. Then he could have kept his palace and his happiness."

"Possibly. However, sometimes we have to have the courage to let go of our attachments to truly understand that we can live with or without them."

By this time the rain had lightened, and Souvik decided to carry on driving. He dropped Sollie off at the airport, and they waved fond farewells. All seemed good until Sollie approached the security gates… When he fished into his bag, it seemed that his passport had been stolen. So had his money. With his loose pocket change he decided to take a taxi back to the Mustard Garden. This time Souvik wouldn't be waiting for him.

EMPEROR HUIZONG'S HELPERS

When he arrived at the Mustard Garden, he walked into the main house. There was no one around. There was, however, something missing; something dramatic. He stared in disbelief. The painting, *Auspicious Cranes,* had either disappeared or been modified. Was the painting that stood in front of him his copy? It appeared to have the same frame. The palace roof was still there; however, there were no longer any cranes. Painted on a lawn, in front of the palace and sitting in a circle, were some very familiar faces. They were all dressed in red, silk kimono-like gowns. Embroidered on the back of their robes were cranes, ancient teapots and inscriptions in Mandarin that said,

Emperor Huizong's Helpers – Make Art and Tea, Not War.

Some of the faces sitting in the circle were so familiar that it beggared belief. One had Gringe's stubble, another resembled Shimla's husband. Of course, there were some that he did not recognise; a very old couple with creamy-white hair and an old man with a nose not unlike Apolline's. The one that popped his buttons wore a huge mop of dark, frizzy hair not unlike the unruly bush that usually sat on Gabriel's head. In the middle of the circle sat an imposing figure. He wore a funny black hat with side flaps; it was Emperor Huizong himself.

INKY EYES AND DISCIPLES

Forgiveness - Deceit - Devotion

Sollie was standing outside the main house when he heard some hypnotic music coming from the direction of Yutika's bedroom window. He decided that he would creep up on her. By standing on his tiptoes, he managed to haul himself up and rest his arms on the window ledge. Yutika was now partially in view, sitting at the end of the bed. Everything else that Sollie witnessed was unfamiliar.

Yutika's once beautiful, long, dark hair sat on the table in a waxy pile. Now her head was bald, save for a few tufts. Sollie watched in disbelief as she dipped her left hand into a bowl of yellow saffron and smeared it on her face. He winced as she grabbed one of her remaining tufts of hair and pulled it out with her hand.

'AGH!' He turned away. 'How could she?' However, she wasn't finished; her right hand dipped into a bowl of red chilli powder. She rubbed it ferociously into her now hairless head.

Sollie pulled himself up the ledge a little further. As he did, Yutika stood up before disappearing out of sight for a few minutes. She returned carrying a small shrine. However, this wasn't the one that they kept at the Mustard Garden. He had not seen this one before. Yutika placed it on the table in front of her. In the middle of the shrine was a green, red and blue altar. Standing in front of it was an idol; a sinister-looking female God. He had not seen that either… but it did push something to the forefront of his mind… a little matter that had upset Ling: 'Ling, why are you so tearful?'… 'It's the idol that we were making, it has disappeared!'

Yutika still had her back to Sollie when she performed the next ritual. What he had always assumed was the embodiment of innocence was provocatively uncloaking before him. The belt around her gown was loosened before it slowly fell to the floor. What he had previously resisted was now naked in front of him: slender, straight-backed and shimmering. He was left motionless with wonder, astonishment and finally fright. He realized what was happening. He recalled one of her jail visits, when she had expressed an unhealthy interest in 'total commitment'. 'Oh my God. It is my fault. It was me that taught her about non-attachment and wrenching your hair out,' he cried out to himself.

Her next ritual confirmed his fears. Whilst stepping into a metal bucket, her right arm lent over to pick up a large, green jug. She poured the milky contents over her head, shoulders and breasts. Then she stretched forward to pick up a neck chain attached to a symbol of devotion: a many-pointed, spinning gold star disc. It was the same design as the one the sadhu had worn on his charm bracelet. However, this one was much larger.

Sollie had a good memory. He recalled her recruitment interview and the chain that had tucked its charms beneath her dress… Then an image of Yutika fighting with Komodo over a photograph came to mind. A picture of a demonic-eyed little girl holding on with all her might to a chain and star symbol. A symbol that he later learned was a Sudarshan chakra. This was a powerful, auspicious spinning disk-like weapon with serrated edges. It was also the name of the PM's sadhu. He felt queasy in the stomach and realised the error of his judgements.

The trance-like music began to play again. Yutika cackled and gave a throaty laugh. Sollie stared in disbelief. Then he spoke to himself again: 'I failed her. She wanted a bigger role in the play. I left her feeling undervalued and overlooked. I rejected her advances, and the devil stepped into the void. He offered her passion, recognition and satanic thrills.'

Then she lit six red candles to make a circle around her and sat cross-legged on the floor. After a short prayer she cupped her hands in supplication. Then she began to coil; rhythmically twisting her body, then raising her arms above her head to clap her hands. Something, it seemed, was now moving through her. It made her stand tall, wave her arms and sway her hips. Then her body began to shake until it was in a frenzy. Finally, she spoke.

"All I ever wanted was a way out of poverty, a frisson of excitement and a blessing from my God. But he overlooked me. My passions went unstirred. I needed a way out. You opened your arms. I set fire to my children and my husband, and you offered me forgiveness... we always love those that forgive us. Then you gave me more: power, trust, lust and responsibility. You became my lover. Now I am ready to prove my devotion. You are my only God. Never doubt that I am here to serve you."

Then Yutika's phone rang. As she turned round to pick it up, her full nakedness stood brazenly in front of him. However, her beauty had diminished. Now, sooty eye makeup had demonized the black swampy pools of her eyes and robbed her of her sparkle. All her innocence had been stripped away and coated over in a mendacious darkness.

'Where is my lovely Yutika?' he wondered.

It appeared that Yutika's true, loving heart had been covered up for a very long time. She held the phone to her ear for a few minutes before replying with a pickled tongue: "Don't worry, Sudarshan. Everything will work out as it should. The new flight path of the albatross will deceive Sollie and give him false hope. You have curdled the mind of the Prime Minister. Durga has completed his tasks. The orphans trust and love me... now we have 13 willing disciples to help us carry out our mission. Soon all our devotion will be rewarded."

Sollie paled. Then all the shadows of all the trees passed over him at the same time.

1963 – A FRENCH PRESIDENT

Fate – Deceit

You are given a role in the play, and you can choose how to play your character. However, you are not able to choose the play.

Apolline Rippe entered Olivia's room. There seemed to be few possessions there, save for two changes of clothes. No jewellery, no gadgets, no mementos. Just a heart-shaped box of her favourite chocolates, wrapped up with yellow ribbons.

She left the room with a little sigh and headed for her own room to lie on the bed and read her journal. She reminded herself of all their pleasant encounters on the train. How Olivia had said, 'How can you expect to fly, if you are weighed down by possessions?' How Olivia always carried a box of chocolates in her bag. 'What was it that she had said? Take as many as you want from the top tray. I only ever buy boxes with two trays, and the bottom layer is all for me; it's my secret compartment.'

Apolline stood up as straight as an arrow and marched back into Olivia's room. For a minute, she just stared at the yellow-ribbon-covered box. Then she nervously took the lid off. The first tray was completely empty. Cautious fingers removed it. In the second tray, there were just two chocolates left. Eating them allowed her to lift this tray up.

There didn't seem to be anything at the bottom other than a brown cardboard base. A tool was needed: her nail scissors. Her heartbeat quickened as she cut around the edge. She pulled the base up… Lying beneath it was a brown paper bag.

Feeling light, she decided to sit down on the rug. Then trembling hands emptied the contents onto the floor. There was a letter… on beautifully-embossed blue paper. At the top was a coat of arms and a date: 1963. Underlining it all was a signature in the pen of a president. She read the letter whilst her stomach swirled.

We agree to each one of your demands. We will close the original Lascaux caves before the end of the year. The newly-discovered bird cave will be completely sealed off, so that it can never be excavated. Replica caves will be constructed where visitors can experience reproductions of the original cave art.

It was addressed to Olivia and Hubert. 'It's not right. I don't want to believe it.' Then the old French newsreels that she had witnessed as a child came to mind… Scientists talking about mould, fungi and crystals on the Lascaux cave walls: 'Now I know that this was all lies! The French government deceived us.' There was a painful pause in her thinking: 'Why? Why did they make up this story?'

Suddenly, her back straightened. 'Am I going to allow everything that I have learnt in India to drain away in an instant? Am I going to permit my fears and the past to paralyse me? No!' Her breathing levelled again. Now Apolline had focus, and the waves of her mind were only splashing. In addition to the old letter, there were two photographs. The most recent photograph, from 2012, was a picture of a Russian president sitting in a hang-glider helping cranes to migrate.

'What made this president put the Siberian cranes under the protection of the Russian government? Is there another reason why Emperor Huizong put the cranes in his painting? What is the secret that the French, Russian and Chinese governments all seem to know?' she asked herself. Now Apolline felt betrayed by the truth. Bongo's musical washing line appeared in her thoughts: 'Was Marcus Aurelius right and Bongo wrong after all?' She took a deep breath: 'Let us hope that there are no more surprises.'

On the second photograph, a group of children were standing on a river-bank in Les Eyzies, a small village near Lascaux. Apolline remembered it well; a school trip to the famous caves and a canoe trip down the river. A pen had been used to draw a circle around a pretty little girl in the front row of the picture; her hair was parted with a grip. The girl wore white socks and had large silver buckles on her shoes. The ones Apolline had always loved.

With intuitive trepidation, Apolline turned the photograph over. At the top in the centre was a simple drawing of a bird's head on a long stick. To the right was a tiny violin and to the left a group of dancing cranes. Below it there were three inscriptions. They were penned in faded, pale-blue ink. They named a place, a date – 50 years on – and a name:

Lascaux Caves, France - 2071 - Apolline Rippe.

Apolline stared into the inscription until she began to shake. Then the blood drained away from her.

THE END

APPEAL

Turn your good intentions into action. Let us help the widows dance. Should you wish to become a pollinator and make this book come alive, you can. Donations to give the widows a proper place to live, a purpose and some joy can be made at:

www.TheTreeMystic.com

EPILOGUE – EXTRACTS FROM THE INNER JOURNEY

Being - Self-approval - God - Self and spiritual development Meditation - Liberation

The beguiling temples at Angkor Wat in Cambodia and Sanchi near Bhopal were covered up and lost to the forest for many years. Then the vines and foliage were cut away to reveal their original beauty. There is another incredible temple that is waiting to be rediscovered; it is called your loving heart. Remove all that is obscuring it and you will find your pure and authentic self.

Tom leaned forward until his nose almost touched Sollie's: "How would you describe the inner journey?"

"It is a journey along a spiritual path to search for the God within you. A path that takes you away from man's profane world and towards the sacred. A path away from your physical reality and towards the world of consciousness."

"What aids do I need?"

"Devotion will melt away the desires and attachments that you must break free from. Meditation will help remove the negative thoughts that prevent you from seeing your own loving heart. Meditation is also one of the spiritual activities that will help you live in the 'present'. It is here that God reveals himself. It is in the present that we see God is in all things."

"Will this journey give me salvation?"

"We are enlightened when we realise that salvation is not achieved in heaven but here on earth. The goal is not to find God so that God can save you. The aim is to find yourself through God and thus create your own salvation."

"Is the inner journey a voyage to find ourselves, change ourselves or find enlightenment?"

"I suggest that you don't try to change or become a different person. Look to rediscover your authentic self, the beating compassionate heart that has been buried beneath a lifetime of false beliefs and clutter.

"We don't travel on the inner journey for enlightenment. The focus should be on the development of your spiritual being, i.e. 'who am I?'"

"What is that?"

"It is based on the premise that we are all capable of our own evolution and that all the resources that we need are already within us. The aim is not to self-develop through experience and knowledge. It is to lighten through non-attachment, downsizing and surrender. This allows you to sink deep into your essence. It is from here that something is borne out of you. This is how we are liberated from striving.

"Read my notes on self-love. Immerse yourself in nature, for it will take you back to your core; to simplicity and your authenticity. It is here that you will resolve your anxiety and suffering."

"What happens when you reach the end of the journey?"

"You will be awake; your inner light will come on and you will enter a state of consciousness – the purest state of mind where everything is clear. Here you will be able to distinguish the wood from the trees. **Here there are no dualities, and you can live in the world without procrastination. Everything can be laughed at and cried at**.

"Most importantly, you will see and feel the consequences of every action before you do them; the effect of every child brought into the world, each mouthful of food, each tree that you fell; in fact, every thought, transaction and extraction that you make.

"Now God's light can be seen, felt and heard in whatever you do, whether it be painting, composing or caring. This is so because it is from our hearts, our minds and our outstretched hands that God is created and revealed. It is at this point that you realise that the only approval that you need is self-approval: the one from within."

(You will find a more complete guide to the inner journey at – TheTreeMystic.com)

THE FRUIT TREE

It sinks deeper and deeper into the soil. It feeds itself from its own roots, tapping into its own essence. All its beautiful gifts, including its perfume and its blossom, come from within. Eventually, something wonderful is borne out of it and the world is showered with fruit.

Printed in Great Britain
by Amazon

62471437R00196